READINGS IN WESTERN CIVILIZATION

—VOLUME THREE—

THIRD EDITION

Fall 2005–Spring 2006

PROVIDENCE COLLEGE

Development of Western Civilization Program

Tapestry Press, Ltd.
Littleton, MA 01720

Front Cover: "The Fighting 'Temeraire' tugged to her . . . Last berth broken up" by Joseph Mallord William Turner, 1838. Copyright © National Gallery, London. Reprinted by permission.

All possible effort has been made to locate the copyright owner or holder of the copyrighted material included in this book. If any rights have been inadvertently infringed upon, the publisher asks to be excused, and agrees to make corrections to any subsequent editions or reprintings.

Acknowledgments:
Pp. 40–62: From *The Confessions* by Jean-Jacques Rousseau. Translated by J. M. Cohen (Penguin Classics, 1953). Copyright 1953 by J. M. Cohen. Reproduced by permission of Penguin Books Ltd.
Pp. 196–201: "Of Bronze—and Blaze," "The Soul Selects Her Own Society," "I Should Have Been Too Glad, I See—," "I Tend My Flowers for Thee," "What Soft—Cherubic Creatures—," "This World Is Not Conclusion," "Nature Is What We See," "Because I Could Not Stop for Death," "She Rose to His Requirement," "Those—Dying Then" by Emily Dickinson. Reprinted by permission of the publishers and the Trustees of Amherst College. From *The Poems of Emily Dickinson*, Thomas H. Johnson, ed., Cambridge, Mass.: The Belknap Press of Harvard University Press, copyright © 1951, 1955, 1979, 1983 by the President and Fellows of Harvard College.

CONTENTS

PROLOGUE

Readings in Western Civilization, volume two, third edition, provides selections for the literature component of Providence College's Development of Western Civilization Program. It is for use in the program's second year which runs, roughly, from France in the middle of the Seventeenth Century with Louis XIV and Descartes, to the present time. The two semesters of the academic year break around 1880. In literature that means that traditionally we end the Fall semester with Dostoevsky and begin the Spring semester with Tolstoy. The course integrates literature with history, theology, philosophy, and the fine arts, so literary works are studied in their historical and intellectual context.

For the most part, *Readings in Western Civilization* consists of shorter pieces and is designed to be supplemented by paperbacks of such fundamental works as *Tartuffe, Gulliver's Travels, Candide* and so on. The western focus of the program, partial as it is, reflects a conscious effort to provide a coherent view of the various western heritages by which we in the modern west have been historically shaped—regardless of our race, ethnicity, or national origin. The program traces that historical development, including its expansion towards greater appreciation of non-western achievements and influences as the past moves to the present and cultural influences are no longer contained in or by geography.

Brian Barbour

1. JONATHAN SWIFT

Jonathan Swift (1667–1745) was born in Ireland to the English ruling class. He was educated in Ireland (Trinity College, Dublin, 1686) and ordained a priest (1695) for the Anglican Church (confusingly called the Church of Ireland), but his ambitions took him to England. He hoped to become a bishop and though he had connections to political influence, Queen Anne was utterly opposed to his promotion. After 1714 he was more or less kept in Ireland where he was the Dean of St. Patrick's (Anglican) Cathedral, and it was there that he wrote Gulliver's Travels *(1726) and* A Modest Proposal *(1729). Swift hated the emerging Enlightenment with its motto that "reason alone is sufficient to govern a rational creature," and he hated the related developments of Deism, benevolence, and the exaltation of science. His work is deeply satirical, but in it he tries to draw in the reader to a quasi-acceptance of what is being satirized so that the reader will have to reconsider his or her own views.*

A MODEST PROPOSAL

FOR PREVENTING THE CHILDREN OF POOR PEOPLE IN IRELAND FROM BEING A BURDEN TO THEIR PARENTS OR COUNTRY, AND FOR MAKING THEM BENEFICIAL TO THE PUBLIC.
(1729)

It is a melancholy object to those who walk through this great town or travel in the country, when they see the streets, the roads, and cabin doors, crowded with beggars of the female sex, followed by three, four, or six children, all in rags and importuning every
5   passenger for an alms. These mothers, instead of being able to work for their honest livelihood, are forced to employ all their time in strolling to beg sustenance for their helpless infants, who, as they grow up, either turn thieves for want of work, or leave their dear native country to fight for the Pretender in Spain, or sell themselves
10 to the Barbadoes.

I think it is agreed by all parties that this prodigious number of children in the arms, or on the backs, or at the heels of their mothers, and frequently of their fathers, is in the present deplorable state of the kingdom a very great additional grievance; and therefore
15 whoever could find out a fair, cheap, and easy method of making

these children sound, useful members of the commonwealth would deserve so well of the public as to have his statue set up for a preserver of the nation.

But my intention is very far from being confined to provide
5   only for the children of professed beggars; it is of a much greater extent, and shall take in the whole number of infants at a certain age who are born of parents in effect as little able to support them as those who demand our charity in the streets.

As to my own part, having turned my thoughts for many years
10 upon this important subject, and maturely weighed the several schemes of other projectors, I have always found them grossly mistaken in their computation. It is true, a child just dropped from its dam may be supported by her milk for a solar year, with little other nourishment; at most not above the value of two shillings, which
15 the mother may certainly get, or the value in scraps, by her lawful occupation of begging; and it is exactly at one year old that I propose to provide for them in such a manner as instead of being a charge upon their parents or the parish, or wanting food and raiment for the rest of their lives, they shall on the contrary contribute
20 to the feeding, and partly to the clothing, of many thousands.

There is likewise another great advantage in my scheme, that it will prevent those voluntary abortions, and that horrid practice of women murdering their bastard children, alas, too frequent among us, sacrificing the poor innocent babes, I doubt, more to avoid the
25 expense than the shame, which would move tears and pity in the most savage and inhuman breast.

The number of souls in this kingdom being usually reckoned one million and a half, of these I calculate there may be about two hundred thousand couple whose wives are breeders; from which
30 number I subtract thirty thousand couples who are able to maintain their own children, although I apprehend there cannot be so many under the present distresses of the kingdom; but this being granted, there will remain an hundred and seventy thousand breeders. I again subtract fifty thousand for those women who miscarry, or
35 whose children die by accident or disease within the year. There only remain an hundred and twenty thousand children of poor parents annually born. The question therefore is, how this number shall be reared and provided for, which, as I have already said, under the present situation of affairs, is utterly impossible by all the methods
40 hitherto proposed. For we can neither employ them in handicraft or agriculture; we neither build houses (I mean in the country) nor cultivate land. They can very seldom pick up a livelihood by stealing till they arrive at six years old, except where they are of towardly parts; although I confess they learn the rudiments much earlier,
45 during which time they can however be looked upon only as pro-

bationers, as I have been informed by a principal gentleman in the county of Cavan, who protested to me that he never knew above one or two instances under the ages of six, even in a part of the kingdom so renowned for the quickest proficiency in that art.

5   I am assured by our merchants that a boy or a girl before twelve years old is no salable commodity; and even when they come to this age they will not yield above three pounds, or three pounds and half a crown at most on the Exchange; which cannot turn to account either to the parents or the kingdom, the charge of nutriment and

10   rags having been at least four times that value.

I shall now therefore humbly propose my own thoughts, which I hope will not be liable to the least objection.

I have been assured by a very knowing American of my acquaintance in London, that a young healthy child well nursed is

15   at a year old a most delicious, nourishing, and wholesome food, whether stewed, roasted, baked, or boiled; and I make no doubt that it will equally serve in a fricassee or a ragout.

I do therefore humbly offer it to public consideration that of the hundred and twenty thousand children, already computed, twenty

20   thousand may be reserved for breed, whereof only one fourth part to be males, which is more than we allow to sheep, black cattle, or swine; and my reason is that these children are seldom the fruits of marriage, a circumstance not much regarded by our savages, therefore one male will be sufficient to serve four females. That the

25   remaining hundred thousand may at a year old be offered in sale to the persons of quality and fortune through the kingdom, always advising the mother to let them suck plentifully in the last month, so as to render them plump and fat for a good table. A child will make two dishes at an entertainment for friends; and when the fam-

30   ily dines alone, the fore or hind quarter will make a reasonable dish, and seasoned with a little pepper or salt will be very good boiled on the fourth day, especially in winter.

I have reckoned upon a medium that a child just born will weigh twelve pounds, and in a solar year if tolerably nursed

35   increaseth to twenty-eight pounds.

I grant this food will be somewhat dear, and therefore very proper for landlords, who, as they have already devoured most of the parents, seem to have the best title to the children.

Infant's flesh will be in season throughout the year, but more

40   plentiful in March, and a little before and after. For we are told by a grave author, an eminent French physician,[1] that fish being a prolific diet, there are more children born in Roman Catholic countries about nine months after Lent than at any other season; therefore,

[1] Rabelais.

reckoning a year after Lent, the markets will be more glutted than usual, because the number of popish infants is at least three to one in this kingdom; and therefore it will have one other collateral advantage, by lessening the number of Papists among us.

5   I have already computed the charge of nursing a beggar's child (in which list I reckon all cottagers, laborers, and four fifths of the farmers) to be about two shillings per annum, rags included; and I believe no gentleman would repine to give ten shillings for the carcass of a good fat child, which, as I have said, will make four dish-

10   es of excellent nutritive meat, when he hath only some particular friend or his own family to dine with him. Thus the squire will learn to be a good landlord, and grow popular among the tenants; the mother will have eight shillings net profit, and be fit for work till she produces another child.

15   Those who are more thrifty (as I must confess the times require) may flay the carcass; the skin of which artificially dressed will make admirable gloves for ladies, and summer boots for fine gentlemen.

As to our city of Dublin, shambles may be appointed for this purpose in the most convenient parts of it, and butchers we may be

20   assured will not be wanting; although I rather recommend buying the children alive, and dressing them hot from the knife as we do roasting pigs.

A very worthy person, a true lover of his country, and whose virtues I highly esteem, was lately pleased in discoursing on this

25   matter to offer a refinement upon my scheme. He said that many gentlemen of this kingdom, having of late destroyed their deer, he conceived that the want of venison might be well supplied by the bodies of young lads and maidens, not exceeding fourteen years of age nor under twelve, so great a number of both sexes in every

30   county being now ready to starve for want of work and service; and these to be disposed of by their parents, if alive, or otherwise by their nearest relations. But with due deference to so excellent a friend and so deserving a patriot, I cannot be altogether in his sentiments; for as to the males, my American acquaintance assured me

35   from frequent experience that their flesh was generally tough and lean, like that of our schoolboys, by continual exercise, and their taste disagreeable; and to fatten them would not answer the charge. Then as to the females, it would, I think with humble submission, be a loss to the public, because they soon would become breeders

40   themselves; and besides, it is not improbable that some scrupulous people might be apt to censure such a practice (although indeed very unjustly) as a little bordering upon cruelty, which I confess, hath always been with me the strongest objection against any project, howsoever well intended.

45   But in order to justify my friend, he confessed that this expedi-

ent was put into his head by the famous Psalmanazar, a native of the island Formosa, who came from thence to London above twenty years ago, and in conversation told my friend that in his country when any young person happened to be put to death, the execu-

5 tioner sold the carcass to persons of quality as a prime dainty; and that in his time the body of a plump girl of fifteen, who was crucified for an attempt to poison the emperor, was sold to his Imperial Majesty's prime minister of state, and other great mandarins of the court, in joints from the gibbet, at four hundred crowns. Neither

10 indeed can I deny that if the same use were made of several plump young girls in this town, who without one single groat to their fortunes cannot stir abroad without a chair, and appear at the playhouse and assemblies in foreign fineries which they never will pay for, the kingdom would not be the worse.

15 Some persons of a desponding spirit are in great concern about that vast number of poor people who are aged, diseased, or maimed, and I have been desired to employ my thoughts what course may be taken to ease the nation of so grievous an encumbrance. But I am not in the least pain upon that matter, because it is

20 very well known that they are every day dying and rotting by cold and famine, and filth and vermin, as fast as can be reasonably expected. And as to the younger laborers, they are now in almost as hopeful a condition. They cannot get work, and consequently pine away for want of nourishment to a degree that if at any time they

25 are accidentally hired to common labor, they have not strength to perform it; and thus the country and themselves are happily delivered from the evils to come.

I have too long digressed, and therefore shall return to my subject. I think the advantages by the proposal which I have made are

30 obvious and many, as well as of the highest importance.

For first, as I have already observed, it would greatly lessen the number of Papists, with whom we are yearly overrun, being the principal breeders of the nation as well as our most dangerous enemies; and who stay at home on purpose to deliver the kingdom to

35 the Pretender, hoping to take their advantage by the absence of so many good Protestants, who have chosen rather to leave their country than stay at home and pay tithes against their conscience to an Episcopal curate.

Secondly, the poorer tenants will have something valuable of

40 their own, which by law may be made liable to distress, and help to pay their landlord's rent, their corn and cattle being already seized and money a thing unknown.

Thirdly, whereas the maintenance of an hundred thousand children, from two years old and upwards, cannot be computed at

45 less than ten shillings a piece per annum, the nation's stock will be

thereby increased fifty thousand pounds per annum, besides the profit of a new dish introduced to the tables of all gentlemen of fortune in the kingdom who have any refinement in taste. And the money will circulate among ourselves, the goods being entirely of
5   our own growth and manufacture.

Fourthly, the constant breeders, besides the gain of eight shillings sterling per annum by the sale of their children, will be rid of the charge of maintaining them after the first year.

Fifthly, this food would likewise bring great custom to taverns,
10   where the vintners will certainly be so prudent as to procure the best receipts for dressing it to perfection, and consequently have their houses frequented by all the fine gentlemen, who justly value themselves upon their knowledge in good eating; and a skillful cook, who understands how to oblige his guests, will contrive to
15   make it as expensive as they please.

Sixthly, this would be a great inducement to marriage, which all wise nations have either encouraged by rewards or enforced by laws and penalties. It would increase the care and tenderness of mothers toward their children, when they were sure of a settlement
20   for life, to the poor babes, provided in some sort by the public, to their annual profit instead of expense. We should see an honest emulation among the married women, which of them could bring the fattest child to the market. Men would become as fond of their wives during the time of their pregnancy as they are now of their
25   mares in foal, their cows in calf, or sows when they are ready to farrow; nor offer to beat or kick them (as is too frequent a practice) for fear of a miscarriage.

Many other advantages might be enumerated. For instance, the addition of some thousand carcasses in our exportation of barreled
30   beef, the propagation of swine's flesh, and improvement in the art of making good bacon, so much wanted among us by the great destruction of pigs, too frequent at our tables, which are no way comparable in taste or magnificence to a well-grown, fat, yearling child, which roasted whole will make a considerable figure at a lord
35   mayor's feast or any other public entertainment. But this and many others I omit, being studious of brevity.

Supposing that one thousand families in this city would be constant customers for infants' flesh, besides others who might have it at merry meetings, particularly weddings and christenings,
40   I compute that Dublin would take off annually about twenty thousand carcasses, and the rest of the kingdom (where probably they will be sold somewhat cheaper) the remaining eighty thousand.

I can think of no one objection that will probably be raised against this proposal, unless it should be urged that the number of
45   people will be thereby much lessened in the kingdom. This I freely

own, and it was indeed one principal design in offering it to the world. I desire the reader will observe, that I calculate my remedy for this one individual kingdom of Ireland and for no other that ever was, is, or I think ever can be upon earth. Therefore let no man

5   talk to me of other expedients: *of taxing our absentees at five shillings a pound: of using neither clothes nor household furniture except what is of our own growth and manufacture: of utterly rejecting the materials and instruments that promote foreign luxury: of curing the expensiveness of pride, vanity, idleness, and gaming in our women: of introducing a vein of*

10   *parsimony, prudence, and temperance: of learning to love our country, in the want of which we differ even from Laplanders and the inhabitants of Topinamboo: of quitting our animosities and factions, nor acting any longer like the Jews, who were murdering one another at the very moment their city was taken: of being a little cautious not to sell our country and*

15   *conscience for nothing: of teaching landlords to have at least one degree of mercy toward their tenants: lastly, of putting a spirit of honesty, industry, and skill into our shopkeepers; who, if a resolution could now be taken to buy only our native goods, would immediately unite to cheat and exact upon us in the price, the measure, and the goodness, nor could ever yet be*

20   *brought to make one fair proposal of just dealing, though often and earnest-ly invited to it.*

    Therefore I repeat, let no man talk to me of these and the like expedients, till he hath at least some glimpse of hope that there will ever be some hearty and sincere attempt to put them in practice.

25   But as to myself, having been wearied out for many years with offering vain, idle, visionary thoughts, and at length utterly despairing of success, I fortunately fell upon this proposal, which, as it is wholly new, so it hath something solid and real, of no expense and little trouble, full in our own power, and whereby we

30   can incur no danger in disobliging England. For this kind of com-modity will not bear exportation, the flesh being of too tender a con-sistence to admit a long continuance in salt, although perhaps I could name a country which would be glad to eat up our whole nation without it.

35   After all, I am not so violently bent upon my own opinion as to reject any offer proposed by wise men, which shall be found equal-ly innocent, cheap, easy, and effectual. But before something of that kind shall be advanced in contradiction to my scheme, and offering a better, I desire the author or authors will be pleased maturely to

40   consider two points. First, as things now stand, how they will be able to find food and raiment for an hundred thousand useless mouths and backs. And secondly, there being a round million of creatures in human figure throughout this kingdom, whose sole subsistence put into a common stock would leave them in debt two

45   millions of pounds sterling, adding those who are beggars by pro-

fession to the bulk of farmers, cottagers, and laborers, with their wives and children who are beggars in effect; I desire those politicians who dislike my overture, and may perhaps be so bold to attempt an answer, that they will first ask the parents of these mor-
5   tals whether they would not at this day think it a great happiness to have been sold for food at a year old in the manner I prescribe, and thereby have avoided such a perpetual sense of misfortunes as they have since gone through by the oppression of landlords, the impossibility of paying rent without money or trade, the want of common
10   sustenance, with neither house nor clothes to cover them from the inclemencies of the weather, and the most inevitable prospect of entailing the like or greater miseries upon their breed forever.

     I profess, in the sincerity of my heart, that I have not the least personal interest in endeavoring to promote this necessary work,
15   having no other motive than the public good of my country, by advancing our trade, providing for infants, relieving the poor, and giving some pleasure to the rich. I have no children by which I can propose to get a single penny; the youngest being nine years old, and my wife past childbearing.

2. ALEXANDER POPE

Alexander Pope (1688–1744) was born with a major civic disability: as a Roman Catholic he could not receive a university education or hold a position under the government, and he could not reside within ten miles of London. Besides this, as a child he contracted tuberculosis of the bone and grew to be only four feet, six inches in stature and was always sickly. Nevertheless, by sheer ability he came to dominate the literary life of his age. He was a great poet, and he was the first successful professional literary man: the first person to make a comfortable living solely by publishing his works. He was the master of the heroic couplet, the basic idiom of the period, and he could express himself with ease, brilliance, and wit. His satiric intention was, like Molière's, to correct vice. He could express both the gap between human ideals and human shortcomings, and he could express the great commonplaces or assumptions of the day: for example, its confidence in the sufficiency of reason, its exaltation of Newton.

EPITAPH FOR SIR ISAAC NEWTON (1730)

Nature and nature's laws lay hid in night;
God said, *Let Newton be!* and all was light.

FROM AN ESSAY ON MAN (1733)

ARGUMENT OF THE FIRST EPISTLE

Of the Nature and State of Man, with respect to the UNIVERSE.

Of Man in the abstract.—I. That we can judge only with regard to our own system, being ignorant of the relations of systems and things, VER. 17, &c. II. That Man is not to be deemed imperfect, but a Being suited to his place and rank in the creation, agreeable to the general Order of things, and conformable to Ends and Relations to him unknown, VER. 35, &c. III. That it is partly upon his ignorance of future events, and partly upon the hope of a future state, that all his happiness in the present depends, VER. 77, &C. IV. The pride of aiming at more knowledge, and pretending to more Perfection, the cause of Man's error and misery. The impiety of putting himself in the

5

place of God, and judging of the fitness or unfitness, perfection or imperfection, justice
10   or injustice of his dispensations, VER. 113, &c. V. The absurdity of conceiting himself
the final cause of the creation, or expecting that perfection in the moral world, which is
not in the natural, VER. 131, &c. VI. The unreasonableness of his complaints against
Providence, while on the one hand he demands the Perfections of the Angels, and on
the other the bodily qualifications of the Brutes; though, to possess any of the sensitive
15   faculties in a higher degree, would render him miserable, VER. 173, &c. VII. That
throughout the whole visible world, an universal order and gradation in the sensual
and mental faculties is observed, which causes a subordination of creature to creature,
and of all creatures to Man. The gradations of sense, instinct, thought, reflection, reason; that Reason alone countervails all the other faculties, VER. 207. VIII. How much
20   farther this order and subordination of living creatures may extend, above and below
us; were any part of which broken, not that part only, but the whole connected creation
must be destroyed. VER. 233. IX. The extravagance, madness, and pride of such a
desire, VER. 259. X. The consequence of all the absolute submission due to Providence,
both as to our present and future state, VER. 281, &c. to the end.

Awake, my ST. JOHN! leave all meaner things
To low ambition, and the pride of Kings.
Let us (since Life can little more supply
Than just to look about us and to die)
5   Expatiate free o'er all this scene of Man;
A mighty maze! but not without a plan;
A Wild, where weeds and flow'rs promiscuous shoot,
Or Garden, tempting with forbidden fruit.
Together let us beat this ample field,
10   Try what the open, what the covert yield;
The latent tracts, the giddy heights explore
Of all who blindly creep, or sightless soar;
Eye Nature's walks, shoot Folly as it flies,
And catch the Manners living as they rise;
15   Laugh where we must, be candid where we can;
But vindicate the ways of God to Man.
        I. Say first, of God above, or Man below,
What can we reason, but from what we know?
Of Man what see we, but his station here
20   From which to reason, or to which refer?
Thro' worlds unnumber'd tho' the God be known,
'Tis ours to trace him only in our own.
He, who thro' vast immensity can pierce,
See worlds on worlds compose one universe,
25   Observe how system into system runs,
What other planets circle other suns,
What vary'd being peoples ev'ry star,
May tell why Heav'n has made us as we are.

But of this frame the bearings, and the ties,
30   The strong connections, nice dependencies,
Gradations just, has thy pervading soul
Look'd thro'? or can a part contain the whole?
     Is the great chain, that draws all to agree,
And drawn, supports, upheld by God, or thee?
35   II. Presumptuous Man! the reason wouldst thou find,
Why form'd so weak, so little, and so blind!
First, if thou canst, the harder reason guess,
Why form'd no weaker, blinder, and no less!
Ask of thy mother earth, why oaks are made
40   Taller or stronger than the weeds they shade?
Or ask of yonder argent fields above,
Why JOVE's Satellites are less than JOVE?
     Of Systems possible, if 'tis confest
That Wisdom infinite must form the best,
45   Where all must full or not coherent be,
And all that rises, rise in due degree;
Then, in the scale of reas'ning life, 'tis plain
There must be, somewhere, such a rank as Man;
And all the question (wrangle e'er so long)
50   Is only this, if God has plac'd him wrong?
     Respecting Man, whatever wrong we call,
May, must be right, as relative to all.
In human works, tho' labour'd on with pain,
A thousand movements scarce one purpose gain;
55   In God's, one single can its end produce;
Yet serves to second too some other use.
So Man, who here seems principal alone,
Perhaps acts second to some sphere unknown,
Touches some wheel, or verges to some goal;
60   'Tis but a part we see, and not a whole.
     When the proud steed shall know why Man restrains
His fiery course, or drives him o'er the plains;
When the dull Ox, why now he breaks the clod,
Is now a victim, and now Ægypt's God:
65   Then shall Man's pride and dulness comprehend
His actions', passions', being's, use and end;
Why doing, suff'ring, check'd, impell'd; and why
This hour a slave, the next a deity.
     Then say not Man's imperfect, Heav'n in fault;
70   Say rather, Man's as perfect as he ought;
His knowledge measur'd to his state and place,
His time a moment, and a point his space.
If to be perfect in a certain sphere,

What matter, soon or late, or here or there?
75   The blest today is as completely so,
As who began a thousand years ago.
      III. Heav'n from all creatures hides the book of Fate,
All but the page prescrib'd, their present state;
From brutes what men, from men what spirits know:
80   Or who could suffer Being here below?
The lamb thy riot dooms to bleed to-day,
Had he thy Reason, would he skip and play?
Pleas'd to the last, he crops the flow'ry food,
And licks the hand just rais'd to shed his blood.
85   Oh blindness to the future! kindly giv'n,
That each may fill the circle mark'd by Heavn;
Who sees with equal eye, as God of all,
A hero perish, or a sparrow fall,
Atoms or systems into ruin hurl'd,
90   And now a bubble burst, and now a world.
      Hope humbly then; with trembling pinions soar;
Wait the great teacher Death, and God adore!
What future bliss, he gives not thee to know,
But gives that Hope to be thy blessing now.
95   Hope springs eternal in the human breast:
Man never Is, but always To be blest:
The soul, uneasy and confin'd from home,
Rests and expatiates in a life to come.
      Lo! the poor Indian, whose untutor'd mind
100   Sees God in clouds, or hears him in the wind;
His soul proud Science never taught to stray
Far as the solar walk, or milky way;
Yet simple Nature to his hope has giv'n,
Behind the cloud-topt hill, an humbler heav'n;
105   Some safer world in depth of woods embrac'd,
Some happier island in the watry waste,
Where slaves once more their native land behold,
No fiends torment, no Christians thirst for gold!
To Be, contents his natural desire,
110   He asks no Angel's wing, no Seraph's fire;
But thinks, admitted to that equal sky,
His faithful dog shall bear him company.
      IV. Go, wiser thou! and in thy scale of sense
Weigh thy Opinion against Providence;
115   Call Imperfection what thou fancy'st such,
Say, here he gives too little, there too much;
Destroy all creatures for thy sport or gust,
Yet cry, If Man's unhappy, God's unjust;

If Man alone ingross not Heav'n's high care,
120   Alone made perfect here, immortal there:
Snatch from his hand the balance and the rod,
Re-judge his justice, be the GOD of GOD!
          In Pride, in reas'ning Pride, our error lies;
All quit their sphere, and rush into the skies.
125   Pride still is aiming at the blest abodes,
Men would be Angels, Angels would be Gods.
Aspiring to be Gods, if Angels fell,
Aspiring to be Angels, Men rebel;
And who but wishes to invert the laws
130   Of ORDER, sins against th' Eternal Cause.
          V. Ask for what end the heav'nly bodies shine,
Earth for whose use? Pride answers, "Tis for mine:
For me kind Nature wakes her genial pow'r,
Suckles each herb, and spreads out ev'ry flow'r;
135   Annual for me, the grape, the rose renew
The juice nectareous, and the balmy dew;
For me, the mine a thousand treasures brings;
For me, health gushes from a thousand springs;
Seas roll to waft me, suns to light me rise;
140   My foot-stool earth, my canopy the skies."
          But errs not Nature from this gracious end,
From burning suns when livid deaths descend,
When earthquakes swallow, or when tempests sweep
Towns to one grave, whole nations to the deep?
145   'No ('tis reply'd) the first Almighty Cause
Acts not by partial, but by gen'ral laws;
Th' exceptions few; some change since all began,
And what created perfect?'—Why then Man?
If the great end be human Happiness,
150   Then Nature deviates; and can Man do less?
As much that end a constant course requires
Of show'rs and sun-shine, as of Man's desires;
As much eternal springs and cloudless skies,
As Men for ever temp'rate, calm, and wise.
155   If plagues or earthquakes break not Heav'n's design,
Why then a Borgia, or a Catiline ?
Who knows but he, whose hand the light'ning forms,
Who heaves old Ocean, and who wings the storms,
160   Pours fierce Ambition in a Caesar's mind,
Or turns young Ammon loose to scourge mankind?
From pride, from pride, our very reas'ning springs;
Account for moral as for nat'ral things:
Why charge we Heav'n in those, in these acquit?

165   In both, to reason right is to submit.
         Better for Us, perhaps, it might appear,
Were there all harmony, all virtue here;
That never air or ocean felt the wind;
That never passion discompos'd the mind:
170   But ALL subsists by elemental strife;
And Passions are the elements of Life.
The gen'ral ORDER, since the whole began,
Is kept in Nature, and is kept in Man.
         VI. What would this Man? Now upward will he soar,
175   And little less than Angel, would be more;
Now looking downwards, just as griev'd appears
To want the strength of bulls, the fur of bears.
Made for his use all creatures if he call,
Say what their use, had he the pow'rs of all?
180   Nature to these, without profusion kind,
The proper organs, proper pow'rs assign'd;
Each seeming want compensated of course,
Here with degrees of swiftness, there of force;
All in exact proportion to the state;
185   Nothing to add, and nothing to abate.
Each beast, each insect, happy in its own;
Is Heav'n unkind to Man, and Man alone?
Shall he alone, whom rational we call,
Be pleas'd with nothing, if not bless'd with all ?
190   The bliss of Man (could Pride that blessing find)
Is not to act or think beyond mankind;
No pow'rs of body or of soul to share,
But what his nature and his state can bear.
Why has not Man a microscopic eye?
195   For this plain reason, Man is not a Fly.
Say what the use, were finer optics giv'n,
T' inspect a mite, not comprehend the heav'n?
Or touch, if tremblingly alive all o'er,
To smart and agonize at ev'ry pore ?
200   Or quick effluvia darting thro' the brain,
Die of a rose in aromatic pain?
If nature thunder'd in his op'ning ears,
And stunn'd him with the music of the spheres,
How would he wish that Heav'n had left him still
205   The whisp'ring Zephyr, and the purling rill?
Who finds not Providence all good and wise,
Alike in what it gives, and what denies?
        VII. Far as Creation's ample range extends,
The scale of sensual, mental pow'rs ascends:

210   Mark how it mounts, to Man's imperial race,
From the green myriads in the peopled grass:
What modes of sight betwixt each wide extreme,
The mole's dim curtain, and the lynx's beam:
Of smell, the headlong lioness between,
215   And hound sagacious on the tainted green:
Of hearing, from the life that fills the flood,
To that which warbles thro' the vernal wood:
The spider's touch, how exquisitely fine!
Feels at each thread, and lives along the line:
220   In the nice bee, what sense so subtly true
From pois'nous herbs extracts the healing dew:
How Instinct varies in the grov'ling swine,
Compar'd, half-reas'ning elephant, with thine:
'Twixt that, and Reason, what a nice barrier;
225   For ever sep'rate, yet for ever near!
Remembrance and Reflection how ally'd;
What thin partitions Sense from Thought divide:
And Middle natures, how they long to join,
Yet never pass th' insuperable line!
230   Without this just gradation, could they be
Subjected these to those, or all to thee?
The pow'rs of all subdu'd by thee alone,
Is not thy Reason all these pow'rs in one ?
         VIII. See, thro' this air, this ocean, and this earth,
235   All matter quick, and bursting into birth.
Above, how high progressive life may go!
Around, how wide! how deep extend below!
Vast chain of being, which from God began,
Natures æthereal, human, angel, man,
240   Beast, bird, fish, insect! what no eye can see,
No glass can reach! from Infinite to thee,
From thee to Nothing!—On superior pow'rs
Were we to press, inferior might on ours:
Or in the full creation leave a void,
245   Where, one step broken, the great scale's destoy'd:
From Nature's chain whatever link you strike,
Tenth or ten thousandth, breaks the chain alike.
         And if each system in gradation roll,
Alike essential to th' amazing whole;
250   The least confusion but in one, not all
That system only, but the whole must fall.
Let Earth unbalanc'd from her orbit fly,
Planets and Suns run lawless thro' the sky,
Let ruling Angels from their spheres be hurl'd,

255   Being on being wreck'd, and world on world,
Heav'n's whole foundations to their centre nod,
And Nature tremble to the throne of God:
All this dread ORDER break—for whom? for thee?
Vile worm!—oh Madness, Pride, Impiety!
260   IX. What if the foot, ordain'd the dust to tread,
Or hand to toil, aspir'd to be the head ?
What if the head, the eye, or ear repin'd
To serve mere engines to the ruling Mind?
Just as absurd for any part to claim
265   To be another, in this gen'ral frame:
Just as absurd, to mourn the tasks or pains
The great directing MIND of ALL ordains.
     All are but parts of one stupendous whole,
Whose body, Nature is, and God the soul;
270   That, chang'd thro' all, and yet in all the same,
Great in the earth, as in th' æthereal frame,
Warms in the sun, refreshes in the breeze,
Glows in the stars, and blossoms in the trees,
Lives thro' all life, extends thro' all extent,
275   Spreads undivided, operates unspent,
Breathes in our soul, informs our mortal part,
As full, as perfect, in a hair as heart;
As full, as perfect, in vile Man that mourns
As the rapt Seraph that adores and burns;
280   To him no high, no low, no great, no small;
He fills, he bounds, connects, and equals all.
     X. Cease then, nor ORDER Imperfection name:
Our proper bliss depends on what we blame.
Know thy own point: This kind, this due degree
285   Of blindness, weakness, Heav'n bestows on thee.
Submit—In this, or any other sphere,
Secure to be as blest as thou canst bear:
Safe in the hand of one disposing Pow'r,
Or in the natal, or the mortal hour.
290   All Nature is but Art, unknown to thee;
All Chance, Direction, which thou canst not see;
All Discord, Harmony, not understood;
All partial Evil, universal Good:
And, spite of Pride, in erring Reason's spite,
295   One truth is clear, 'Whatever IS, is RIGHT.'

EPISTLE II

Know then thyself, presume not God to scan;
The proper study of Mankind is Man.
Plac'd on this isthmus of a middle state,
A being darkly wise, and rudely great:
300 With too much knowledge for the Sceptic side,
With too much weakness for the Stoic's pride,
He hangs between; in doubt to act, or rest,
In doubt to deem himself a God, or Beast;
In doubt his Mind or Body to prefer,
305 Born but to die, and reas'ning but to err;
Alike in ignorance, his reason such,
Whether he thinks too little, or too much:
Chaos of Thought and Passion, all confus'd;
Still by himself abus'd, or disabus'd;
310 Created half to rise, and half to fall;
Great lord of all things, yet a prey to all;
Sole judge of Truth, in endless Error hurl'd:
The glory, jest, and riddle of the world! . . .

FROM THE DUNCIAD, BOOK IV (1743)

* * *

In vain, in vain,—the all-composing Hour
Resistless falls: The Muse obeys the Pow'r.
She comes! she comes! the sable Throne behold
Of Night Primæval, and of *Chaos* old!
5 Before her, *Fancy's* gilded clouds decay,
And all its varying Rain-bows die away.
Wit shoots in vain its momentary fires,
The meteor drops, and in a flash expires.
As one by one, at dread Medea's strain,
10 The sick'ning stars fade off th' ethereal plain;
As Argus' eyes by Hermes' wand opprest,
Clos'd one by one to everlasting rest;
Thus at her felt approach, and secret might
Art after *Art* goes out, and all is Night.
15 See skulking *Truth* to her old Cavern fled,
Mountains of Casuistry heap'd o'er her head!
Philosophy, that lean'd on Heav'n before,
Shrinks to her second cause, and is no more.
Physic of *Metaphysic* begs defence,
20 And *Metaphysic* calls for aid on *Sense!*

See *Mystery* to *Mathematics* fly!
In vain! they gaze, turn giddy, rave, and die.
Religion blushing veils her sacred fires,
And unawares *Morality* expires.
25 Nor *public* Flame, nor *private*, dares to shine;
Nor *human* Spark is left, nor Glimpse *divine!*
Lo! thy dread Empire, CHAOS! is restor'd;
Light dies before thy uncreating word:
Thy hand, great Anarch! lets the curtain fall;
30 And Universal Darkness buries All.

3. DIDEROT AND THE PHILOSOPHES

The Encyclopédie *was one of the greatest yet most characteristic achievements of the eighteenth century. The period was fascinated with systematizing knowledge. Newton, Buffon and Linnaeus brought classification and order to the world of nature. Johnson conceived and constructed the* Dictionary. *Blackstone organized the Laws of England. And the* philosophes *led by Diderot made the* Encyclopédie. *The project took over twenty years, from 1751 to 1772, and was monumental: twelve volumes of text, four of supplements, and eleven of striking illustrations. The idea was to present systematically all human knowledge, and though the work was in the hands of the* philosophes *there was to be no direct attack on the Church (the problem of censorship was too real). Instead, there was to be a straightforward presentation of useful information. Nevertheless, the project took its place in that great effort to* ecrasez l'infame. *This was managed in several ways. One was through tone or insinuation. The general attitude was that religion is a matter of superstition, taken seriously only by fanatics. The alternative is to live by "reason."*

FROM THE ENCYCLOPÉDIE
(1751–1772)

THE COWL

Type of robe used by the followers of St. Bernard, the Benedictines, etc. There are two kinds of cowls, one white and very full, used on ceremonial occasions; the other black, which is part of the ordinary habit.

5   Father Mabillon claims that originally the cowl was the same thing as the scapular. But the author of the Apologia for Emperor Henry IV distinguishes two types of cowls; one was really a robe that reached from the head down to the feet, with sleeves, worn on special occasions, the other was a kind of hood, for every day. The
10   latter is properly called a scapular, because it covers only the head and the shoulders.

Cowl is also commonly used to designate a rough piece of cloth, cut and sewn together in a conical shape, or rounded at one end, which the Capuchins, the Recollects, the Franciscans, and other
15   mendicant orders use as a head covering.

The cowl was once the cause of a major war among the Franciscans. The order split into two factions, the spiritual friars and the conventuals. One group wanted a narrow cowl, the other a wide one. The quarrel lasted more than a century and was fought
5   with a great deal of heat and animosity. Four papal bulls, issued by Nicolas IV, Clement V, John XXII, and Benedict XII, were barely able to put an end to the quarrel. Today the members of the order can only recall this dispute with the most contempt.

Nevertheless, if anyone should venture today to treat the
10   thought of Scotus as it deserves, such an aggressor would have a lively fight on his hands and become the object of a great many insults, even though the qualities of the clever doctor are even less important than the shape of his disciples' hoods.

Could not, however, a great Grey Friar endowed with common
15   sense say with good reason to the others: "It seems to me, fathers, that we are making a good deal of noise for nothing; our insults will not improve Scotus' quibbling. If we wait until sound philosophy, which is spreading its light everywhere, has penetrated into our cloisters, then maybe we shall come to consider the dreams of our
20   doctor as ridiculous as the stubbornness of our predecessors about the size of our cowls."

HAPPINESS

Is taken here to mean a state or situation which we would like to see continue forever unchanged. This is what distinguishes happiness from pleasure, which is no more than a feeling that is agree-
25   able but short and fleeting. Pleasure can never be a state, while it is possible to speak of a state of pain.

All men are one in their desire for happiness. Nature has made happiness a law of our being, and all that is not happiness is alien to our disposition. It alone has unmistakable power over our hearts,
30   it attracts us all through an instant inclination, a powerful charm, and an irresistible attraction. Happiness is the charm and perfection of Nature and she has indelibly engraved it on our hearts.

All men also agree on the nature of happiness which they identify with pleasure, or at least they agree that it owes to pleasure its
35   greatest delight and stimulation. If happiness is not enlivened from time to time by pleasure, it is not so much true happiness as a state of tranquility, a very sorry kind of happiness indeed! If we are left in a state of lazy indolence that offers no stimulus to our activity, we cannot be happy; our desires can only be fulfilled by our being
40   transported out of this listlessness in which we languish. Joy must flow into the innermost recesses of our hearts, it must be stimulated by pleasant feelings, kept in motion by gentle shocks, filled with delightful variety, it must intoxicate us with a pure pleasure that

nothing can spoil. But man's condition does not allow for such a state: pleasures cannot accompany every moment of our life and the most delightful state includes many periods of languor; once the first flame of feeling has died down, the best we can hope for is
5   tranquility. As we stated at the beginning of this article, our most perfect happiness in this life is only a state of tranquility that is enlivened from time to time by moments of pleasure.

Thus the differences of opinion between philosophers regarding happiness touch not on its nature but on its efficient cause. Their
10   opinion is basically the same as that of Epicurus for whom felicity consisted essentially in pleasure. Possession of goods is the foundation of our happiness but it is not happiness itself, for what would we gain if we had power over possessions and did not know it? The madman of Athens who believed that he owned all the ships arriv-
15   ing at Piraeus enjoyed the happiness of riches without having any; yet it may be that those who really owned the ships had ownership without pleasure. When Aristotle defines happiness as the knowledge and love of the highest good, he apparently intended to define only the basis of happiness. Otherwise he would be grossly in error,
20   for if one were to separate pleasure from this knowledge and love, one would see something more is needed to make men happy. Stoics who taught that happiness consisted in the possession of wisdom were not so unreasonable as to imagine that the idea of happiness should be separated from the inner satisfaction which they
25   gained from this wisdom. Their joy flowed from the exaltation of their soul which complimented itself on an inner strength it did not possess. All men are in general agreement on this principle and I do not know why some authors have preferred to show them in disagreement when it is indubitable that men have never thought more
30   alike on any other point. The miser delights only in the anticipation of enjoying his riches, that is, in feeling the pleasure he derives from owning them. It is true he makes no use of them, but that is because his pleasure consists in preserving them. The miser loses himself in the feeling of ownership, he finds happiness in this fashion. Since he
35   is happy, why should we deny his happiness? Does not everyone have the right to be happy according to his whims? The ambitious man seeks honors only for the pleasure of seeing himself elevated above others, the vindictive man would not seek revenge if he did not hope to find his satisfaction in it.
40   This undisputed maxim is not in contradiction with the moral commandments and the religion of Jesus Christ, our legislator and our God, who has come to perfect nature, not to destroy it. He does not ask us to renounce love of pleasure and does not condemn virtue to an unhappy existence on earth; His law charms and
45   attracts us and consists entirely in the love of God and of one's

neighbor. The well of legitimate pleasures flows no less for the Christian than for the unbeliever, but in the order of grace the hope of future blessings brings the Christian infinitely more happiness than his present possessions. The happiness he enjoys on earth is to
5   him only the seed of an eternal happiness. He finds his pleasures in moderation, good works, temperance, and a good conscience. These are noble, pure, spiritual pleasures, far superior to sensual pleasure.

     Certainly anyone who preached that virtue was so rarefied that it excluded all feelings of joy and pleasure would only repel our
10 hearts. The heart opens only to pleasure—that is in its nature—only pleasure can reach all its secret recesses. We may possibly respect a virtue that is not accompanied by pleasure, but we will not be drawn to it. I admit that the same pleasure is not suited to all of us: some prefer vulgar pleasures, others the pleasures of refinement,
15 some keen, others lasting pleasures, some sensual and others spiritual pleasures, and yet again some prefer the pleasures of feeling and others the pleasures of reflection. But all without exception seek pleasure.

     In the works of M. de Fontenelle we find judicious and well-
20 founded reflections on happiness. It is true that our happiness does not entirely depend on ourselves since it is not within our power to have fortune place us in humble station, where we would be most likely to enjoy a tranquil existence and thus be happy. Yet our way of thinking does have a certain effect on our condition.

THE PHILOSOPHER

25   Nothing is easier to acquire today than the name of philosopher. If a man leads an unobtrusive and withdrawn life, gives the appearance of wisdom, and has read a little, that is enough for him to become known as a philosopher and to gain undeserved distinction.

30   Others, for whom free thought takes the place of reasoning, look on themselves as the only true philosophers because they have dared to overthrow the sacred bounds set down by religion and have broken the fetters that faith placed on their reason. They are proud of having rid themselves of the prejudices concerning reli-
35 gion which their upbringing instilled in them, and they look with disdain on their fellows as being weak men, slavish spirits and pusillanimous souls who let themselves be frightened by the consequences of unbelief, who do not dare for an instant to step outside the circle of established truths or follow new paths, and whose
40 minds are dulled by the yoke of superstition.

     But there should be a more accurate conception of a philosopher, and here is how we characterize him.

Other men are impelled to act without either feeling or knowing the causes of their actions; they do not think that there might be
such causes. The philosopher, on the contrary, discerns these causes
to the best of his ability, often even anticipates them and conscious-
5   ly allows himself to be moved by them: he is a clock which, so to
speak, sometimes winds itself. Consequently, he avoids subjects
that can produce sentiments in him that are contrary to well-being
and a reasonable life, and he seeks those subjects that can arouse
feelings suited to the condition in which he finds himself. Reason is
10 to a philosopher what grace is to a Christian. Grace impels the
Christians to act, reason impels the philosopher.

Other men are carried away by their passions; their actions are
not preceded by reflection: they are men who walk in darkness. A
philosopher, on the other hand, even in moments of passion, acts
15 only after reflection; he walks through the night, but he is preceded
by a torch.

The philosopher forms his principles from an infinity of individual observations. The common people adopt a principle without
thinking of the observations that have produced it; they believe that
20 a maxim exists, so to speak, by itself. The philosopher, however,
takes a maxim from its source, he examines its origin, he knows its
true worth and uses it only where it is suitable.

For the philosopher truth is not a mistress that corrupts his
imagination and therefore appears to him everywhere. He is satis-
25 fied if he can bring it to light where he catches a glimpse of it. He
does not confuse it with verisimilitude: he accepts as true what is
true, as false what is false, as doubtful what is doubtful, and as
probable what is merely probable. He goes even further: when he
does not have any proper basis, he knows how to suspend judg-
30 ment, and this is the most perfect trait of the philosopher.

The world is full of very intelligent persons who are always
judging. In effect, they are always guessing; for we guess when we
judge without knowing whether or not we have sound grounds for
judgment. Such people do not know the reach of the human mind
35 and think it can know everything. Thus they think it shameful not
to arrive at a decision and imagine that intelligence consists in having opinions. The philosopher believes that it consists in judging
well: he is more pleased with himself when he is able to withhold
conclusions than he would be if he had made up his mind before
40 perceiving the proper grounds for coming to a decision. Therefore,
he judges and speaks less, but he judges more accurately and
speaks better. He does not avoid the brilliant flashes that naturally
come to the mind through a sudden and frequently surprising connection of ideas. This sudden connection is what we commonly call
45 wit. Yet the philosopher in no way actively seeks wit. Instead of

such brilliance, he prefers to proceed carefully to perceive his ideas clearly, to know accurately their scope and the connections between them, and thus to avoid taking a wrong turn by carrying too far some particular link between them. It is this ability to distinguish

5   which we call judgment and precise thinking, and this precision is combined with flexibility and clarity. The philosopher is not so attached to a system as to be unable to understand the strength of the objections that can be raised against it. The majority of men are so strongly committed to their opinions that they do not even take

10   the trouble to inquire into the opinions of others. The philosopher understands the point of view he rejects, as clearly and to the same extent as his own.

    The philosopher's spirit is thus characterized by observation and precision and relates everything to its true principles. However,

15   the philosopher cultivates not only the mind; his attention and his preoccupations extend further.

    Man is not a monster who should live only in the depths of the sea or the farthest reaches of the forest. The very necessities of life make intercourse with others essential for him. In whatever condi-

20   tion he finds himself, his needs and the desire for well-being oblige him to live in society. Reason demands that he know and study the qualities of sociability and endeavor to acquire them.

    Our philosopher does not think that he lives in exile in this world; he does not believe himself to be in enemy territory; he wish-

25   es to enjoy as a frugal steward the goods that nature offers him; he wishes to find pleasure in the company of others, and to find pleasure he has to give pleasure, so that he seeks to adapt himself to those with whom he lives by chance or by choice. At the same time he finds what suits him: he is an *honnête homme* who wishes to

30   please others and to render himself useful.

    Most nobles, whose dissipations do not leave them enough time for reflection, are without indulgence toward those whom they do not consider their equals. The common run of philosophers who reflect too much, or rather reflect badly, behave in the same manner

35   toward everyone: they flee men, and men avoid them. But our philosopher, who knows how to divide his time between solitude and social intercourse, is full of humanity. He is like the Chremes of Terence who feels that he is human and that humanity itself impels him to take an interest in the good or bad fortune of his neighbor.

40   *Homo sum, humani a me nihil alienum puto* [I am a man, and I believe that nothing human is alien to me].

    There is no need to point out here how scrupulous the philosopher is in all matters of honor and probity. One might say that he looks on civil society as a divinity on earth: he offers it incense and

45   honors it with probity, with a painstaking devotion to his duties and

a sincere desire not to be a useless or troublesome member of society. Feelings of probity are as much part of the make-up of a philosopher as an enlightened mind. The more reason you find in a man, the more probity you will find in him. In contrast, wherever
5   fanaticism and superstition reign, uncontrolled passions reign too. The temperament of the philosopher is to act out of a feeling for order or according to reason. Because he loves society profoundly, he is concerned, far more than other men, with directing all his efforts toward achieving the ideal of the *honnête homme*. Do not fear
10   that he will engage in acts contrary to probity, when no eyes are watching him. No! Such an action is not in accord with the make-up of the wise man: one might say that he is kneaded with the leaven of rule and order, that he is filled with concern for the good of civil society and that he knows its principles far better than other men.
15   Crime would find too much resistance in him, it would have to destroy too many natural and acquired ideas. His capacity for action resembles, so to speak, the string of a musical instrument that is tuned for a certain tone and could not produce its opposite. He is afraid to fall out of tune with himself, and this reminds me of
20   Velleius' description of Cato of Utica: "he has never done good deeds in order to show that he has done them, but only because it was not in him to do otherwise."

Moreover, in all their actions men seek only their own immediate satisfaction: they are impelled to act by the good, or rather by
25   their present inclination that depends on the elements that constitute their make-up at the moment. Now the philosopher more than anyone else is disposed by his reflections to find a greater attraction and pleasure in living with you, in gaining your trust and esteem, and in fulfilling the duties imposed by friendship and gratitude.
30   These feelings are also nourished in his heart by religion to which he has been brought by the natural light of his reason. To put it another way, wickedness is just as incompatible with the idea of a philosopher as is stupidity, and experience shows us every day that the more rational and enlightened a man is, the more reliable he is
35   and suited to life in society. A fool, said La Rochefoucauld, does not have what it takes to be good. We sin only because the light of our reason is not as strong as our passions, and there is a certain truth in the theological maxim that all sinners are ignorant.

This love of society which is so essential in the philosopher
40   proves the truth of the remark made by the Emperor Antoninus: "How happy the people will be when kings will be philosophers, or philosophers kings!"

The philosopher is thus an *honnête homme* who follows reason in all his actions and who combines a reflective and precise mind
45   with the manners and qualities of a sociable man. Graft a prince

onto a philosopher of this stamp and you will have a perfect sovereign.

From this it is easy to conclude how far removed the impassive sage of the Stoics is from our philosopher: the philosopher is a man while their sage was only a phantom. They were ashamed of their humanity, he takes pride in his. Their foolish desire was to destroy the passions and raise us above our nature by means of an illusory impassivity; whereas he does not reach out for the illusory honor of destroying the passions, because that is impossible; rather he strives not to be tyrannized by them, to use them to good advantage and reasonably, because that is possible and because reason commands him to do it.

One can see moreover, by all that we have said, how far from being true philosophers are those indolent men who give themselves over to idle meditation and neglect their temporal affairs and everything that we know as fortune. The true philosopher is not tormented by ambition; he merely desires the comforts of life. He needs, over and above the bare necessities, the modest superfluity which is a necessity for an *honnête homme* and which alone brings happiness, for it is the foundation of all proprieties and amenities. Only counterfeit philosophers, with their dazzling maxims, have propagated the false notion that the barest necessities suffice for a philosopher, and they have done so to justify their own indolence.

4. SAMUEL JOHNSON

Samuel Johnson—"Dr. Johnson,"—(1709–1784) was the greatest writer and the greatest conversationalist of his age. Indeed, he was the greatest Englishman of the eighteenth century and yet his achievements are not easy to summarize or state. Johnson's range was enormous: he wrote a novel; he was a great poet; he wrote outstanding moral essays; he wrote the first real dictionary of the English language; he was one of the half dozen greatest literary critics who have ever lived; he edited the works of Shakespeare; he invented the genre of literary biography; and he became the subject of the greatest of all biographies, The Life of Samuel Johnson, L.L.D., by James Boswell. Johnson was the voice of Christian humanism in opposition to the Enlightenment and its general drift towards secularism and naturalism. His central moral theme is distilled in two lines, one from The Vanity of Human Wishes: "How rarely reason guides the stubborn choice," and one from The Preface to Shakespeare: "He who thinks reasonably must think morally." He was a moralist who "saw life steadily and saw it whole" and who expressed what he saw with courageous honesty. The following selections exhibit his range, his depth, and his good sense.

FROM THE VANITY OF HUMAN WISHES
or The Tenth Satire of Juvenal Imitated

Let Observation with extensive View,
Survey Mankind from China to Peru;
Remark each anxious Toil, each eager Strife,
And watch the busy Scenes of crowded Life;
5   Then say how Hope and Fear, Desire and Hate
O'erspread with Snares the clouded Maze of Fate,
Where wavering Man, betrayed by venturous Pride,
To tread the dreary Paths without a Guide;
As treacherous Phantoms in the Mist delude,
10   Shuns fancied Ills, or chases airy Good;
How rarely Reason guides the stubborn Choice,
Rules the bold hand, or prompts the suppliant Voice;
How nations sink, by darling schemes oppressed,
When Vengeance listens to the fool's request.

* * *

Where then shall Hope and Fear their objects find?
Must dull Suspense corrupt the stagnant mind?
Must helpless man, in ignorance sedate,
Roll darkling down the torrent of his fate?
5   Must no dislike alarm, no wishes rise,
No cries invoke the mercies of the skies?
Inquirer, cease; petitions yet remain,
Which Heaven may hear, nor deem religion vain.
Still raise for good the supplicating voice,
10   But leave to heaven the measure and the choice,
Safe in his power, whose eyes discern afar
The secret ambush of a specious prayer.
Implore his aid, in his decisions rest,
Secure whate'er he gives, he gives the best.
15   Yet when the sense of sacred presence fires,
And strong devotion to the skies aspires,
Pour forth thy fervors for a healthful mind,
Obedient passions, and a will resigned;
For love, which scarce collective man can fill;
20   For patience, sovereign o'er transmuted ill;
For faith, that panting for a happier seat,
Counts death kind Nature's signal of retreat:
These goods for man, the laws of Heaven ordain,
These goods He grants, who grants the power to gain;
25   With these celestial Wisdom calms the mind,
And makes the happiness she does not find.

1749

FROM THE LIFE OF
SAMUEL JOHNSON
(1791)

After we came out of the church, we stood talking for some
time together of Bishop Berkeley's ingenious sophistry to prove the
non-existence of matter, and that everything in the universe is merely ideal. I observed that though we are satisfied his doctrine is not
5 true, it is impossible to refute it. I never shall forget the alacrity with
which Johnson answered, striking his foot with mighty force
against a large stone, till he rebounded from it, "I refute it *thus*."

JOHNSON: "Hume, and other skeptical innovators, are vain
men and will gratify themselves at any expence. Truth will not
10 afford sufficient food to their vanity; so they have betaken themselves to errour. Truth, Sir, is a cow which will yield such people no

more milk, and so they are gone to milk the bull."

JOHNSON: "Rousseau, Sir, is a very bad man. I would sooner sign a sentence for his transportation than that of any felon who has gone from the Old Bailey these many years."

5   BOSWELL: "Sir, do you think him as bad a man as Voltaire?"

JOHNSON: "Why, Sir, it is difficult to settle the proportion of iniquity between them."

QUOTES AND DICTA

Patriotism is the last refuge of a scoundrel.

No man but a blockhead ever wrote except for money.

10   Depend upon it, Sir, when a man knows he is to be hanged in a fort-
    night, it concentrates his mind wonderfully.

A decent provision for the poor is the true test of a civilization.

I am willing to love all mankind, except an American.

He who tires of London has tired of life.

15   He who thinks reasonably must think morally.

To prevent evil is the great end of government.

To be happy at home is the end of all labour.

The great end of learning is to enable us better to enjoy life, or bet-
    ter to endure it.

20   Never permit your mind to confuse virtue with vice. The woman's
    a whore and there's an end on it.

Life has no pleasure higher or nobler than that of friendship

Marriage has many pains, but celibacy has few pleasures.

SPECIMEN ENTRIES FROM
JOHNSON'S *DICTIONARY*
(1755)

CANT. 3. A whining pretension to goodness, in formal and affected
25   terms.

ENTHUSIASM. 1. A vain belief of private revelation; a vain confi-
    dence of divine favor or communication. 2. Heat of imagina-
    tion; violence of passion; confidence of opinion.

EXCISE. A hateful tax levied upon commodities and adjudged not
30   by the common judges of property, but wretches hired by those
    to whom the excise is paid.

LEXICOGRAPHER. A writer of dictionaries; a harmless drudge that
    busies himself on tracing the original, and detailing the signifi-
    cation, of words.

NETWORK. Anything reticulated or decussated, at equal distances, with interstices between the intersections.

OATS. A grain, which in England is generally given to horses, but in Scotland supports the people.

5   PENSION. An allowance made to anyone without an equivalent. In England it is generally understood to mean pay given to a state hireling for treason to his country.

PURITAN. A sectary pretending to eminent purity of religion.

TORY. One who adheres to the ancient constitution of the state, and
10   the apostolical hierarchy of the Church of England; opposed to a Whig.

WHIG. The name of a faction.

FROM THE LIFE OF MILTON
(1779)

JOHNSON ON EDUCATION

But the truth is that the knowledge of external nature, and the sciences which that knowledge requires or includes, are not the
15   great or the frequent business of the human mind. Whether we provide for action or conversation, whether we wish to be useful or pleasing, the first requisite is the religious and moral knowledge of right and wrong; the next is an acquaintance with the history of mankind and with those examples which may be said to embody
20   truth and prove by events the reasonableness of opinions. Prudence and Justice are virtues, and excellences, of all times and of all places; we are perpetually moralists, but we are geometricians only by chance. Our intercourse with intellectual nature is necessary; our speculations upon matter are voluntary and at leisure.
25   Physiological learning is of such rare emergence that one man may know another half his life without being able to estimate his skill in hydrostaticks or astronomy; but his moral and prudential character immediately appears.

Those authors, therefore, are to be read at schools that supply
30   most axioms of prudence, most principles of moral truth, and most materials for conversation; and these purposes are best served by poets, orators, and historians.

Let me not be censured for this digression as pedantick or paradoxical; for if I have Milton against me, I have Socrates on my side.
35   It was his labour to turn philosophy from the study of nature to speculations upon life; but the innovators whom I oppose are turning off attention from life to nature. They seem to think that we are placed here to watch the growth of plants or the motions of the

stars. Socrates was rather of opinion that what we had to learn was, how to do good, and avoid evil.

FROM THE ADVENTURER
(1753)

NUMBER 120, 29 DECEMBER 1753

> *But no frail man, however great or high,*
> *Can be concluded blest before he die.*

—Addison

The numerous miseries of human life have extorted in all ages an universal complaint. The wisest of men [Solomon] terminated all
5   his experiments in search of happiness by the mournful confession that "all is vanity;"[1] and the ancient patriarchs lamented that "the days of their pilgrimage were few and evil."[2]

There is, indeed, no topic on which it is more superfluous to accumulate authorities, nor any assertion of which our own eyes
10   will more easily discover, or our sensations more frequently impress the truth than that misery is the lot of man, that our present state is a state of danger and infelicity.

When we take the most distant prospect of life, what does it present us but a chaos of unhappiness, a confused and tumultuous
15   scene of labor and contest, disappointment and defeat? If we view past ages in the reflection of history, what do they offer to our meditation but crimes and calamities? One year is distinguished by a famine, another by an earthquake; kingdoms are made desolate, sometimes by wars, sometimes by pestilence; the peace of the world
20   is interrupted at one time by the caprices of a tyrant, at another by the rage of a conqueror. The memory is stored only with vicissitudes of evil; and the happiness, such as it is, of one part of mankind is found to arise commonly from sanguinary success, from victories which confer upon them the power, not so much of improving life
25   by any new enjoyment, as of inflicting misery on others and gratifying their own pride by comparative greatness.

But by him that examines life with a more close attention, the happiness of the world will be found still less than it appears. In

---

[1]Ecclesiastes 12:8. And compare the title and theme of Johnson's greatest poem, "The Vanity of Human Wishes."

[2][Genesis 47:9]

some intervals of public prosperity, or, to use terms more proper, in some intermissions of calamity, a general diffusion of happiness may seem to overspread a people; all is triumph and exultation, jollity and plenty; there are no public fears and dangers, and "no com-
5 plaining in the streets."[3] But the condition of individuals is very little mended by this general calm; pain and malice and discontent still continue their havoc, the silent depredation goes incessantly forward, and the grave continues to be filled by the victims of sorrow.

10 He that enters a gay assembly, beholds the cheerfulness displayed in every countenance, and finds all sitting vacant and disengaged, with no other attention than to give or to receive pleasure; would naturally imagine that he had reached at last the metropolis of felicity, the place sacred to gladness of heart, from whence all fear
15 and anxiety were irreversibly excluded. Such, indeed, we may often find to be the opinion of those who from a lower station look up to the pomp and gaiety which they cannot reach; but who is there of those who frequent these luxurious assemblies that will not confess his own uneasiness, or cannot recount the vexations and distresses
20 that prey upon the lives of his gay companions.

The world, in its best state, is nothing more than a larger assembly of beings, combining to counterfeit happiness which they do not feel, employing every art and contrivance to embellish life, and to hide their real condition from the eyes of one another.

25 The species of happiness most obvious to the observation of others is that which depends upon the goods of fortune; yet even this is often fictitious. There is in the world more poverty than is generally imagined; not only because many whose possessions are large have desires still larger and many measure their wants by the
30 gratifications which others enjoy; but great numbers are pressed by real necessities which it is their chief ambition to conceal and are forced to purchase the appearance of competence and cheerfulness at the expense of many comforts and conveniences of life.

Many, however, are confessedly rich and many more are suffi-
35 ciently removed from all danger of real poverty: but it has been long ago remarked that money cannot purchase quiet; the highest of mankind can promise themselves no exemption from that discord or suspicion by which the sweetness of domestic retirement is destroyed; and must always be even more exposed, in the same
40 degree as they are elevated above others, to the treachery of dependents, the calumny of defamers, and the violence of opponents.

---

[3][Psalm 144]

4. *Samuel Johnson*

Affliction is inseparable from our present state; it adheres to all the inhabitants of this world in different proportions indeed, but with an allotment which seems very little regulated by our own conduct. It has been the boast of some swelling moralists that every
5   man's fortune was in his own power, that prudence supplied the place of all other divinities, and that happiness is the unfailing consequence of virtue. But surely the quiver of Omnipotence is stored with arrows against which the shield of human virtue, however adamantine it has been boasted, is held up in vain: we do not
10   always suffer by our crimes; we are not always protected by our innocence.

A good man is by no means exempt from the danger of suffering by the crimes of others; even his goodness may raise him enemies of implacable malice and restless perseverance: the good man
15   has never been warranted by Heaven from the treachery of friends, the disobedience of children, or the dishonesty of a wife: he may see his cares made useless by profusion, his instructions defeated by perverseness, and his kindness rejected by ingratitude; he may languish under the infamy of false accusations or perish reproachfully
20   by an unjust sentence.

A good man is subject, like other mortals, to all the influences of natural evil: his harvest is not spared by the tempest, nor his cattle by the murrain; his house flames like the others in a conflagration; nor have his ships any peculiar power of resisting hurricanes:
25   his mind, however elevated, inhabits a body subject to innumerable casualties, of which he must always share the dangers and the pains; he bears about him the seeds of disease and may linger away a great part of his life under the tortures of the gout or stone; at one time groaning with insufferable anguish, at another dissolved in
30   listlessness and languor.

From this general and indiscriminate distribution of misery the moralists have always derived one of their strongest moral arguments for a future state; for since the common events of the present life happen alike to the good and bad, it follows from the justice of
35   the Supreme Being that there must be another state of existence in which a just retribution shall be made and every man shall be happy and miserable according to his works.

The miseries of life, may, perhaps, afford some proof of a future state compared as well with the mercy as the justice of God. It is
40   scarcely to be imagined that Infinite Benevolence would create a being capable of enjoying so much more than is here to be enjoyed, and qualified by nature to prolong pain by remembrance and anticipate it by terror, if he was not designed for something nobler and better than a state in which many of his faculties can serve only for
45   his torment, in which he is to be importuned by desires that never

can be satisfied, to feel many evils which he had no power to avoid, and to fear many which he shall never feel: there will surely come a time when every capacity of happiness shall be filled and none shall be wretched but by his own fault.

5   In the mean time, it is by affliction chiefly that the heart of man is purified and that the thoughts are fixed upon a better state. Prosperity, allayed and imperfect as it is, has power to intoxicate the imagination, to fix the mind upon the present scene, to produce confidence and elation, and to make him who enjoys affluence and

10 honors forget the hand by which they were bestowed. It is seldom that we are otherwise, than by affliction, awakened to a sense of our own imbecility or taught to know how little all our acquisitions can conduce to safety or to quiet; and how justly we may ascribe to the superintendence of a Higher Power those blessings which in the

15 wantonness of success we considered as the attainments of our policy or courage.

    Nothing confers so much ability to resist the temptations that perpetually surround us as an habitual consideration of the shortness of life and the uncertainty of those pleasures that solicit our

20 pursuit; and this consideration can be inculcated only by affliction. "O Death! how bitter is the remembrance of thee to a man that lives at ease in his possessions."[4] If our present state were one continued succession of delights, or one uniform flow of calmness and tranquility, we should never willingly think upon its end; death would

25 then surely surprise us as "a thief in the night;"[5] and our task of duty would remain unfinished till "the night came when no man can work."[6]

    While affliction thus prepares us for felicity, we may console ourselves under its pressures by remembering that they are no par-

30 ticular marks of divine displeasure; since all the distresses of persecution have been suffered by those "of whom the world was not worthy;"[7] and the Redeemer of mankind himself was "a man of sorrows and acquainted with grief."[8]

---

[4][Ecclesiasticus 41:1]
[5][I Thessalonians 5:2]
[6][John 9:4]
[7][Hebrews 11:38]
[8][Isaiah 53:3]

4. *Samuel Johnson*

FROM RASSELAS
(1759)

CHAPTER 18: THE PRINCE FINDS A WISE AND
HAPPY MAN

As he [Rasselas] was one day walking in the street, he saw a
spacious building which all were, by the open doors, invited to
enter: he followed the stream of people and found it a hall or school
of declamation in which professors read lectures to their auditory.
5   He fixed his eye upon a sage raised above the rest who discoursed
with great energy on the government of the passions. His look was
venerable, his action graceful, his pronunciations clear, and his diction elegant. He showed, with great strength of sentiment and variety of illustration, that human nature is degraded and debased
10   when the lower faculties predominate over the higher; that when
fancy, the parent of passion, usurps the dominion of the mind nothing ensues but the natural effect of unlawful government, perturbation and confusion; that she betrays the fortresses of intellect to
rebels and excites her children to sedition against reason their law-
15   ful sovereign. He compared reason to the sun, of which the light is
constant, uniform, and lasting; and fancy to a meteor, of bright but
transitory lustre, irregular in its motion, and delusive in its direction.

He then communicated the various precepts given from time to
20   time for the conquest of passion and displayed the happiness of
those who had obtained the important victory, after which man is
no longer the slave of fear nor the fool of hope; is no more emaciat-
ed by envy, inflamed by anger, emasculated by tenderness, or
depressed by grief; but walks on calmly through the tumults or pri-
25   vacies of life, as the sun pursues alike his course through the calm
or the stormy sky.

He enumerated many examples of heroes immovable by pain
or pleasure, who looked with indifference on those modes or acci-
dents to which the vulgar give the names of good and evil. He
30   exhorted his hearers to lay aside their prejudices and arm themselves against the shafts of malice or misfortune by invulnerable
patience; concluding that this state only was happiness, and that
this happiness was in every one's power.

Rasselas listened to him with the veneration due to the instruc-
35   tions of a superior being, and, waiting for him at the door, humbly
implored the liberty of visiting so great a master of true wisdom.
The lecturer hesitated a moment, when Rasselas put a purse of gold
into his hand, which he received with a mixture of joy and wonder.

"I have found," said the prince at his return to Imlac, "a man who can teach all that is necessary to be known, who, from the unshaken throne of rational fortitude looks down on the scenes of life changing beneath him. He speaks, and attention watches his
5   lips. He reasons, and conviction closes his periods [sentences]. This man shall be my future guide: I will learn his doctrines and imitate his life."

"Be not too hasty," said Imlac, "to trust or to admire the teachers of morality: they discourse like angels, but they live like men."
10   Rasselas, who could not conceive how any man could reason so forcibly without feeling the cogency of his own arguments, paid his visit in a few days and was denied admission. He had now learned the power of money and made his way by a piece of gold to the inner apartment where he found the philosopher in a room half
15   darkened, with eyes misty, and his face pale. "Sir," said he, "you are come at a time when all human friendship is useless; what I suffer cannot be remedied, what I have lost cannot be supplied. My daughter, my only daughter, from whose tenderness I expected all the comforts of my age, died last night of a fever. My views, my
20   purposes, my hopes are at an end: I am now a lonely being disunited from society."

"Sir," said the prince, "mortality is an event by which a wise man can never be surprised; we know that death is always near, and it should therefore always be expected."
25   "Young man," answered the philosopher, "you speak like one that has never felt the pangs of separation."

"Have you then forgot the precepts," said Rasselas, "which you so powerfully enforced? Has wisdom no strength to arm the heart against calamity? Consider that external things are naturally vari-
30   able, but truth and reason are always the same."

"What comfort," said the mourner, "can truth and reason afford me? Of what effect are they now, but to tell me that my daughter will not be restored?"

The prince, whose humanity would not suffer him to insult
35   misery with reproof, went away convinced of the emptiness of rhetorical sound and the inefficacy of polished periods and studied sentences.

CHAPTER 34: THEY RETURN TO CAIRO WITHOUT PEKUAH

There was nothing to be hoped from longer stay. They returned to Cairo repenting of their curiosity, censuring the negligence of the
40   government, lamenting their own rashness which had neglected to

procure a guard, imagining many expedients by which the loss of Pekuah might have been prevented, and resolving to do something for her recovery, though none could find any thing proper to be done.

5   Nekayah retired to her chamber, where her women attempted to comfort her by telling her that all had their troubles, and that lady Pekuah had enjoyed much happiness in the world for a long time, and might reasonably expect a change of fortune. They hoped that some good would befall her wheresoever she was, and that their
10 mistress would find another friend who might supply her place.

The princess made them no answer, and they continued the form of condolence, not much grieved in their hearts that the favourite was lost.

Next day the prince presented to the Bassa a memorial of the
15 wrong which he had suffered, and a petition for redress. The Bassa threatened to punish the robbers, but did not attempt to catch them, nor, indeed, could any account or description be given by which he might direct the pursuit.

It soon appeared that nothing would be done by authority.
20 Governors, being accustomed to hear of more crimes than they can punish, and more wrongs than they can redress, set themselves at ease by indiscriminate negligence, and presently forget the request when they lose sight of the petitioner.

Imlac then endeavoured to gain some intelligence by private
25 agents. He found many who pretended to an exact knowledge of all the haunts of the Arabs, and to regular correspondence with their chiefs, and who readily undertook the recovery of Pekuah. Of these, some were furnished with money for their journey, and came back no more; some were liberally paid for accounts which a few days
30 discovered to be false. But the princess would not suffer any means, however improbable, to be left untried. While she was doing something she kept her hope alive. As one expedient failed, another was suggested; when one messenger returned unsuccessful, another was despatched to a different quarter.

35   Two months had now passed, and of Pekuah nothing had been heard; the hopes which they had endeavoured to raise in each other grew more languid, and the princess, when she saw nothing more to be tried, sunk down inconsolable in hopeless dejection. A thousand times she reproached herself with the easy compliance by
40 which she permitted her favourite to stay behind her. "Had not my fondness," said she, "lessened my authority, Pekuah had not dared to talk of her terrors. She ought to have feared me more than spectres. A severe look would have overpowered her; a peremptory command would have compelled obedience. Why did foolish
45 indulgence prevail upon me? Why did I not speak and refuse to

hear?"

"Great princess," said Imlac, "do not reproach yourself for your virture, or consider that as blameable by which evil has accidentally been caused. Your tenderness for the timidity of Pekuah
5 was generous and kind. When we act according to our duty, we commit the event to him by whose laws our actions are governed, and who will suffer none to be finally punished for obedience. When, in prospect of some good, whether natural or moral, we break the rules prescribed us, we withdraw from the direction of
10 superior wisdom, and take all consequences upon ourselves. Man cannot so far know the connexion of causes and events as that he may venture to do wrong in order to do right. When we pursue our end by lawful means, we may always console our miscarriage by the hope of future recompense. When we consult only our own pol-
15 icy, and attempt to find a nearer way to good, by overleaping the settled boundaries of right and wrong, we cannot be happy even by success, because we cannot escape the consciousness of our fault; but, if we miscarry, the disappointment is irremediably embittered. How comfortless is the sorrow of him who feels at once the pangs
20 of guilt, and the vexation of calamity which guilt has brought upon him!

"Consider, princess, what would have been your condition, if the lady Pekuah had entreated to accompany you, and, being compelled to stay in the tents, had been carried away; or how would
25 you have borne the thought, if you had forced her into the pyramid, and she had died before you in agonies of terror."

"Had either happened," said Nekayah, "I could not have endured life till now: I should have been tortured to madness by the remembrance of such cruelty, or must have pined away in abhor-
30 rence of myself."

"This at least," said Imlac, "is the present reward of virtuous conduct, that no unlucky consequence can oblige us to repent it."

ON THE DEATH OF
DR. ROBERT LEVET

Condemned to hope's delusive mine
    As on we toil from day to day,
By sudden blasts or slow decline,
    Our social comforts drop away.

5 Well tried through many a varying year,
    See *Levet* to the grave descend;
Officious, innocent, sincere,

4. *Samuel Johnson*

Of every friendless name the friend.

Yet still he fills affection's eye,
10   Obscurely wise and coarsely kind;
Nor, lettered arrogance, deny
      Thy praise to merit unrefined.

When fainting nature called for aid,
      And hovering death prepared the blow,
15 His vigorous remedy displayed
      The power of art without the show.

In misery's darkest cavern known,
      His useful care was ever nigh,
Where hopeless anguish poured his groan,
20   And lonely want retired to die.

No summons mocked by chill delay,
      No petty gain disdained by pride,
The modest wants of every day
      The toil of every day supplied.

25 His virtues walked their narrow round,
      Nor made a pause, nor left a void;
And sure the Eternal Master found
      The single talent well employed.

The busy day, the peaceful night,
30   Unfelt, uncounted, glided by;
His frame was firm, his powers were bright,
      Though now his eightieth year was nigh.

Then with no throbbing fiery pain,
      No cold gradations of decay,
35 Death broke at once the vital chain,
      And forced his soul the nearest way.   1783

5. JEAN-JACQUES ROUSSEAU

Rousseau was and is one of the most controversial men of the eighteenth century. Although he moved within the orbit of the philosophes, *he was pulled in a new direction that would later be called Romanticism. His work exhibits considerable range: in music, in social and political theory, and in the general life of the mind. His emphasis on feeling and on his own uniqueness are typically modern. His social thought seems to elevate the individual to primacy over society; but his political thought seems to subordinate the individual to the General Will. His influence has been enormous: on the French Revolution, on Romanticism, on modernity. His* Confessions *are a deliberate secular inversion of the* Confessions *of St. Augustine.*

FROM THE CONFESSIONS
(1781)

BOOK ONE: 1712–1719

I have resolved on an enterprise which has no precedent, and which, once complete, will have no imitator. My purpose is to display to my kind a portrait in every way true to nature, and the man I shall portray will be myself.

5   Simply myself. I know my own heart and understand my fellow man. But I am made unlike any one I have ever met; I will even venture to say that I am like no one in the whole world. I may be no better, but at least I am different. Whether Nature did well or ill in breaking the mould in which she formed me, is a question which
10 can only be resolved after the reading of my book.

Let the last trump sound when it will, I shall come forward with this work in my hand, to present myself before my Sovereign Judge, and proclaim aloud: "Here is what I have done, and if by chance I have used some immaterial embellishment it has been only
15 to fill a void due to a defect of memory. I may have taken for fact what was no more than probability, but I have never put down as true what I knew to be false. I have displayed myself as I was, as vile and despicable when my behaviour was such, as good, generous, and noble when I was so. I have bared my secret soul as Thou

thyself hast seen it, Eternal Being! So let the numberless legion of my fellow men gather round me, and hear my confessions. Let them groan at my depravities, and blush for my misdeeds. But let each one of them reveal his heart at the foot of Thy throne with equal sin-
5   cerity, and may any man who dares, say 'I was a better man than he.'"

I was born at Geneva in 1712, the son of Isaac Rousseau, a citizen of that town, and Susanne Bernard, his wife. My father's inheritance, being a fifteenth part only of a very small property which
10 had been divided among as many children, was almost nothing, and he relied for his living entirely on his trade of watchmaker, at which he was very highly skilled. My mother was the daughter of a minister of religion and rather better-off. She had besides both intelligence and beauty, and my father had not found it easy to win her.
15 Their love had begun almost with their birth; at eight or nine they would walk together every evening along La Treille, and at ten they were inseparable. Sympathy and mental affinity strengthened in them a feeling first formed by habit. Both, being affectionate and sensitive by nature, were only waiting for the moment when they
20 would find similar qualities in another; or rather the moment was waiting for them, and both threw their affections at the first heart that opened to receive them. Fate, by appearing to oppose their passion, only strengthened it. Unable to obtain his mistress, the young lover ate out his heart with grief, and she counselled him to travel
25 and forget her. He traveled in vain, and returned more in love than ever, to find her he loved still faithful and fond. After such a proof, it was inevitable that they should love one another for all their lives. They swore to do so, and Heaven smiled on their vows.

Gabriel Bernard, one of my mother's brothers, fell in love with
30 one of my father's sisters, and she refused to marry him unless her brother could marry my mother at the same time. Love overcame all obstacles, and the two pairs were wedded on the same day. So it was that my uncle married my aunt, and their children became my double first cousins. Within a year both couples had a child, but at
35 the end of that time each of them was forced to separate.

My uncle Bernard, who was an engineer, went to serve in the Empire and Hungary under Prince Eugène, and distinguished himself at the siege and battle of Belgrade. My father, after the birth of my only brother, left for Constantinople, where he had been called
40 to become watchmaker to the Sultan's Seraglio. While he was away my mother's beauty, wit, and talents brought her admirers, one of the most pressing of whom was M. de la Closure, the French Resident in the city. His feelings must have been very strong, for thirty years later I have seen him moved when merely speaking to
45 me about her. But my mother had more than her virtue with which

to defend herself; she deeply loved my father, and urged him to come back. He threw up everything to do so, and I was the unhappy fruit of his return. For ten months later I was born, a poor and sickly child, and cost my mother her life. So my birth was the first
5   of my misfortunes.

     I never knew how my father stood up to his loss, but I know that he never got over it. He seemed to see her again in me, but could never forget that I robbed him of her; he never kissed me that I did not know by his sighs and his convulsive embrace that there
10 was a bitter grief mingled with his affection, a grief which nevertheless intensified his feeling for me. When he said to me, "Jean-Jacques, let us talk of your mother," I would reply: "Very well, father, but we are sure to cry." "Ah," he would say with a groan; "Give her back to me, console me for her, fill the void she has left in
15 my heart! Should I love you so if you were not more to me than a son?" Forty years after he lost her he died in the arms of a second wife, but with his first wife's name on his lips, and her picture imprinted upon his heart.

     Such were my parents. And of all the gifts with which Heaven
20 endowed them, they left me but one, a sensitive heart. It had been the making of their happiness, but for me it has been the cause of all the misfortunes in my life.

     I was almost born dead, and they had little hope of saving me. I brought with me the seed of a disorder which has grown stronger
25 with the years, and now gives me only occasional intervals of relief in which to suffer more painfully in some other way. But one of my father's sisters, a nice sensible woman, bestowed such care on me that I survived; and now, as I write this, she is still alive at the age of eighty, nursing a husband rather younger than herself but ruined
30 by drink. My dear aunt, I pardon you for causing me to live, and I deeply regret that I cannot repay you in the evening of your days all the care and affection you lavished on me at the dawn of mine. My nurse Jacqueline is still alive too, and healthy and strong. Indeed the fingers that opened my eyes at birth may well close them at my
35 death.

     I felt before I thought: which is the common lot of man, though more pronounced in my case than in another's. I know nothing of myself till I was five or six. I do not know how I learnt to read. I only remember my first books and their effect upon me; it is from my
40 earliest reading that I date the unbroken consciousness of my own existence. My mother had possessed some novels, and my father and I began to read them after supper. At first it was only to give me some practice in reading. But soon my interest in this entertaining literature became so strong that we read by turns continuously, and
45 spent whole nights so engaged. For we could never leave off till the

end of the book. Sometimes my father would say with shame as we heard the morning larks: "Come, let us go to bed. I am more of a child than you are."

In a short time I acquired by this dangerous method, not only
5 an extreme facility in reading and expressing myself, but a singular insight for my age into the passions. I had no idea of the facts, but I was already familiar with every feeling. I had grasped nothing; I had sensed everything. These confused emotions which I experienced one after another, did not warp my reasoning powers in any
10 way, for as yet I had none. But they shaped them after a special pattern, giving me the strangest and most romantic notions about human life, which neither experience nor reflection has ever succeeded in curing me of.

* * *

... So I have spent my days in silent longing in the presence of
15 those I most loved. I never dared to reveal my strange taste, but at least I got some pleasure from situations which pandered to the thought of it. To fall on my knees before a masterful mistress, to obey her commands, to have to beg for her forgiveness, have been to me the most delicate of pleasures; and the more my vivid imagi-
20 nation heated my blood the more like a spellbound lover I looked. As can be imagined, this way of making love does not lead to rapid progress, and is not very dangerous to the virtue of the desired object. Consequently I have possessed few women, but I have not failed to get a great deal of satisfaction in my own way, that is to say
25 imaginatively. So it is that my sensibility, combined with my timidity and my romantic nature, have preserved the purity of my feelings and my morals, by the aid of those same tastes which might, with a little more boldness, have plunged me into the most brutal sensuality.

* * *

30 My passions are extremely strong, and while I am under their sway nothing can equal my impetuosity. I am amenable to no restraint, respect, fear, or decorum. I am cynical, bold, violent, and daring. No shame can stop me, no fear of danger alarm me. Except for the one object in my mind the universe for me is non-existent.
35 But all this lasts only a moment; and the next moment plunges me into complete annihilation. Catch me in a calm mood, I am all indolence and timidity. Everything alarms me, everything discourages me. I am frightened by a buzzing fly. I am too lazy to speak a word or make a gesture. So much am I a slave to fears and shames that I
40 long to vanish from mortal sight. If action is necessary I do not know what to do; if I must speak I do not know what to say; if anyone looks at me I drop my eyes. When roused by passion, I can sometimes find the right words to say, but in ordinary conversation

I can find none, none at all. I find conversation unbearable owing to the very fact that I am obliged to speak.

Furthermore, none of my dominant desires are for things that can be bought. All I need are simple pleasures, and money poisons
5 them all. I am fond, for example, of a good meal, but cannot stand the boredom of polite company or the gross manners of an inn. I can only enjoy eating with a friend; when I am alone it is impossible, because my imagination is always busy with something else and I take no pleasure in my food. If the fire in my blood demands
10 women, the emotion in my heart cries more loudly for love. Women who could be bought would lose all their charm with me. I doubt whether I could even take advantage of the situation. It is the same with all pleasures within my reach. If they are not to be had for nothing, they have no attraction for me. The only things I like are
15 things that belong to no one but the first person who knows how to enjoy them. . . . .

*　*　*

. . . I love liberty; I hate embarrassment, worry, and constraint. So long as the money lasts in my purse, it assures me of independence and relieves me of the need of plotting to obtain more, a need
20 which has always appalled me. So afraid am I to see it end that I treasure it. Money in one's possession is the instrument of liberty; money one pursues is the symbol of servitude. That is why I hold fast to what I have, but covet no more.

My disinterestedness, therefore, is a sign of indolence; the
25 pleasure of possession is not worth the trouble involved in acquisition. And my mad spending is a sign of indolence too; when the occasion for spending agreeably arises, too much use cannot be made of it. I am less tempted by money than by things, because between money and the desired object there is always an interme-
30 diary, whereas between a thing and its enjoyment, there is none. If I see something, it tempts me. But if all I see is the way of acquiring it, I am not tempted. I have been a thief, and sometimes I still steal trifles that tempt me, and that I had rather take than ask for. But, in youth or age, I do not remember ever having taken a farthing from
35 anyone, except on one occasion, almost fifteen years ago, when I stole seven *livres* ten *sous*. . . .

*　*　*

. . . Since my imagination was rich enough to embellish any state with illusions, and powerful enough to transport me, so to speak, according to my whim, from one state to another, it mattered
40 very little to me in what walk of life I actually was. Never mind how great the distance between my position and the nearest castle in Spain, I had no difficulty in taking up residence there. It followed, therefore, that the simplest of situations, the one that demanded the

least trouble and exertion, the one that left the mind most free, was the most suitable for me; and that was precisely the situation I was then in. I should have passed a calm and peaceful life in the security of my faith, in my own country, among my family and friends.

5　That was what my peculiar character required, a life spent in the uniform pursuit of a trade I had chosen, and in a society after my own heart. I should have been a good Christian, a good citizen, a good father, a good friend, a good workman, a good man in every way. I should have been happy in my condition, and should per-

10　haps have been respected. Then, after a life—simple and obscure, but also mild and uneventful—I should have died peacefully in the bosom of my family. Soon, no doubt, I should have been forgotten, but at least I should have been mourned for as long as I was remembered.

15　But instead . . . what a picture I have to paint! But do not let us anticipate the miseries of my life. I shall have only too much to say to my readers on that melancholy subject.

BOOK TWO: 1728–1731

* * *

My father was not only an honorable man, but was a man of scrupulous integrity, and possessed that strength of mind that

20　makes for true virtue. What is more he was a good father, at least to me. He loved me very dearly, but he also loved his pleasures, and other affections had somewhat cooled his paternal feelings since I had been living away. He had married again at Nyon; and though his wife was no longer of an age to give me brothers, she had rela-

25　tions; and that made another family, other surroundings, and a new household, which caused him to think of me less often. My father was aging, and had not the means to support his old age. My brother and I had inherited some property from my mother, the income from which would fall to my father in our absence. The thought of

30　this did not affect him directly, or prevent his doing his duty. But it acted upon him obscurely without his being conscious of it himself and sometimes restrained his zeal, which otherwise would have been more extreme. That, I think, is the reason why, having traced me as far as Annecy, he did not pursue me to Chambéry, where he

35　was morally certain to catch me up. That is the reason why, though I have often been to see him since I ran away, and have always been received with paternal affection, he has never made any great effort to keep me with him.

This behavior in a father of whose goodness and affection I am

40　convinced, has caused me to reflect on my own conduct; and my reflections have had no small share in preserving the integrity of my conduct. They have taught me one great maxim of morality, the only one perhaps which is of practical use: to avoid situations which place our duties in opposition to our interests, and show us

5   where another man's loss spells profit to us. For I am sure that, in such situations, however sincere and virtuous the motives we start with, sooner or later and unconsciously we weaken, and become wicked and unjust in practice, though still remaining good and just in our hearts.

10   I have carried this maxim firmly imprinted on my heart and applied it, although somewhat late in the day, to all my conduct. It has been one of the principal causes, indeed, of my seeming so foolish and strange in public, particularly in the eyes of my acquaintances. I have been accused of trying to be original and of acting

15   unlike other people, though really I have hardly even thought whether I was acting like others or unlike them. My sincere wish has been to do what was right, and I have strenuously avoided all situations which might set my interests in opposition to some other man's, and cause me, even despite myself, to wish him ill.

* * *

20   . . . I have loved with too much sincerity—too perfectly, I might even say—to attain easy success. No passions were ever at once so pure and so strong as mine. Never was love more tender, genuine, and disinterested. On countless occasions I would have sacrificed my happiness to that of the woman I loved. Her reputation has been

25   dearer to me than my life, and never for all the joys of gratification have I been willing to risk her peace of mind for a single moment. Therefore I have brought so much care, so much secrecy, and so many precautions to my affairs that not one of them has ever been successful. My lack of success with women has always come from

30   loving them too much.

* * *

But alas, I have not said all that I have to say about my time at Mme de Vercellis's. For though my condition was apparently unchanged I did not leave her house as I had entered it. I took away with me lasting memories of a crime and the unbearable weight of

35   a remorse which, even after forty years, still burdens my conscience. In fact the bitter memory of it, far from fading, grows more painful with the years. Who would suppose that a child's wickedness could have such cruel results? It is for these only two probable consequences that I can find no consolation. I may have ruined a nice,

40   honest, and decent girl, who was certainly worth a great deal more than I, and doomed her to disgrace and misery.

It is almost inevitable that the breaking up of an establishment should cause some confusion in the house, and that various things

should be mislaid. But so honest were the servants and so vigilant were M. and Mme Lorenzi that nothing was found missing when the inventory was taken. Only Mlle Pontal lost a little pink and silver ribbon, which was quite old. Plenty of better things were with-
5   in my reach, but this ribbon alone tempted me. I stole it, and as I hardly troubled to conceal it it was soon found. They inquired how I had got hold of it. I grew confused, stammered, and finally said with a blush that it was Marion who had given it to me. Marion was a young girl from the Maurienne whom Mme de Vercellis had taken
10 as her cook when she had ceased to give dinners and had discharged her chef, since she had more need of good soup than of fine stews. Marion was not only pretty. She had that fresh complexion that one never finds except in the mountains, and such a sweet and modest air that one had only to see her to love her. What is more she
15 was a good girl, sensible and absolutely trustworthy. They were extremely surprised when I mentioned her name. But they had no less confidence in me than in her, and decided that it was important to find which of us was a thief. She was sent for, to face a considerable number of people, including the Comte de la Roque himself.
20 When she came she was shown the ribbon. I boldly accused her. She was confused, did not utter a word, and threw me a glance that would have disarmed the devil, but my cruel heart resisted. In the end she firmly denied the theft. But she did not get indignant. She merely turned to me, and begged me to remember myself and not
25 disgrace an innocent girl who had never done me any harm. But, with infernal impudence, I repeated my accusation, and declared to her face that she had given me the ribbon. The poor girl started to cry, but all she said to me was, 'Oh, Rousseau, I thought you were a good fellow. You make me very sad, but I should not like to be in
30 your place.' That is all. She continued to defend herself with equal firmness and sincerity, but never allowed herself any reproaches against me. This moderation, contrasted with my decided tone, prejudiced her case. It did not seem natural to suppose such diabolical audacity on one side and such angelic sweetness on the
35 other. They seemed unable to come to a definite decision, but they were prepossessed in my favour. In the confusion of the moment they had not time to get to the bottom of the business; and the Comte de la Roque, in dismissing us both, contented himself with saying that the guilty one's conscience would amply avenge the
40 innocent. His prediction was not wide of the mark. Not a day passes on which it is not fulfilled.

     I do not know what happened to the victim of my calumny, but she cannot possibly have found it easy to get a good situation after that. The imputation against her honor was cruel in every respect.
45 The theft was only a trifle, but after all, it was a theft and, what is

worse, had been committed in order to lead a boy astray. Theft, lying and obstinacy—what hope was there for a girl in whom so many vices were combined? I do not even consider misery and friendlessness the worst dangers to which she was exposed. Who

5   can tell to what extremes the depressed feeling of injured innocence might have carried her at her age? And if my remorse at having perhaps made her unhappy is unbearable, what can be said of my grief at perhaps having made her worse than myself?

This cruel memory troubles me at times and so disturbs me that

10   in my sleepless hours I see this poor girl coming to reproach me for my crime, as if I had committed it only yesterday. So long as I have lived in peace it has tortured me less, but in the midst of a stormy life it deprives me of that sweet consolation which the innocent feel under persecution. It brings home to me indeed what I think I have

15   written in one of my books, that remorse sleeps while fate is kind but grows sharp in adversity. Nevertheless I have never been able to bring myself to relieve my heart by revealing this in private to a friend. Not with the most intimate friend, not even with Mme de Warens, has this been possible. The most that I could do was to con-

20   fess that I had a terrible deed on my conscience, but I have never said in what it consisted. The burden, therefore, has rested till this day on my conscience without any relief; and I can affirm that the desire to some extent to rid myself of it has greatly contributed to my resolution of writing these *Confessions*.

25   I have been absolutely frank in the account I have just given, and no one will accuse me, I am certain, of palliating the heinousness of my offence. But I should not fulfil the aim of this book if I did not at the same time reveal my inner feelings and hesitated to put up such excuses for myself as I honestly could. Never was

30   deliberate wickedness further from my intention than at that cruel moment. When I accused that poor girl, it is strange but true that my friendship for her was the cause. She was present in my thoughts, and I threw the blame on the first person who occurred to me. I accused her of having done what I intended to do myself. I

35   said that she had given the ribbon to me because I meant to give it to her. When afterwards I saw her in the flesh my heart was torn. But the presence of all those people prevailed over my repentance. I was not much afraid of punishment, I was only afraid of disgrace. But I feared more than death, more than crime, more than anything

40   in the world. I should have rejoiced if the earth had swallowed me up and stifled me in the abyss. But my invincible sense of shame prevailed over everything. It was my shame that made me impudent, and the more wickedly I behaved the bolder my fear of confession made me. I saw nothing but the horror of being found out,

45   of being publicly proclaimed, to my face, as a thief, a liar, and a slan-

derer. Utter confusion robbed me of all other feeling. If I had been allowed time to come to my senses, I should most certainly have admitted everything. If M. de la Roque had taken me aside and said: 'Do not ruin that poor girl. If you are guilty tell me so,' I should

5   immediately have thrown myself at his feet, I am perfectly sure. But all they did was to frighten me, when what I needed was encouragement. My age also should be taken into account. I was scarcely more than a child. Indeed I still was one. In youth real crimes are even more reprehensible than in riper years; but what is no more

10   than weakness is much less blameworthy, and really my crime amounted to no more than weakness. So the memory tortures me less on account of the crime itself than because of its possible evil consequences. But I have derived some benefit from the terrible impression left with me by the sole offence I have committed. For it

15   has secured me for the rest of my life against any act that might prove criminal in its results. I think also that my loathing of untruth derives to a large extent from my having told that one wicked lie. If this is a crime that can be expiated, as I venture to believe, it must have been atoned for by all the misfortunes that have crowded the

20   end of my life, by forty years of honest and upright behaviour under difficult circumstances. Poor Marion finds so many avengers in this world that, however great my offence against her may have been, I have little fear of carrying the sin on my conscience at death. . . .

BOOK THREE: 1731–1732

* * *

25   In me are united two almost irreconcilable characteristics, though in what way I cannot imagine. I have a passionate temperament, and lively and headstrong emotions. Yet my thoughts arise slowly and confusedly, and are never ready till too late. It is as if my heart and my brain did not belong to the same person. Feelings

30   come quicker than lightning and fill my soul, but they bring me no illumination; they burn me and dazzle me. I feel everything and I see nothing; I am excited but stupid; if I want to think I must be cool. The astonishing thing is, though, that I have considerable tact, some understanding, and a certain skill with people so long as they

35   will wait for me. I can make excellent replies impromptu, if I have a moment to think, but on the spur of the moment I can never say or do anything right. I could conduct a most delightful conversation by post, as they say the Spaniards play chess. When I read the story

40   of that Duke of Savoy who turned round on his homeward journey to cry, "Mind out, my fine Paris merchant!" I recognize myself.

But I do not suffer from this combination of quick emotion and

slow thoughts only in company. I know it too when I am alone and
when I am working. Ideas take shape in my head with the most
incredible difficulty. They go round in dull circles and ferment, agi-
tating me and overheating me till my heart palpitates. During this
5   stir of emotion I can see nothing clearly, and cannot write a word; I
have to wait. Insensibly all this tumult grows quiet, the chaos sub-
sides, and everything falls into place, but slowly, and after long and
confused perturbations. . . .

* * *

. . . The view of the Lake of Geneva and its lovely shores had
10 always a particular attraction in my eyes, which I cannot explain
and which does not depend only on the beauty of the sight, but on
something more compelling which moves and stimulates me. Every
time I visit the Canton of Vaud, I experience an impression composed of memories of Mme de Warens, who was born there, of my
15 father, who lived there, of Mlle de Vulson who reaped the first fruits
of my love, of several expeditions I made in my childhood and of
some from another source still more secret and still more powerful
than all those. When a burning desire for that mild and happy existence which eludes me and for which I was born, comes to fire my
20 imagination, it is always associated with the Canton of Vaud, with
its lake shores and its lovely countryside. I cannot live without an
orchard on the shores of that lake, and no other; I must have a constant friend, a charming wife, a cow, and a little boat. I shall not
enjoy perfect happiness upon earth until I have all these. I am
25 amused by the simplicity with which I have gone several times to
that country solely to seek that imaginary happiness. Each time I
have been surprised to find its inhabitants, particularly its women,
of an entirely different character from that which I had expected.
What an anomaly this seemed to me! The country and the people
30 who inhabit it have never seemed to me to have been made for one
another.

On this trip to Vevay, walking along that lovely shore, I gave
myself up to the sweetest of melancholy. My heart darted eagerly
after a thousand innocent delights. I indulged my feelings. I sighed
35 and cried like a child. How often I would stop to weep at my leisure
and, sitting on a large stone, would be amused to see my tears fall
into the water!

* * *

How greatly did my first sight of Paris belie the idea I had
formed of it! The exterior decoration that I had seen at Turin, the
40 beauty of the streets, the symmetry and alignment of the houses,
had led me to expect something even finer in Paris. I had imagined
a city of a most imposing appearance, as beautiful as it was large,
where nothing was to be seen but splendid streets and palaces of

marble or gold. As I entered through the Faubourg Saint-Marceau, I saw nothing but dirty, stinking little streets, ugly black houses, a general air of squalor and poverty, beggars, carters, menders of clothes, sellers of herb drinks and old hats. All this so affected me at
5   the outset that all the real magnificence I have since seen in Paris has not been sufficient to efface my first impression, and I have always retained a secret aversion against living in the capital. I may say that all the time I did, subsequently, reside there was entirely devoted to seeking means which would enable me to live else-
10 where. Such is the fruit of an over-lively imagination, which exaggerates beyond the common measure and always sees more than it is told to expect. I had heard such praise of Paris that I had imagined it like ancient Babylon, which, had I visited it, I should no doubt have found falling equally short of the picture I had formed
15 of it. The same thing happened to me at the opera, which I hastened to visit on the day after my arrival; the same thing happened to me later at Versailles; and later still when I saw the sea; and the same thing will always happen to me when I see sights of which I have heard too much. For it is impossible for men, and difficult for
20 Nature herself, to surpass the riches of my imagination.

* * *

BOOK SEVEN: 1741

After two years of patient silence, in spite of my resolutions I take up the pen once more. Suspend your judgement, reader, as to the reasons that force me to it. You cannot judge them till you have read me to the end.
25 You have seen my peaceful youth flow by in a uniform and pleasant enough way, without great set-backs or remarkable spells of prosperity. This middling state of things was largely the result of my ardent but feeble nature, which was more easily discouraged than roused to activity, which quitted its repose when rudely
30 shocked but soon relapsed into it again out of lassitude and natural inclination, and which, whilst keeping me far from the great virtues and even farther from the great vices, always brought me back to the quiet and idle life for which I felt I had been born, never allowing me to achieve anything of importance, either good or bad.
35 What a different picture I shall soon have to fill in! After favouring my wishes for thirty years, for the next thirty fate opposed them; and from this continual opposition between my situation and my desires will be seen to arise great mistakes, incredible misfortunes, and every virtue that can do credit to adversity
40 except strength of character.
My first part has been entirely written from memory, and I

must have made many mistakes in it. Being compelled to write the second from memory also, I shall now probably make still more. The sweet memories of my best years, passed in equal innocence and calm, have left me a thousand charming impressions that I love
5   ceaselessly to recall. It will speedily be seen how different are the recollections of the rest of my life. To recall them is to relive their bitterness. Far from increasing the painfulness of my situation by such sad retrospects, I dismiss them in so far as I can; and I often succeed so well that I cannot recapture them when I need them. This ease
10 with which I forget misfortunes is a consolation contrived for me by Heaven in the midst of all those evils that fate was one day to pile upon my head. Since my memory calls up only pleasant objects, it acts as the happy counterpoise to my fearful imagination, which makes me foresee nothing in the future but cruel disasters.
15   The papers that I had collected to make good the defects in my memory and to guide me in this undertaking have all passed into other hands and will never return into mine. I have only one faithful guide on which I can count; the succession of feelings which have marked the development of my being, and thereby recall the
20 events that have acted upon it as cause or effect. I easily forget my misfortunes, but I cannot forget my faults, and still less my genuine feelings. The memory of them is too dear ever to be effaced from my heart. I may omit or transpose facts, or make mistakes in dates; but I cannot go wrong about what I have felt, or about what my feelings
25 have led me to do; and these are the chief subjects of my story. The true object of my confessions is to reveal my inner thoughts exactly in all situations of my life. It is the history of my soul that I have promised to recount, and to write it faithfully I have need of no other memories; it is enough if I enter again into my inner self, as I
30 have done till now.

* * *

BOOK EIGHT: 1750–1752

In the following year (1750) when I had given up thinking about my essay I learned that it had won the prize at Dijon. The news reawakened all the ideas that it had suggested to me, endowed them with fresh vigour, and set that first leavening of
35 heroism and virtue working in my heart that my father, my native land, and Plutarch had implanted there in my childhood. I could no longer see any greatness or beauty except in being free and virtuous, superior to fortune and man's opinion, and independent of all external circumstances. Although false shame and a fear of oppro-
40 brium prevented me at first from acting on these principles and from openly defying the conventions of my age, my mind was made up from that moment, and I only delayed the execution of my

resolve until such time as contradiction provoked it and rendered it victorious.

Whilst I was philosophizing on the duties of man an event occurred which made me reflect more deeply upon my own. Thérèse became pregnant for the third time. Too sincere with myself, too proud in my heart, to be willing to belie my principles by my actions, I began to consider the fate of my children and my relationship with their mother, by reference to the laws of nature, justice, and reason, and of that religion—pure, sacred, and eternal as its Author—which men have soiled whilst pretending they were trying to purify it, and which they have turned by their formulas into no more than a religion of words, seeing that it is not costly to prescribe the impossible if you excuse yourself from performing it.

If I was mistaken in my conclusions, nothing can be more remarkable than the calm spirit in which I surrendered to them. If I were one of those low-born men, deaf to the gentle voice of Nature, a man in whose breast no real feeling of justice and humanity ever arose, this hardness of heart would have been quite easy to explain. But my warm-heartedness, my acute sensibility, the ease with which I formed friendships, the hold they exercised over me, and the cruel wrench when they had to be broken; my innate goodwill towards my fellow men; my burning love for the great, the true, the beautiful, and the just; my horror of evil in every form, my inability to hate, to hurt, or even to wish to; that softening, that sharp and sweet emotion I feel at the sight of all that is virtuous, generous, and lovable: is it possible that all these can ever dwell in the same soul along with depravity which, quite unscrupulously, tramples the dearest of obligations underfoot? No, I feel, and boldly declare—it is impossible. Never for a moment in his life could Jean-Jacques have been a man without feelings or compassion, an unnatural father. I may have been mistaken, but I could never be callous. If I were to state my reasons, I should say too much. For since they were strong enough to seduce me, they would seduce many others; and I do not wish to expose any young people who may read me to the risk of being misled by the same error. I will be content with a general statement that in handing my children over for the State to educate, for lack of means to bring them up myself, by destining them to become workers and peasants instead of adventurers and fortune-hunters, I thought I was acting as a citizen and a father, and looked upon myself as a member of Plato's Republic. More than once since then the regret in my heart has told me that I was wrong. But far from my reason having told me the same story, I have often blessed Heaven for having thus safeguarded them from their father's fate, and from that which would have overtaken them at the moment when I should have been compelled to abandon them.

If I had left them to Mme d'Épinay or to Mme de Luxembourg who, out of friendship or generosity, or from some other motive, offered to take charge of them at a later date, would they have been happier, would they have been brought up at least as honest people? I do
5   not know; but I am sure that they would have been led to hate, and perhaps to betray, their parents. It is a hundred times better that they have never known them.

     My third child, therefore was taken to the Foundling Hospital like all the others, and the next two were disposed of in the same
10 way, for I had five in all. This arrangement seemed so good and sensible and right to me that if I did not boast of it openly it was solely out of regard for their mother. But I told everyone whom I had told of our relationship; I told Diderot and Grimm. Later I informed Mme d'Épinay, and still later Mme de Luxembourg, and this freely,
15 frankly, and under no kind of compulsion, at a time when I might easily have concealed the matter from everybody; for Mlle Gouin was an honest woman and most discreet, and I could utterly rely upon her. The only one of my friends in whom I had some reason to confide was Thierry the doctor, who attended my poor 'aunt' in one
20 of her confinements during which she was very ill. In a word, I made no mystery about my conduct, not only because I have never been able to conceal anything from my friends, but because I really saw nothing wrong in it. All things considered, I made the best choice for my children, or what I thought was the best. I could have
25 wished, and still do wish, that I had been brought up and nurtured as they have been.

     Whilst I made my confidences in my way, Mme Le Vasseur did the same in hers, but from far less disinterested motives. I had introduced her and her daughter to Mme Dupin, who out of friendship
30 to me had done them many kindnesses. The mother let her into the daughter's secret. Mme Dupin is kind and generous, and Mme Le Vasseur did not tell her how carefully I provided for everything despite the modesty of my resources. She therefore made some provision herself with a liberality which Thérèse always concealed
35 from me, on her mother's orders, all the while I was in Paris, and which she only admitted to me at the Hermitage, as a sequel to several other confessions. I did not know that Mme Dupin, who never showed the least sign of being so, was so well informed; and I do not know to this day whether her daughter-in-law, Mme de
40 Chenonceaux, knew also. But Mme de Francueil, her stepdaughter, certainly did and could not keep quiet. She talked about it to me in the next year, when I had already left their house. This compelled me to write her a letter on the subject, which will be found in my collection. In it I reveal such of my reasons as I could give without
45 compromising Mme Le Vasseur and her family; for the most deci-

sive of them came from that quarter, and about those I was silent.

I can rely on Mme Dupin's discretion and on Mme de Chenonceaux's friendship; I was also able to trust Mme de Francueil who, anyhow, died long before my secret was noised abroad. It could never have been disclosed except by those in whom I had confided, and indeed it was not until after my break with them that it became public. By that fact alone they are judged. Without wishing to disown the blame which I deserve, I would rather have that on my conscience than have to answer, like them, for sheer maliciousness. My fault is great, but it was an error; I neglected my duties, but the desire to do harm never entered my head, and a father's feelings cannot speak very loudly for children he has never seen. But to betray a friend's confidences, to violate the most sacred of all bonds, to publish secrets entrusted to our bosom, deliberately to dishonour the friends we have deceived and who still respect us as they say good-bye—those are not faults; they are utter baseness and infamy.

I have promised to write my confessions, but not to make my apologies; so I will stop here. My duty is to tell the truth; my readers' to be just, and that is all that I shall ever ask of them.

* * *

. . . Precipitated against my will into the world without possessing its manners, and in no state to learn them or conform to them, I decided to adopt manners of my own which would excuse me from the necessity. Since my foolish and tiresome silence, which I could not overcome, arose from my fear of making social blunders I elected, in order to give myself courage, to trample all courtesies underfoot. I became cynical and sarcastic out of awkwardness, and affected to despise the manners I did not know how to practise. It is true that, to harmonize this rudeness with my new principles, I embodied it in my mind until it assumed the shape of dauntless virtue; and it is because of this exalted basis, I venture to assert, that it persisted more strongly and for a longer time than might have been expected of a behaviour so contrary to my nature. However, despite the misanthropic reputation which my appearance and a few happy phrases gained for me in the world, in private I always sustained the part badly. Certainly my friends and acquaintances led this unsociable bear around like a lamb. I limited my sarcasms to unwelcome but general truths, and never could say an unkind word to anybody.

* * *

BOOK NINE: 1756

So impatient was I to live at the Hermitage that I could not wait
for the return of the fine weather; and as soon as my quarters were
ready I hastily moved in amidst the loud derision of the Holbach
circle, who loudly predicted that I should not be able to stand three
5 months of solitude, and that in a little while they would see me
come back with my tail between my legs to live like them in Paris.
For my part, having been out of my element for fifteen years and
finding myself now on the point of returning to it, I did not even
pay any attention to their jeers. Ever since I had unwillingly
10 plunged into the world I had not ceased to regret my dear
Charmettes and the pleasant life I had led there. I felt that I was
born for retirement and the country; it was impossible for me to live
happily anywhere else. At Venice amidst the stir of public business,
in a dignified and more or less diplomatic position, and proud in
15 my hopes of promotion; at Paris, in the whirl of high society, at luxurious suppers, amidst the glitter of the theatre, in a cloud of vain-
glory; always the memory of my woods and streams and solitary
walks would come to distract and sadden me, and draw from me
sighs of longing and desire. None of the labours to which I had been
20 able to subject myself, none of the ambitious projects which had fit-
fully roused my energy, had any other purpose but that one day I
should enjoy the happy rural ease which I now flattered myself I
was on the point of attaining. Although I had not acquired the honest independence which I had thought alone might lead me to it, I
25 considered that my peculiar situation enabled me to dispense with
it and that I might arrive at the same end by an entirely opposite
way. I had not the slightest income; but I had a name and talents. I
was temperate and had rid myself of my expensive wants—all
those that depended upon public opinion. Moreover, although lazy,
30 I was industrious when I wished to be and my indolence was not so
much that of an idler as of an independent man, who only likes to
work in his own time. My trade of music-copying was neither brilliant nor lucrative; but it was certain. The world approved my
courage in having chosen it. I could reckon never to be short of
35 work, and if I worked hard I could earn enough to live on. Two
thousand francs which remained over from the profits of *The Village
Soothsayer* and of my other writings left me sufficient reserves to
prevent my being pushed for money; and several works which
were then in hand promised me sufficient in addition, without
40 resort to the booksellers, to enable me to work in peace without
exhausting myself, and even to profit from my leisure and my
walks. My little household, made up of three people, all usefully
employed, was not very costly to keep up. Indeed my resources,

being proportionate to my needs and my desires, might reasonably promise me a long and happy life in the condition that my tastes had led me to choose.

* * *

. . . Although for some years I had fairly frequently gone into
5 the country, I had hardly tasted its pleasures. Indeed my trips, generally made in the company of pretentious people and always ruined by a feeling of constraint, had merely whetted my appetite for rural delights; the closer the glimpse I got of them the more I felt the want of them. I was so tired of reception rooms, fountains,
10 shrubberies, and flower-beds, and of those most tiresome people who made a show of them; I was so weary of pamphlets, clavichords, wool-sorting, and making knots, of stupid witticisms and tedious affections, of tellers of little tales and great suppers, that when I spied a poor simple thorn bush, a hedge, a barn, or a mead-
15 ow, when walking through a village I smelt a good chervil omelette, when I heard in the distance the rustic refrain of the goat-women's song, I consigned all rouge, flounces, and perfumes to the devil, and in my longing for the housewife's dinner and the local wine, I would gladly have slapped the faces of the chef and his master for
20 making me dine at the hour I take my supper, and sup at the hour when I go to bed. But even more gladly would I have slapped the footmen who feasted their eyes on what I ate and compelled me, if I was not to die of thirst, to buy their master's doctored wine from them at ten times the price I should have had to pay for better drink
25 at an inn.

Here I was then at last, at home in a pleasant and solitary retreat, at liberty to pass my days in this independent, unvarying, and peaceful life for which I felt I was born. Before I record the effect of this unprecedented state of things upon my heart I must recapit-
30 ulate and tell once more of my secret affections, so that the effect of my new change of circumstances may be traced to its source.

I have always regarded the day which united me to my Thérèse as the one that determined my moral being. I needed an attachment, for the one that should have sufficed me had been so cruelly broken.
35 The longing for happiness is never quenched in the heart of a man. Mamma was ageing and deteriorating. I saw clearly that she could never be happy again on earth. I was left to seek a happiness of my own, having lost all hope of ever sharing hers. I drifted for some time from idea to idea, from plan to plan. My journey to Venice
40 would have launched me into public life if the man with whom I tied myself up had possessed any commonsense. I am easily discouraged, particularly in difficult and lengthy enterprises. My failure in that one put me off all others; and since, following my old maxim, I looked on distant objectives as decoys for fools, I deter-

mined to live henceforth from day to day, and no longer saw anything in life that tempted me to strain after it.

It was at that precise moment that we came to know one another. That good girl's sweet nature seemed to me so well suited to my
5   own that I joined myself to her in an attachment that has defied time
and injuries. Indeed, every trial that might have broken it has only
served to make it stronger. The strength of this attachment will
appear in the sequel when I will reveal the wounds and heart-burn-
ings which I suffered for her when my miseries were at their height,
10 without a word of complaint to anyone ever passing my lips up to
the moment of my writing these lines.

When it becomes known that after having made every effort
and braved every danger in order not to be parted from her, after
having lived with her for twenty-five years in defiance of fate and
15 mankind, I finally married her in my old age, without any expectation or entreaties on her part or any engagement or promise on
mine, it may be supposed that a mad passion turned my head from
the first day and led me by degrees to this last extravagance: a
hypothesis which will appear even more credible when the special
20 and powerful reasons are known which should have prevented me
from ever reaching that point. What will the reader think when I tell
him, with all the sincerity that he has come to expect of me, that
from the first moment I saw her till this day I have never felt the
least glimmering of love for her; that I no more desired to possess
25 her than I had desired Mme de Warens, and that the sensual needs
I satisfied with her were for me purely sexual and had nothing to do
with her as an individual? He will believe that I was not made like
other men, and that I was incapable of feeling love, since love did
not enter into the feelings that attached me to the woman who has
30 been dearest to me. Patience, my dear reader, the fatal moment is
approaching when you will be only too rudely undeceived.

I am repeating myself, and I know it; but it is necessary. The
first, the greatest, the strongest, the most inextinguishable of all my
needs was entirely one of the heart. It was the need for intimate
35 companionship, for a companionship as intimate as possible, which
was the chief reason why I needed a woman rather than a man, a
woman friend rather than a man friend. This singular need was
such that the most intimate physical union could not fulfil it; only
two souls in the same body would have sufficed. Failing that, I
40 always felt a void. I believed that the moment had come when I
should feel it no longer. This young person who had so many qualities to make her lovable—even good looks at that time—and was
without a trace of artifice or coquetry, would have absorbed my
whole existence within herself if I could have absorbed hers in me,
45 as I had hoped. I had nothing to fear so far as other men were con-

cerned. I am sure that I am the only one she has truly loved, and so cool are her passions that she has seldom felt the want of a man even when I have ceased to be one for her in that respect. Unlike myself, she had a family, every member of which so differed from
5   her in character that it was impossible for me to adopt them as my own. Therein lay the first cause of my misfortunes. What would I not have given to be a son to her mother? I did all I could to that end, but I never succeeded. It was in vain that I tried to unite all our interests; it was impossible. Mme Le Vasseur always set up interests
10   that differed from mine, that were opposite to mine, and even to her daughter's, which were already inseparable from mine. She and her other children and grandchildren became so many bloodsuckers, and the least injury they did to Thérèse was to steal from her. The poor girl, accustomed to give in, even to her nieces, allowed herself
15   to be robbed and ordered about without saying a word; and I saw to my distress that though I lavished money and advice upon her I could do nothing to help her. I tried to get her away from her mother; she always resisted. I respected her reluctance and esteemed her the more for it, but her refusal was none the less harmful to her
20   interests and mine. In the power of her mother and her family, she was more theirs than mine, belonged to them more than to herself. Their greed was ruinous to her, but even more pernicious was their advice. In short, if thanks to her love for me and her own good character she was not completely their slave, she was so at least to the
25   extent that the good principles I endeavored to instil into her were largely deprived of their effect, and that never mind what efforts I made to overcome it, we always remained separate people.

So it was that in a sincere and mutual attachment into which I put all the affection of my heart, the void in that heart was never-
30   theless never really filled. Children came, who might have filled it; but that made things even worse. I trembled at the thought of entrusting them to that badly brought-up family, to be brought up even more badly. The risks of their upbringing by the Foundling Hospital were considerably less. This reason for the course I adopt-
35   ed was stronger than all those I set out in my letter to Mme de Francueil. It was, however, the only one that I dared not tell. I preferred to be less completely absolved from so grave a charge and so spare the family of the woman I loved. But it can be judged by the conduct of her wretched brother whether, whatever may be said on
40   the subject, I should have been right in exposing my children to the risk of receiving an education like this.

Being unable to taste to the full the intimate companionship of which I felt the need, I looked for something in addition, which would not fill the void but which would make me less conscious of
45   it. Lacking a single friend who would be entirely mine, I required

friends whose energies would overcome my inertia. It was for this reason that I cultivated and strengthened my relationship with Diderot and the Abbè de Condillac, that I entered into a new and even more intimate relationship with Grimm, and that in the end,
5 through that unlucky essay, the story of which I have told, I found myself unexpectedly thrown back into literature, which I thought I had abandoned for ever.

These fresh beginnings led me by a new path into a different intellectual world, possessing a simple and dignified economy
10 which I could not look upon without enthusiasm. Soon, as I continued to explore it, I could see only foolishness and error in the doctrines of our sages, nothing but oppression and misery in our social order. Deluded by my stupid conceit, I thought that I was born to destroy all these deceits; and judging that in order to gain a hearing
15 I must reconcile my actions to my principles, I adopted that singular course which I have not been allowed to pursue, and which my pretended friends have never been able to pardon, since it set an example which at first made me ridiculous, but which would finally have earned me respect if it had been possible for me to persevere
20 with it.

Until then I had been good; from that moment I became virtuous, or at least intoxicated with virtue. This intoxication had begun in my head, but it had passed to my heart. The noblest pride sprang up there on the ruins of uprooted vanity. I played no part; I became
25 indeed what I appeared; and for the four years at least that this exhilaration lasted in its full strength there was nothing great or beautiful that can enter into the heart of man, between earth and heaven, of which I was not capable. This was the origin of my sudden eloquence, and of the truly celestial fire which burned in me
30 and spread to my early books, a fire which had not emitted the tiniest spark in forty years, because it was not yet kindled.

I was truly transformed; my friends and acquaintances no longer recognized me. I had ceased to be that shy creature, who was shamefaced rather than modest and who had not the courage to
35 show himself or even to speak. I had ceased to be a man who was put out by a joking word and blushed at a woman's glance. Bold, proud, and fearless, I now carried with me wherever I went a self-assurance which owed its firmness to its simplicity and which dwelt in my soul rather than in my outward bearing. The contempt
40 which my deep reflections had inspired in me for the customs, principles, and the prejudices of my age made me insensible to the mockery of those who followed them; and I crushed their little witticisms with my observations, as I might crush an insect between my fingers. What a change! All Paris repeated the sharp and biting
45 sarcasms of that same man who two years before—and again ten

years afterwards—could never find the right thing to say or the right word to use. No state of being could be found on earth more contrary to my true nature than this one. If ever there was a moment in my life in which I became another man and ceased to be myself,
5   it was at the time I am speaking of. But instead of lasting six days or six weeks it lasted nearly six years, and would have endured to this day but for the particular circumstances that put an end to it and restored me to Nature, out of whose realm I had been trying to soar.

This change began as soon as I left Paris and the sight of that
10   great city's vices ceased to feed the indignation it aroused in me. . . .

* * *

At the supreme height of my exaltation I was suddenly pulled down, like a kite on a string, and restored to my place by Nature by the agency of a fairly sharp attack of my complaint. I used the only remedy which afforded me any relief, the catheters, and they put a
15   stop to my celestial amours. For not only is one seldom in love when in pain, but my imagination, which only thrives in the country and under trees, languishes and dies in a room beneath the rafters of a ceiling. I have often regretted that dryads do not exist; for among them I should assuredly have found an object for my
20   love.

Other domestic upsets came simultaneously to increase my annoyances. Mme Le Vasseur paid me the prettiest compliments in the world, but alienated her daughter from me in every way she could. I received letters from my old neighbourhood informing me
25   that the good old woman had behind my back incurred several debts in Thérèse's name. Thérèse had known this, but she had not told me of it. The payment of the debts annoyed me much less than the secret that had been made of them. How could a woman from whom I had never kept a secret keep one from me? Can one hide
30   things from the person one loves? The Holbach circle, who saw that I never came to Paris, began to be positively afraid that I enjoyed the country and might be fool enough to stay there. Then began those intrigues, the object of which was to get me back to the city by indirect means. Diderot, who did not want to show his own hand so
35   soon, began by detaching Deleyre from me, whom I had just introduced to him. Deleyre received and handed on to me such thoughts as Diderot chose to impart to him, without perceiving the real purpose of it all.

Everything seemed to combine to arouse me from my sweet
40   and foolish reverie. I had not recovered from my attack when I received a copy of the poem on the destruction of Lisbon which I supposed to have been sent me by the author. This put me under the obligation of writing to him and speaking of his play, which I did in a letter that was printed a long time afterwards, without my

consent, as will be told hereafter.

Struck by seeing that poor man, weighed down, so to speak, by fame and prosperity, bitterly complaining, nevertheless, against the wretchedness of this life and finding everything invariably bad, I
5   formed the insane plan of bringing him back to himself and proving to him that all was well. Though Voltaire has always appeared to believe in God, he has really only believed in the Devil, because his so-called God is nothing but a malicious being who, according to his belief, only takes pleasure in doing harm. The absurdity of
10   this doctrine leaps to the eye, and it is particularly revolting in a man loaded with every kind of blessing who, living in the lap of luxury, seeks to disillusion his fellow-men by a frightening and cruel picture of all the calamities from which he is himself exempt. I who had a better right to count up and weigh the evils of human
15   life, examined them impartially and proved to him that there was not one of all those evils that could be blamed on Providence, not one that has not its source rather in the misuse that man has made of his faculties than in Nature herself. I treated him in that letter with all the deference, consideration, and circumspection possible,
20   indeed I think with the utmost respect. However, since I knew that his vanity was most easily offended, I did not send it straight to him but to Doctor Tronchin, his physician and friend, giving him full authority to pass it on or destroy it, whichever should seem to him the better course. Tronchin gave him the letter, and Voltaire replied
25   to me in a few lines that, being both an invalid and a sick-nurse himself, he would postpone his answer till another time. . . .

* * *

6. THE DECLARATION OF INDEPENDENCE

When the Continental Congress, meeting in Philadelphia in 1776, decided to declare a break with Great Britain, it appointed a committee of five to draft a document. Robert Livingston and Roger Sherman took no part, and John Adams and Benjamin Franklin had the good sense to leave the writing to Thomas Jefferson. His restrained but deeply moving prose combines an American adaptation of Locke's political theory with a catalogue of abuses by the Crown, justifying the revolutionary action. The finished document was presented to Congress on 28 June 1776 and signed on 4 July.

In CONGRESS, July 4, 1776
The unanimous Declaration of the thirteen united STATES of
AMERICA,

When in the course of human events, it becomes necessary for one people to dissolve the political bands which have connected them with another, and to assume among the Powers of the earth, the separate and equal station to which the Laws of Nature and of
5   Nature's God entitle them, a decent respect to the opinions of mankind requires that they should declare the causes which impel them to the separation.

We hold these truths to be self-evident, that all men are created equal, that they are endowed by their Creator with certain unalien-
10   able Rights, that among these are Life, Liberty, and the pursuit of Happiness. That to secure these rights, Governments are instituted among Men, deriving their just powers from the consent of the governed. That whenever any Form of Government becomes destructive of these ends, it is the Right of the People to alter or to abolish
15   it, and to institute new Government, laying its foundation on such principles and organizing its powers in such form, as to them shall seem most likely to affect their Safety and Happiness. Prudence, indeed, will dictate that Governments long established should not be changed for light and transient causes; and accordingly all expe-
20   rience hath shown, that mankind are more disposed to suffer, while evils are sufferable, than to right themselves by abolishing the forms to which they are accustomed. But when a long train of abuses and usurpations, pursuing invariably the same Object evinces a design to reduce them under absolute Despotism, it is their right, it

is their duty, to throw off such Government, and to provide new Guards for their future security.—Such has been the patient sufferance of these Colonies; and such is now the necessity which constrains them to alter their former Systems of Government. The his-
5   tory of the present King of Great Britain is a history of repeated injuries and usurpations, all having in direct object the establishment of an absolute Tyranny over these States. To prove this, let Facts be submitted to a candid world.

He has refused his Assent to Laws, the most wholesome and
10   necessary for the public good.

He has forbidden his governors to pass Laws of immediate and pressing importance, unless suspended in their operation till his Assent should be obtained; and when so suspended, he has utterly neglected to attend to them.

15   He has refused to pass other Laws for the accommodation of large districts of people, unless those people would relinquish the right of Representation in the Legislature, a right inestimable to them and formidable to tyrants only.

He has called together legislative bodies at places unusual,
20   uncomfortable, and distant from the depository of their public Records, for the sole purpose of fatiguing them into compliance with his measures.

He has dissolved Representative Houses repeatedly, for opposing with manly firmness his invasions on the rights of the people.

25   He has refused for a long time, after such dissolutions, to cause others to be elected; whereby the Legislative powers, incapable of Annihilation, have returned to the People at large for their exercise; the State remaining in the mean time exposed to all dangers of invasion from without, and convulsions within.

30   He has endeavored to prevent the population of these States; for that purpose obstructing the Laws of Naturalization of Foreigners; refusing to pass others to encourage their migrations hither, and raising the conditions of new Appropriations of Lands.

He has obstructed the Administration of Justice, by refusing his
35   Assent to Laws for establishing Judiciary powers.

He has made Judges dependent on his Will alone, for the tenure of their offices, and the amount and payment of their salaries.

He has erected a multitude of New Offices, and sent hither swarms of Officers to harass our People, and eat out their substance.

40   He has kept among us, in times of peace, Standing Armies without the Consent of our legislature.

He has affected to render the Military independent of and superior to the Civil Power.

He has combined with others to subject us to a jurisdiction for-
45   eign to our constitution, and unacknowledged by our laws; giving

his Assent to their Acts of pretended Legislation:

For quartering large bodies of armed troops among us:

For protecting them, by a mock Trial, from Punishment for any Murders which they should commit on the Inhabitants of these

5 States:

For cutting off our Trade with all parts of the world:

For imposing taxes on us without our Consent:

For depriving us of many cases, of the benefits of Trial by jury:

For transporting us beyond Seas to be tried for pretended

10 offences:

For abolishing the free System of English Laws in a neighbouring Province, establishing therein an Arbitrary government, and enlarging its Boundaries so as to render it at once an example and fit instrument for introducing the same absolute rule into these

15 colonies:

For taking away our Charters, abolishing our most valuable laws, and altering fundamentally the Forms of our Governments:

For suspending our own Legislatures, and declaring themselves invested with Power to legislate for us in all cases whatsoev-

20 er.

He has abdicated Government here, by declaring us out of his Protection and waging War against us.

He has plundered our seas, ravaged our Coasts, burnt our towns, and destroyed the lives of our people.

25 He is at this time transporting large armies of foreign mercenaries to complete the works of death, desolation, and tyranny, already begun with circumstances of Cruelty & Perfidy scarcely paralleled in the most barbarous ages, and totally unworthy of the Head of a civilized nation.

30 He has constrained our fellow Citizens taken Captive on the high Seas to bear Arms against their Country, to become the executioners of their friends and Brethren, or to fall themselves by their Hands.

He has excited domestic insurrections amongst us, and has

35 endeavoured to bring on the inhabitants of our frontiers, the merciless Indian Savages, whose known rule of warfare is an undistinguished destruction of all ages, sexes, and conditions.

In every stage of these Oppressions We have Petitioned for Redress in the most humble terms: Our repeated Petitions have

40 been answered only by repeated injury. A Prince, whose character is thus marked by every act which may define a Tyrant, is unfit to be the ruler of a free people.

Nor have We been wanting in attention to our British brethren. We have warned them from time to time of attempts by their legis-

45 lature to extend an unwarrantable jurisdiction over us. We have

reminded them of the circumstances of our emigration and settlement here. We have appealed to their native justice and magnanimity, and we have conjured them by the times of our common kindred to disavow these usurpations, which, would inevitably inter-
5   rupt our connections and correspondence. They too must have been
deaf to the voice of justice and of consanguinity. We must, therefore,
acquiesce in the necessity, which denounces our Separation, and
hold them, as we hold the rest of mankind, Enemies in War, in Peace
Friends.

10   We, therefore, the Representatives of the United States of
America, in General Congress Assembled, appealing to the
Supreme Judge of the world for the rectitude of our intentions, do,
in the Name, and by Authority of the good People of these Colonies,
solemnly publish and declare, That these United Colonies are, and
15   of Right ought to be Free and Independent States; that they are
Absolved from all Allegiance to the British Crown, and that all
political connection between them and the State of Great Britain, is
and ought to be totally dissolved; and that as Free and Independent
States, they have full Power to levy War, conclude Peace, contract
20   Alliances, establish Commerce, and to do all other Acts and Things
which Independent States may of right do. And for the support of
this Declaration, with a firm reliance on the Protection of divine
Providence, we mutually pledge to each other our Lives, our
Fortunes, and our sacred Honor.

7. WILLIAM BLAKE

William Blake (1757–1827) was a poet, a painter, and a mystic. He was one of the most original figures of the Romantic age and, if he was largely obscure in his own time, posterity has recognized his genius. His contempt for the Enlightenment is easily seen in his famous painting of Newton, and it is also expressed in his marginalia. Thomas Jefferson, as a good philosophe, thought that Francis Bacon, John Locke, and Isaac Newton were "the three greatest men who have ever lived." Blake thought they were diabolic agents introduced to destroy the human race. His famous lyrics are divided into two sets of dramatic voices, one of Innocence and the other, Experience. Both types of Song present a powerful criticism of the Enlightenment.

SONGS OF INNOCENCE

PIPING DOWN THE VALLEYS WILD

Piping down the valleys wild
Piping songs of pleasant glee
On a cloud I saw a child,
And he laughing said to me,

5   "Pipe a song about a Lamb";
So I piped with merry chear;
"Piper pipe that song again"—
So I piped, he wept to hear.

"Drop thy pipe thy happy pipe
10   Sing thy songs of happy chear";
So I sung the same again
While he wept with joy to hear.

"Piper sit thee down and write
In a book that all may read"—
15   So he vanished from my sight.
And I plucked a hollow reed,

And I made a rural pen
And I stained the water clear,
And I wrote my happy songs
20   Every child may joy to hear.

THE LAMB

Little Lamb, who made thee?
    Dost thou know who made thee?
Gave thee life & bid thee feed,
By the stream & o'er the mead;
5   Gave thee clothing of delight,
Softest clothing wooly bright;
Gave thee such a tender voice,
Making all the vales rejoice!
    Little Lamb who made thee?
10   Dost thou know who made thee?

Little Lamb I'll tell thee,
Little Lamb I'll tell thee!
He is called by thy name,
For he calls himself a Lamb:
15   He is meek & he is mild,
He became a little child:
I a child & thou a lamb,
We are called by his name.
    Little Lamb God bless thee.
20   Little Lamb God bless thee.

THE LITTLE BLACK BOY

My mother bore me in the southern wild,
And I am black, but O! my soul is white;
White as an angel is the English child:
But I am black as if bereav'd of light.

5   My mother taught me underneath a tree,
And sitting down before the heat of day,
She took me on her lap and kissed me,
And pointing to the east, began to say:

"Look on the rising sun: there God does live,
10   And gives his light, and gives his heat away;
And flowers and trees and beasts and men receive
Comfort in the morning, joy in the noon day.

"And we are put on earth a little space,
15   that we may learn to bear the beams of love,
And these black bodies and this sun-burnt face
Is but a cloud, and like a shady grove.

"For when our souls have learned the heat to bear,
The cloud will vanish; we shall hear his voice,
20   Saying: 'Come out from the grove, my love & care,
And round my golden tent like lambs rejoice.'"

Thus did my mother say, and kissed me;
And this I say to little English boy:
When I from black and he from white cloud free,
And round the tent of God like lambs we joy,
25

I'll shade him from the heat til he can bear
To lean in joy upon our father's knee;
And then I'll stand and stroke his silver hair,
And be like him, and he will then love me.

SONGS OF EXPERIENCE

HEAR THE VOICE OF THE BARD!

Hear the voice of the Bard!
Who Present, Past & Future sees;
Whose ears have heard
5   The Holy Word
That walked among the ancient trees;

Calling the lapsed Soul
And weeping in the evening dew;
That might control
10   The starry pole,
And fallen, fallen light renew!

"O Earth, O Earth, return!
Arise from out the dewy grass;
Night is worn,
15   And the morn
Rises from the slumberous mass.

"Turn away no more;
Why wilt thou turn away?
The starry floor
The watery shore
20   Is given thee till the break of day."

THE TYGER

Tyger! Tyger! burning bright
In the forest of the night,
What immortal hand or eye
Could frame thy fearful symmetry?

5   In what distant deeps or skies
Burnt the fire of thine eyes?
On what wings dare he aspire?
What the hand dare seize the fire?

And what shoulder, & what art,
10   Could twist the sinews of thy heart?
And when thy heart began to beat,
What dread hand? & what dread feet?

What the hammer? what the chain?
In what furnace was thy brain?
15   What the anvil? what dread grasp
Dare its deadly terrors clasp?

When the stars threw down their spears,
And watered heaven with their tears,
Did he smile his work to see?
20   Did he who made the Lamb make thee?

Tyger! Tyger! burning bright
In the forests of the night,
What immortal hand or eye
Dare frame thy fearful symmetry?

THE CHIMNEY SWEEPER

A little black thing among the snow
Crying "'weep, 'weep" in notes of woe!
"Where are thy father & mother? say?"
"They are both gone up to the church to pray.

5   "Because I was happy upon the heath,
And smiled among the winter's snow;
They clothed me in the clothes of death,
And taught me to sing the notes of woe.

"And because I am happy, & dance & sing,
They think they have done me no injury,
And are gone to praise God & his Priest & King,
Who make up a heaven of our misery."

LONDON

I wander thro' each charter'd street,
Near where the charter'd Thames does flow,
And mark in every face I meet
Marks of weakness, marks of woe.

5   In every cry of every Man,
In every Infant's cry of fear,
In every voice, in every ban,
The mind-forg'd manacles I hear.

How the Chimney-sweeper's cry
10   Every black'ning Church appalls;
And the hapless Soldier's sigh
Runs in blood down Palace walls.

But most thro' midnight streets I hear
How the youthful Harlot's curse
15   Blasts the new-born Infant's tear,
And blights with plagues the Marriage hearse.

OTHER LYRICS

MOCK ON, MOCK ON, VOLTAIRE, ROUSSEAU

Mock on, Mock on, Voltaire, Rousseau;
Mock on, Mock on, 'tis all in vain!
You throw the sand against the wind,
And the wind blows it back again;

5   And every sand becomes a Gem
Reflected in the beams divine;
Blown back, they blind the mocking Eye,
But still in Israel's paths they shine.

The Atoms of Democritus
10   And Newton's Particles of light
Are sands upon the Red sea shore,
Where Israel's tents do shine so bright.

AND DID THOSE FEET

And did those feet in ancient time
Walk upon England's mountains green?
And was the holy Lamb of God
On England's pleasant pastures seen?

5   And did the Countenance Divine
Shine forth upon our clouded hills?
And was Jerusalem builded here,
Among these dark Satanic Mills?

Bring me my Bow of burning gold,
10   Bring me my Arrows of desire,
Bring me my Spear; O clouds unfold!
Bring me my Chariot of fire!

I will not cease from Mental Fight,
Nor shall my Sword sleep in my hand,
15   Till we have built Jerusalem
In England's green & pleasant Land.

8. WILLIAM WORDSWORTH

It is Wordsworth (1770–1850) who more than anyone else defined the major element in Romantic poetry, Nature, or more properly, the interaction of Man and Nature and the effect of Nature on the feelings and the Imagination. The philosopher David Hume had argued that only the feelings could properly ground the moral life (abandoning the traditional view that morality was accessible to Right Reason), and Wordsworth followed Hume in this new moral understanding. Thus our interactions with Nature are more than just a pleasant and momentary stimulus. Rather, Nature arouses the feelings and this in turn awakens the Imagination. In this complexus Wordsworth tells us that he found,

> The anchor of my purest thoughts, the nurse
> The guide, the guardian of my heart, and soul
> Of all my moral being.

For the Romantics Nature is mystical, not sacramental. That is, its "meaning" is endowed by the poet from within; the poet does not usually see Nature as a sign of a transcendent reality. No Romantic could say what Gerard Manley Hopkins says, "The world is charged with the grandeur of God"; or "He fathers-forth whose beauty is past change:/Praise him."

Although Wordsworth lived the longest of all the Romantics and was still writing poetry in his eightieth year, his great work was all done in a ten-year period ending about 1807. His famous "Ode: Intimations of Immortality" is a recognition of his waning poetical powers.

In his poem, "I Wander'd Lonely as a Cloud," Wordsworth dramatizes what he mostly talks about in "Tintern Abbey"—the transforming power of nature upon the human mind. Here we see the optimism of the early Romantic period, its bold confidence that Nature would provide all of that which the Enlightenment seemed to have robbed Man.

LINES COMPOSED A FEW MILES ABOVE TINTERN ABBEY

Five years have past; five summers, with the length
Of five long winters! and again I hear
These waters, rolling from their mountain-springs
With a soft inland murmur.—Once again
5   Do I behold these steep and lofty cliffs,

That on a wild secluded scene impress
Thoughts of more deep seclusion; and connect
The landscape with the quiet of the sky.
The day is come when I again repose
10 Here, under this dark sycamore, and view
These plots of cottage-ground, these orchard-tufts,
Which at this season, with their unripe fruits,
Are clad in one green hue, and lose themselves
'Mid groves and copses. Once again I see
15 These hedge-rows, hardly hedge-rows, little lines
Of sportive wood run wild: these pastoral farms,
Green to the very door; and wreaths of smoke
Sent up, in silence, from among the trees!
With some uncertain notice, as might seem
20 Of vagrant dwellers in the houseless woods,
Or of some Hermit's cave, where by his fire
The Hermit sits alone.
                              These beauteous forms,
Through a long absence, have not been to me
25 As is a landscape to a blind man's eye:
But oft, in lonely rooms, and 'mid the din
Of towns and cities, I have owed to them
In hours of weariness, sensations sweet,
Felt in the blood, and felt along the heart;
30 And passing even into my purer mind,
With tranquil restoration:—feelings too
Of unremembered pleasure: such, perhaps,
As have no slight or trivial influence
On that best portion of a good man's life,
35 His little, nameless, unremembered acts
Of kindness and of love. Nor less, I trust,
To them I may have owed another gift,
Of aspect more sublime; that blessed mood,
In which the burthen of the mystery,
40 In which the heavy and the weary weight
Of all this unintelligible world,
Is lightened:—that serene and blessed mood,
In which the affections gently lead us on,—
Until, the breath of this corporeal frame
45 And even the motion of our human blood
Almost suspended, we are laid asleep
In body, and become a living soul:
While with an eye made quiet by the power
Of harmony, and the deep power of joy,
50 We see into the life of things.

8. *William Wordsworth*

If this
Be but a vain belief, yet, oh! how oft—
In darkness and amid the many shapes
Of joyless daylight; when the fretful stir
55　Unprofitable, and the fever of the world,
Have hung upon the beatings of my heart—
How oft, in spirit, have I turned to thee,
O sylvan Wye! thou wanderer through the woods,
How often has my spirit turned to thee!

60　　　　　And now, with gleams of half-extinguished thought,
With many recognitions dim and faint,
And somewhat of a sad perplexity,
The picture of the mind revives again:
While here I stand, not only with the sense
65　Of present pleasure, but with pleasing thoughts
That in this moment there is life and food
For future years. And so I dare to hope,
Though changed, no doubt, from what I was when first
I came among these hills; when like a roe
70　I bounded o'er the mountains, by the sides
Of the deep rivers, and the lonely streams,
Wherever nature led: more like a man
Flying from something that he dreads, than one
Who sought the thing he loved. For nature then
75　(The coarser pleasures of my boyish days,
And their glad animal movements all gone by)
To me was all in all.—I cannot paint
What then I was. The sounding cataract
Haunted me like a passion: the tall rock,
80　The mountain, and the deep and gloomy wood,
Their colors and their forms, were then to me
An appetite; a feeling and a love,
That had no need of a remoter charm,
By thought supplied, nor any interest
85　Unborrowed from the eye.—That time is past,
And all its aching joys are now no more,
And all its dizzy raptures. Not for this
Faint I, nor mourn nor murmur; other gifts
Have followed; for such loss, I would believe,
90　Abundant recompense. For I have learned
To look on nature, not as in the hour
Of thoughtless youth; but hearing oftentimes
The still, sad music of humanity,
Nor harsh nor grating, though of ample power

95 To chasten and subdue. And I have felt
    A presence that disturbs me with the joy
    Of elevated thoughts; a sense sublime
    Of something far more deeply interfused,
    Whose dwelling is the light of setting suns,
100 And the round ocean and the living air,
    And the blue sky, and in the mind of man:
    A motion and a spirit, that impels
    All thinking things, all objects of all thought,
    And rolls through all things. Therefore am I still
105 A lover of the meadows and the woods,
    And mountains; and of all the mighty world
    Of eye, and ear,—both what they half create,
    And what perceive; well pleased to recognize
    In nature and the language of the sense
110 The anchor of my purest thoughts, the nurse,
    The guide, the guardian of my heart, and soul
    Of all my moral being.
                                    Nor perchance,
    If I were not thus taught, should I the more
115 Suffer my genial spirits to decay:
    For thou art with me here upon the banks
    Of this fair river; thou my dearest Friend,
    My dear, dear Friend; and in thy voice I catch
    The language of my former heart, and read
120 My former pleasures in the shooting lights
    Of thy wild eyes. Oh! yet a little while
    May I behold in thee what I was once,
    My dear, dear Sister! and this prayer I make,
    Knowing that Nature never did betray
125 The heart that loved her; 'tis her privilege,
    Through all the years of this our life, to lead
    From joy to joy: for she can so inform
    The mind that is within us, so impress
    With quietness and beauty, and so feed
130 With lofty thoughts, that neither evil tongues,
    Rash judgments, nor the sneers of selfish men,
    Nor greetings where no kindness is, nor all
    The dreary intercourse of daily life,
    Shall e'er prevail against us, or disturb
135 Our cheerful faith, that all which we behold
    Is full of blessings. Therefore let the moon
    Shine on thee in thy solitary walk;
    And let the misty mountain-winds be free
    To blow against thee: and, in after years,

140 When these wild ecstasies shall be matured
     Into a sober pleasure; when thy mind
     Shall be a mansion for all lovely forms,
     Thy memory be as a dwelling-place
     For all sweet sounds and harmonies; oh! then,
145 If solitude, or fear, or pain, or grief,
     Should by thy portion, with what healing thoughts
     Of tender joy wilt thou remember me,
     And these my exhortations! Nor, perchance—
     If I should be where I no more can hear
150 Thy voice, nor catch from thy wild eyes these gleams
     Of past existence—wilt thou then forget
     That on the banks of this delightful stream
     We stood together; and that I, so long
     A worshipper of Nature, hither came
155 Unwearied in that service: rather say
     With warmer love—oh! with far deeper zeal
     Of holier love. Nor wilt thou then forget,
     That after many wanderings, many years
     Of absence, these steep woods and lofty cliffs,
160 And this green pastoral landscape, were to me
     More dear, both for themselves and for thy sake!   1798

THE WORLD IS TOO MUCH WITH US

The world is too much with us; late and soon,
Getting and spending, we lay waste our powers:
Little we see in Nature that is ours;
We have given our hearts away, a sordid boon!
5   This Sea that bares her bosom to the moon;
The winds that will be howling at all hours,
And are up-gathered now like sleeping flowers;
For this, for everything, we are out of tune,
It moves us not.—Great God! I'd rather be
10 A Pagan suckled in a creed outworn;
So might I, standing on this pleasant lea,
Have glimpses that would make me less forlorn;
Have sight of Proteus rising from the sea;
Or hear old Triton blow his wreathèd horn.   1802

COMPOSED UPON
WESTMINSTER BRIDGE

Earth has not anything to show more fair:
Dull would he be of soul who could pass by
A sight so touching in its majesty:
This City now doth, like a garment, wear
5   The beauty of the morning; silent, bare,
Ships, towers, domes, theatres, and temples lie
Open unto the fields, and to the sky;
All bright and glittering in the smokeless air.
Never did sun more beautifully steep
10   In his first splendour, valley, rock, or hill;
Ne'er saw I, never felt, a calm so deep!
The river glideth at his own sweet will:
Dear God! the very houses seem asleep;
And all that mighty heart is lying still!   September 3, 1802

I WANDER'D LONELY AS A CLOUD

I wander'd lonely as a cloud
That floats on high o'er vales and hills,
When all at once I saw a crowd,
A host, of golden daffodils;
5   Beside the lake, beneath the trees,
Fluttering and dancing in the breeze.

Continuous as the stars that shine
And twinkle on the milky way,
They stretched in never-ending line
10   Along the margin of a bay:
Ten thousand saw I at a glance,
Tossing their heads in sprightly dance.

The waves beside them danced; but they
Outdid the sparkling waves in glee;
15   A poet could not but be gay,
In such a jocund company;
I gazed—and gazed—but little thought
What wealth the show to me had brought:

For oft, when on my couch I lie
20   In vacant or in pensive mood,
They flash upon that inward eye
Which is the bliss of solitude;
And then my heart with pleasure fills,
And dances with the daffodils.   1804

ODE ON INTIMATIONS OF IMMORTALITY FROM RECOLLECTIONS OF EARLY CHILDHOOD

The Child is father of the Man;
And I could wish my days to be
Bound each to each by natural piety.

I

There was a time when meadow, grove, and stream,
5   The earth, and every common sight,
                To me did seem
            Apparelled in celestial light,
The glory and the freshness of a dream.
It is not now as it hath been of yore;—
10   Turn wheresoe'er I may,
                By night or day,
The things which I have seen I now can see no more.

II

The Rainbow comes and goes,
            And lovely is the Rose,
15   The Moon doth with delight
Look round her when the heavens are bare,
Waters on a starry night
                Are beautiful and fair;
The sunshine is a glorious birth;
20   But yet I know, where'er I go,
That there hath past away a glory from the earth.

III

Now, while the birds thus sing a joyous song,
            And while the young lambs bound

As to the tabor's sound,
25 To me alone there came a thought of grief:
A timely utterance gave that thought relief,
    And I again am strong:
The cataracts blow their trumpets from the steep;
    No more shall grief of mine the season wrong;
30   I hear the Echoes through the mountains throng,
The winds come to me from the fields of sleep,
        All the earth is gay;
            Land and sea
Give themselves up to jollity,
35   And with the heart of May
Doth every Beast keep holiday;—
            Thou child of joy,
Shout round me, let me hear thy shouts, thou happy Shepherd-boy!

IV

Ye blessèd Creatures, I have heard the call
40   Ye to each other make; I see
The heavens laugh with you in your jubilee;
        My heart is at your festival,
        My head hath its coronal,
The fulness of your bliss, I feel—I feel it all.
45   Oh evil day! if I were sullen
            While Earth herself is adorning,
                This sweet May-morning,
            And the Children are culling
                On every side,
50   In a thousand valleys far and wide,
            Fresh flowers; while the sun shines warm,
And the Babe leaps up on his Mother's arm;—
            I hear, I hear, with joy I hear!
            —But there's a Tree, of many, one,
55 A single Field which I have looked upon,
Both of them speak of something that is gone:
                The Pansy at my feet
                Doth the same tale repeat:
Whither is fled the visionary gleam?
60 Where is it now, the glory and the dream?

8. *William Wordsworth*

V

Our birth is but a sleep and a forgetting:
The Soul that rises with us, our life's Star,
    Hath had elsewhere its setting,
      And cometh from afar:
65   Not in entire forgetfulness,
     And not in utter nakedness,
But trailing clouds of glory do we come
      From God, who is our home:
Heaven lies about us in our infancy!
70 Shades of the prison-house begin to close
      Upon the growing Boy,
But He beholds the light, and whence it flows,
      He sees it in his joy;
The Youth, who daily farther from the east
75   Must travel, still is Nature's Priest,
     And by the vision splendid
     Is on his way attended;
At length the Man perceives it die away,
And fade into the light of common day.

VI

80 Earth fills her lap with pleasures of her own;
Yearnings she hath in her own natural kind,
And, even with something of a Mother's mind,
     And no unworthy aim,
    The homely Nurse doth all she can
85 To make her Foster-child, her Inmate Man,
     Forget the glories he hath known,
And that imperial palace whence he came.

VII

Behold the Child among his new-born blisses,
   A six years' Darling of a pigmy size!
90   See, where 'mid work of his own hand he lies,
Fretted by sallies of his mother's kisses,
   With light upon him from his father's eyes!
See, at his feet, some little plan or chart,
Some fragment from his dream of human life,
95 Shaped by himself with newly-learned art;
    A wedding or a festival,

A mourning or a funeral;

And this hath now his heart,

And unto this he frames his song:

100 Then will he fit his tongue

To dialogues of business, love, or strife:

But it will not be long

Ere this be thrown aside,

And with new joy and pride

105 The little Actor cons another part;

Filling from time to time his "humorous stage"

With all the Persons, down to palsied Age,

That life brings with her in her equipage;

As if his whole vocation

110 Were endless imitation.

VIII

Thou, whose exterior semblance doth belie

Thy Soul's immensity;

Thou best Philosopher who yet dost keep

Thy heritage, thou Eye among the blind,

115 That, deaf and silent, read'st the eternal deep,

Haunted for ever by the eternal mind,—

Mighty Prophet! Seer blest!

On whom those truths do rest,

Which we are toiling all our lives to find,

120 In darkness lost, the darkness of the grave;

Thou, over whom thy Immortality

Broods like the Day, a Master o'er a Slave,

A presence which is not to be put by;

To whom the grave

125 Is but a lonely bed without the sense or sight

Of day or the warm light,

A place of thought where we in waiting lie;

Thou little child, yet glorious in the might

Of heaven-born freedom on thy being's height,

130 Why with such earnest pains dost thou provoke

The years to bring the inevitable yoke,

Thus blindly with thy blessedness at strife?

Full soon thy Soul shall have her earthly freight,

And custom lie upon thee with a weight,

135 Heavy as frost, and deep almost as life!

IX

O joy! that in our embers
           Is something that doth live,
That nature yet remembers
           What was so fugitive!
140 The thought of our past years in me doth breed
Perpetual benediction: not indeed
For that which is most worthy to be blest;
Delight and liberty, the simple creed
Of Childhood, whether busy or at rest,
145 With new-fledged hope still fluttering in his breast:—
           Not for these I raise
                The song of thanks and praise;
           But for those obstinate questionings
           Of sense and outward things,
150   Fallings from us, vanishings;
           Blank misgivings of a Creature
Moving about in worlds not realized,
High instincts before which our mortal Nature
Did tremble like a guilty Thing surprised:
155   But for those first affections,
           Those shadowy recollections,
                Which, be they what they may,
Are yet the fountain-light of all our day,
Are yet a master-light of all our seeing;
160   Uphold us, cherish, and have power to make
Our noisy years seem moments in the being
           Of the eternal Silence: truths that wake,
                To perish never:
Which neither listlessness, nor mad endeavor,
165   Nor man nor Boy,
Nor all that is at enmity with joy,
Can utterly abolish or destroy!
           Hence in a season of calm weather
                Though inland far we be,
170 Our souls have sight of that immortal sea
                Which brought us hither,
                Can in a moment travel thither,
And see the Children sport upon the shore,
And hear the mighty waters rolling evermore.

X

Then sing, ye Birds, sing, sing, a joyous song!
175   And let the young Lambs bound
                  As to the tabor's sound!
We in thought will join your throng,
                  Ye that pipe and ye that play,
                  Ye that through your hearts to-day
180   Feel the gladness of the May!
What though the radiance which was once so bright
Be now for ever taken from my sight,
                  Though nothing can bring back the hour
Of splendour in the grass, of glory in the flower;
185   We will grieve not, rather find
                  Strength in what remains behind;
                  In the primal sympathy
                  Which having been must ever be;
                  In the soothing thoughts that spring
190   Out of human suffering;
                  In the faith that looks through death,
In years that bring the philosophic mind.

XI

And O, ye Fountains, Meadows, Hills, and Groves,
Forebode not any severing of our loves!
195 Yet in my heart of hearts I feel your might;
I only have relinquished one delight
To live beneath your more habitual sway.
I love the Brooks which down their channels fret,
Even more than when I tripped lightly as they;
200 The innocent brightness of a new-born Day
                           Is lovely yet;
The Clouds that gather round the setting sun
Do take a sober colouring from an eye
That hath kept watch o'er man's mortality;
205 Another race hath been, and other palms are won.
Thanks to the human heart by which we live,
Thanks to its tenderness, its joys, and fears,
To me the meanest flower that blows can give
Thoughts that do often lie too deep for tears. 1807

FROM THE PRELUDE BOOK X: THE FRENCH REVOLUTION

    O pleasant exercise of hope and joy!
For great were the auxiliars which then stood
Upon our side, we who were strong in love;
Bliss was it in that dawn to be alive,
5   But to be young was very heaven; O times,
In which the meagre, stale, forbidding ways
Of custom, law, and statute took at once
The attraction of a Country in Romance;
When Reason seem'd the most to assert her rights
10 When most intent on making herself
A prime Enchanter to assist the work,
Which then was going forwards in her name.
Not favour'd spots alone, but the whole earth
The beauty wore of promise, that which sets,
15 To take an image which was felt, no doubt,
Among the bowers of paradise itself,
The budding rose above the rose full blown.
What temper at the prospect did not wake
To happiness unthought of? The inert
20 Were rouz'd, and lively natures rapt away:
They who had fed their childhood upon dreams,
The Play-fellows of Fancy, who had made
All powers of swiftness, subtlety, and strength
Their ministers, used to stir in lordly wise
25 Among the grandest objects of the sense,
And deal with whatsoever they found there
As if they had within some lurking right
To wield it; they too, who, of gentle mood
Had watch'd all gentle motions, and to these
30 Had fitted their own thoughts, schemers more mild,
And in the region of their peaceful selves,
Did now find helpers to their hearts' desire,
And stuff at hand, plastic as they could wish,
Were call'd upon to exercise their skill,
35 Not in Utopia, subterraneous Fields,
Or some secreted Island, Heaven knows where,
But in the very world which is the world
Of all of us, the place in which, in the end,
We find our happiness, or not at all.   1805

PREFACE TO *LYRICAL BALLADS*

THE FIRST volume of these Poems has already been submitted to general perusal. It was published, as an experiment, which, I hoped, might be of some use to ascertain, how far, by fitting to metrical arrangement a selection of the real language of men in a state
5 of vivid sensation, that sort of pleasure and that quantity of pleasure may be imparted, which a Poet may rationally endeavour to impart.

I had formed no very inaccurate estimate of the probable effect of those Poems: I flattered myself that they who should be pleased
10 with them would read them with more than common pleasure: and, on the other hand, I was well aware, that by those who should dislike them, they would be read with more than common dislike. The result has differed from my expectation in this only, that a greater number have been pleased than I ventured to hope I should please.
15 Several of my Friends are anxious for the success of these Poems, from a belief, that, if the views with which they were composed were indeed realized, a class of Poetry would be produced, well adapted to interest mankind permanently, and not unimportant in the quality, and in the multiplicity of its moral relations: and
20 on this account they have advised me to prefix a systematic defence of the theory upon which the Poems were written. But I was unwilling to undertake the task, knowing that on this occasion the Reader would look coldly upon my arguments, since I might be suspected of having been principally influenced by the selfish and foolish
25 hope of *reasoning* him into an approbation of these particular Poems: and I was still more unwilling to undertake the task, because, adequately to display the opinions, and fully to enforce the arguments, would require a space wholly disproportionate to a preface. For, to treat the subject with the clearness and coherence of
30 which it is susceptible, it would be necessary to give a full account of the present state of the public taste in this country, and to determine how far this taste is healthy or depraved; which, again, could not be determined, without pointing out in what manner language and the human mind act and re-act on each other, and without
35 retracing the revolutions, not of literature alone, but likewise of society itself. I have therefore altogether declined to enter regularly upon this defence; yet I am sensible, that there would be something like impropriety in abruptly obtruding upon the Public, without a few words of introduction, Poems so materially different from those
40 upon which general approbation is at present bestowed.

It is supposed, that by the act of writing in verse an Author makes a formal engagement that he will gratify certain known habits of association; that he not only thus apprises the Reader that

certain classes of ideas and expressions will be found in his book, but that others will be carefully excluded. This exponent or symbol held forth by metrical language must in different eras of literature have excited very different expectations: for example, in the age of
5 Catullus, Terence, and Lucretius, and that of Statius or Claudian; and in our own country, in the age of Shakespeare and Beaumont and Fletcher, and that of Donne and Cowley, or Dryden, or Pope. I will not take upon me to determine the exact import of the promise which, by the act of writing in verse, an Author in the present day
10 makes to his reader: but it will undoubtedly appear to many persons that I have not fulfilled the terms of an engagement thus voluntarily contracted. They who have been accustomed to the gaudiness and inane phraseology of many modern writers, if they persist in reading this book to its conclusion, will, no doubt, frequently
15 have to struggle with feelings of strangeness and awkwardness: they will look round for poetry, and will be induced to inquire by what species of courtesy these attempts can be permitted to assume that title. I hope therefore the reader will not censure me for attempting to state what I have proposed to myself to perform; and
20 also (as far as the limits of a preface will permit) to explain some of the chief reasons which have determined me in the choice of my purpose: that at least he may be spared any unpleasant feeling of disappointment, and that I myself may be protected from one of the most dishonourable accusations which can be brought against an
25 Author, namely, that of an indolence which prevents him from endeavouring to ascertain what is his duty, or, when his duty is ascertained, prevents him from performing it.

The principal object, then, proposed in these Poems was to choose incidents and situations from common life, and to relate or
30 describe them, throughout, as far as was possible in a selection of language really used by men, and, at the same time, to throw over them a certain colouring of imagination, whereby ordinary things should be presented to the mind in an unusual aspect; and, further, and above all, to make these incidents and situations interesting by
35 tracing in them, truly though not ostentatiously, the primary laws of our nature: chiefly, as far as regards the manner in which we associate ideas in a state of excitement. Humble and rustic life was generally chosen, because, in that condition, the essential passions of the heart find a better soil in which they can attain their maturity,
40 are less under restraint, and speak a plainer and more emphatic language; because in that condition of life our elementary feelings coexist in a state of greater simplicity, and, consequently, may be more accurately contemplated, and more forcibly communicated; because the manners of rural life germinate from those elementary
45 feelings, and, from the necessary character of rural occupations, are

more easily comprehended, and are more durable; and, lastly,
because in that condition the passions of men are incorporated with
the beautiful and permanent forms of nature. The language, too, of
these men has been adopted (purified indeed from what appear to
5 be its real defects, from all lasting and rational causes of dislike or
disgust) because such men hourly communicate with the best
objects from which the best part of language is originally derived;
and because, from their rank in society and the sameness and narrow circle of their intercourse, being less under the influence of
10 social vanity, they convey their feelings and notions in simple and
unelaborated expressions. Accordingly, such a language, arising out
of repeated experience and regular feelings, is a more permanent,
and a far more philosophical language, than that which is frequently substituted for it by Poets, who think that they are conferring
15 honour upon themselves and their art, in proportion as they separate themselves from the sympathies of men, and indulge in arbitrary and capricious habits of expression, in order to furnish food
for fickle tastes, and fickle appetites, of their own creation.[1]

I cannot, however, be insensible to the present outcry against
20 the triviality and meanness, both of thought and language, which
some of my contemporaries have occasionally introduced into their
metrical compositions; and I acknowledge that this defect, where it
exists, is more dishonourable to the Writer's own character than
false refinement or arbitrary innovation, though I should contend at
25 the same time, that it is far less pernicious in the sum of its consequences. From such verses the Poems in these volumes will be
found distinguished at least by one mark of difference, that each of
them has a worthy *purpose*. Not that I always began to write with a
distinct purpose formerly conceived; but habits of meditation have,
30 I trust, so prompted and regulated my feelings, that my descriptions of such objects as strongly excite those feelings, will be found
to carry along with them a *purpose*. If this opinion be erroneous, I
can have little right to the name of a Poet. For all good poetry is the
spontaneous overflow of powerful feelings: and though this be true,
35 Poems to which any value can be attached were never produced on
any variety of subjects but by a man who, being possessed of more

---

[1] I here use the word 'Poetry' (though against my own judgement) as
opposed to the word Prose, and synonymous with metrical composition.
But much confusion has been introduced into criticism by this contradis-
tinction of Poetry and Prose, instead of the more philosophical one of Poetry
and Matter of Fact, or Science. The only strict antithesis to Prose is Metre; nor
is this, in truth, a strict antithesis, because lines and passages of metre so naturally occur in writing prose, that it would be scarcely possible to avoid
them, even were it desirable.

than usual organic sensibility, had also thought long and deeply. For our continued influxes of feeling are modified and directed by our thoughts, which are indeed the representatives of all our past feelings; and, as by contemplating the relation of these general repre-
5 sentatives to each other, we discover what is really important to men, so, by the repetition and continuance of this act, our feelings will be connected with important subjects, till at length, if we be originally possessed of much sensibility, such habits of mind will be produced, that, by obeying blindly and mechanically the impulses
10 of those habits, we shall describe objects, and utter sentiments, of such a nature, and in such connexion with each other, that the understanding of the Reader must necessarily be in some degree enlightened, and his affections strengthened and purified.

It has been said that each of these poems has a purpose.
15 Another circumstance must be mentioned which distinguishes these Poems from the popular Poetry of the day; it is this, that the feeling therein developed gives importance to the action and situation, and not the action and situation to the feeling.

A sense of false modesty shall not prevent me from asserting,
20 that the Reader's attention is pointed to this mark of distinction, far less for the sake of these particular Poems than from the general importance of the subject. The subject is indeed important! For the human mind is capable of being excited without the application of gross and violent stimulants; and he must have a very faint percep-
25 tion of its beauty and dignity who does not know this, and who does not further know, that one being is elevated above another, in proportion as he possesses this capability. It has therefore appeared to me, that to endeavour to produce or enlarge this capability is one of the best services in which, at any period, a Writer can be engaged;
30 but this service, excellent at all times, is especially so at the present day. For a multitude of causes, unknown to former times, are now acting with a combined force to blunt the discriminating powers of the mind, and, unfitting it for all voluntary exertion, to reduce it to a state of almost savage torpor. The most effective of these causes
35 are the great national events which are daily taking place, and the increasing accumulation of men in cities, where the uniformity of their occupations produces a craving for extraordinary incident, which the rapid communication of intelligence hourly gratifies. to this tendency of life and manners the literature and theatrical exhi-
40 bitions of the country have conformed themselves. The invaluable works of our elder writers, I had almost said the works of Shakespeare and Milton, are driven into neglect by frantic novels, sickly and stupid German Tragedies, and deluges of idle and extravagant stories in verse.—When I think upon this degrading
45 thirst after outrageous stimulation, I am almost ashamed to have

spoken of the feeble endeavour made in these volumes to counter-
act it; and, reflecting upon the magnitude of the general evil, I
should be oppressed with no dishonourable melancholy, had I not
a deep impression of certain inherent and indestructible qualities of
5   the human mind, and likewise of certain powers in the great and
permanent objects that act upon it, which are equally inherent and
indestructible; and were there not added to this impression a belief,
that the time is approaching when the evil will be systematically
opposed, by men of greater powers, and with far more distin-
10 guished success.

Having dwelt thus long on the subjects and aim of these
Poems, I shall request the Reader's permission to apprise him of a
few circumstances relating to their *style*, in order, among other reasons, that he may not censure me for not having performed what I
15 never attempted. The Reader will find that personifications of
abstract ideas rarely occur in these volumes; and are utterly rejected, as an ordinary device to elevate the style, and raise it above
prose. My purpose was to imitate, and, as far as possible, to adopt
the very language of men; and assuredly such personifications do
20 not make any natural or regular part of that language. They are,
indeed, a figure of speech occasionally prompted by passion, and I
have made use of them as such; but have endeavoured utterly to
reject them as a mechanical device of style, or as a family language
which Writers in metre seem to lay claim to by prescription. I have
25 wished to keep the Reader in the company of flesh and blood, persuaded that by so doing I shall interest him. Others who pursue a
different track will interest him likewise; I do not interfere with
their claim, but wish to prefer a claim of my own. There will also be
found in these volumes little of what is usually called poetic diction;
30 as much pains has been taken to avoid it as is ordinarily taken to
produce it; this has been done for the reason already alleged, to
bring my language near to the language of men; and further,
because the pleasure which I have proposed to myself to impart, is
of a kind very different from that which is supposed by many per-
35 sons to be the proper object of poetry. Without being culpably particular, I do not know how to give my Reader a more exact notion
of the style in which it was my wish and intention to write, than by
informing him that I have at all times endeavoured to look steadily
at my subject; consequently, there is I hope in these Poems little
40 falsehood of description, and my ideas are expressed in language
fitted to their respective importance. Something must have been
gained by this practice, as it is friendly to one property of all good
poetry, namely, good sense: but it has necessarily cut me off from a
large portion of phrases and figures of speech which from father to
45 son have long been regarded as the common inheritance of Poets. I

have also thought it expedient to restrict myself still further, having abstained from the use of many expressions, in themselves proper and beautiful, but which have been foolishly repeated by bad Poets, till such feelings of disgust are connected with them as it is scarcely
5 possible by any art of association to overpower.

If in a poem there should be found a series of lines, or even a single line, in which the language, though naturally arranged, and according to the strict laws of metre, does not differ from that of prose, there is a numerous class of critics, who, when they stumble
10 upon these prosaisms, as they call them, imagine that they have made a notable discovery, and exult over the Poet as over a man ignorant of his own profession. Now these men would establish a canon of criticism which the Reader will conclude he must utterly reject, if he wishes to be pleased with these volumes. and it would
15 be a most easy task to prove to him, that not only the language of a large portion of every good poem, even of the most elevated character, must necessarily, except with reference to the metre, in no respect differ from that of good prose, but likewise that some of the most interesting parts of the best poems will be found to be strictly the language of prose when prose is well written. The truth of this
20 assertion might be demonstrated by innumerable passages from almost all the poetical writings, even of Milton himself. To illustrate the subject in a general manner, I will here adduce a short composition of Gray, who was at the head of those who, by their reasonings, have attempted to widen the space of separation betwixt Prose and
25 Metrical composition, and was more than any other man curiously elaborate in the structure of his own poetic diction.

In vain to me the smiling mornings shine,
And reddening Phœbus lifts his golden fire:
30 The birds in vain their amorous descant join,
Or cheerful fields resume their green attire.
These ears, alas! for other notes repine;
A different object do these eyes require;
My lonely anguish melts no heart but mine;
And in my breast the imperfect joys expire;
35 Yet morning smiles the busy race to cheer,
And new-born pleasure brings to happier men;
The fields to all their wonted tribute bear;
To warm their little loves the birds complain.
I fruitless mourn to him that cannot hear,
40 *And weep the more because I weep in vain.*

It will easily be perceived, that the only part of this Sonnet which is of any value is the lines printed in Italics; it is equally obvious, that, except in the rhyme, and in the use of the single word 'fruitless' for fruitlessly, which is so far a defect, the language of these lines does in no respect differ from that of prose.

5   By the foregoing quotation it has been shown that the language of Prose may yet be well adapted to Poetry; and it was previously asserted, that a large portion of the language of every good poem can in no respect differ from that of good Prose. We will go further. It may be safely affirmed, that there neither is, nor can be, any *essential* difference between the language of prose and metrical composi-

10 tion. We are fond of tracing the resemblance between Poetry and Painting, and, accordingly, we call them Sisters: but where shall we find bonds of connexion sufficiently strict to typify the affinity betwixt metrical and prose composition? They both speak by and to the same organs; the bodies in which both of them are clothed may

15 be said to be of the same substance, their affections are kindred, and almost identical, not necessarily differing even in degree; Poetry[2] sheds no tears 'such as Angels weep,' but natural and human tears; she can boast of no celestial choir that distinguishes her vital juices from those of prose; the same human blood circulates through the

20 veins of them both.

    If it be affirmed that rhyme and metrical arrangement of themselves constitute a distinction which overturns what has just been said on the strict affinity of metrical language with that of prose, and paves the way for other artificial distinctions which the mind

25 voluntarily admits, I answer that the language of such Poetry as is here recommended is, as far as is possible, a selection of the language really spoken by men; that this selection, wherever it is made with true taste and feeling, will of itself form a distinction far greater than would at first be imagined, and will entirely separate

30 the composition from the vulgarity and meanness of ordinary life; and, if metre be superadded thereto, I believe that a dissimilitude will be produced altogether sufficient for the gratification of a rational mind. What other distinction would we have? Whence is it to come? and where is it to exist? Not, surely, where the Poet speaks

35 through the mouths of his characters: it cannot be necessary here, either for elevation of style, or any of its supposed ornaments: for, if the Poet's subject be judiciously chosen, it will naturally, and upon fit occasion, lead him to passions the language of which, if selected truly and judiciously, must necessarily be dignified and variegated,

40 and alive with metaphors and figures. I forbear to speak of an in-

---

[2]As sensibility to harmony of numbers, and the power of producing it, are invariably attendants upon the faculties above specified, nothing has been said upon those requisites.

congruity which would shock the intelligent Reader, should the Poet interweave any foreign splendour of his own with that which the passion naturally suggests: it is sufficient to say that such addition is unnecessary. and, surely, it is more probable that those pas-
5   sages, which with propriety abound with metaphors and figures, will have their due effect, if, upon other occasions where the passions are of a milder character, the style also be subdued and temperate.

But, as the pleasure which I hope to give by the Poems now
10   presented to the Reader must depend entirely on just notions upon this subject, and, as it is in itself of high importance to our taste and moral feelings, I cannot content myself with these detached remarks. and if, in what I am about to say, it shall appear to some that my labour is unnecessary, and that I am like a man fighting a
15   battle without enemies, such persons may be reminded, that, whatever be the language outwardly holden by men, a practical faith in the opinions which I am wishing to establish is almost unknown. If my conclusions are admitted, and carried as far as they must be carried if admitted at all, our judgements concerning the works of the
20   greatest Poets both ancient and modern will be far different from what they are at present, both when we praise, and when we censure: and our moral feelings influencing and influenced by these judgements will, I believe, be corrected and purified.

Taking up the subject, then, upon general grounds, let me ask,
25   what is meant by the word Poet? What is a Poet? to whom does he address himself? and what language is to be expected from him?— He is a man speaking to men: a man, it is true, endowed with more lively sensibility, more enthusiasm and tenderness, who has a greater knowledge of human nature, and a more comprehensive
30   soul, than are supposed to be common among mankind; a man pleased with his own passions and volitions, and who rejoices more than other men in the spirit of life that is in him; delighting to contemplate similar volitions and passions as manifested in the goings-on of the Universe, and habitually impelled to create them where he
35   does not find them. To these qualities he has added a disposition to be affected more than other men by absent things as if they were present; an ability of conjuring up in himself passions, which are indeed far from being the same as those produced by real events, yet (especially in those parts of the general sympathy which are
40   pleasing and delightful) do more nearly resemble the passions produced by real events, than anything which, from the motions of their own minds merely, other men are accustomed to feel in themselves:—whence, and from practice, he has acquired a greater readiness and power in expressing what he thinks and feels, and espe-
45   cially those thoughts and feelings which, by his own choice, or from

the structure of his own mind, arise in him without immediate external excitement.

But whatever portion of this faculty we may suppose even the greatest Poet to possess, there cannot be a doubt that the language
5 which it will suggest to him, must often, in liveliness and truth, fall short of that which is uttered by men in real life, under the actual pressure of those passions, certain shadows of which the Poet thus produces, or feels to be produced, in himself.

However exalted a notion we would wish to cherish of the
10 character of a Poet, it is obvious, that while he describes and imitates passions, his employment is in some degree mechanical, compared with the freedom and power of real and substantial action and suffering. So that it will be the wish of the Poet to bring his feelings near to those of the persons whose feelings he describes, nay,
15 for short spaces of time, perhaps, to let himself slip into an entire delusion, and even confound and identify his own feelings with theirs; modifying only the language which is thus suggested to him by a consideration that he describes for a particular purpose, that of giving pleasure. Here, then, he will apply the principle of selection
20 which has been already insisted upon. He will depend upon this for removing what would otherwise be painful or disgusting in the passion; he will feel that there is no necessity to trick out or to elevate nature: and, the more industriously he applies this principle, the deeper will be his faith that no words, which *his* fancy or imag-
25 ination can suggest, will be to be compared with those which are the emanations of reality and truth.

But it may be said by those who do not object to the general spirit of these remarks, that, as it is impossible for the Poet to produce upon all occasions language as exquisitely fitted for the pas-
30 sion as that which the real passion itself suggests, it is proper that he should consider himself as in the situation of a translator, who does not scruple to substitute excellencies of another kind for those which are unattainable by him; and endeavours occasionally to surpass his original, in order to make some amends for the general
35 inferiority to which he feels that he must submit. But this would be to encourage idleness and unmanly despair. Further, it is the language of men who speak of what they do not understand; who talk of Poetry as of a matter of amusement and idle pleasure; who will converse with us as gravely about a *taste* for Poetry, as they express
40 it, as if it were a thing as indifferent as a taste for rope-dancing, or Frontiniac or Sherry. Aristotle, I have been told, has said, that Poetry is the most philosophic of all writing: it is so: its object is truth, not individual and local, but general, and operative; not standing upon external testimony, but carried alive into the heart by passion; truth
45 which is its own testimony, which gives competence and confidence

to the tribunal to which it appeals, and receives them from the same tribunal. Poetry is the image of man and nature. The obstacles which stand in the way of the fidelity of the Biographer and Historian, and of their consequent utility, are incalculably greater

5   than those which are to be encountered by the Poet who comprehends the dignity of his art. The Poet writes under one restriction only, namely, the necessity of giving immediate pleasure to a human Being possessed of that information which may be expected from him, not as a lawyer, a physician, a mariner, an astronomer, or

10 a natural philosopher, but as a Man. Except this one restriction, there is no object standing between the Poet and the image of things; between this, and the Biographer and Historian, there are a thousand.

      Nor let this necessity of producing immediate pleasure be con-
15 sidered as a degradation of the Poet's art. It is far otherwise. It is an acknowledgement of the beauty of the universe, an acknowledgement the more sincere, because not formal, but indirect; it is a task light and easy to him who looks at the world in the spirit of love: further, it is a homage paid to the native and naked dignity of man,

20 to the grand elementary principle of pleasure, by which he knows, and feels, and lives, and moves. We have no sympathy but what is propagated by pleasure: I would not be misunderstood; but wherever we sympathize with pain, it will be found that the sympathy is produced and carried on by subtle combinations with pleasure. We

25 have no knowledge, that is, no general principles drawn from the contemplation of particular facts, but what has been built up by pleasure, and exists in us by pleasure alone. The Man of science, the Chemist and Mathematician, whatever difficulties and disgusts they may have had to struggle with, know and feel this. However

30 painful may be the objects with which the Anatomist's knowledge is connected, he feels that his knowledge is pleasure; and where he has no pleasure he has no knowledge. What then does the Poet? He considers man and the objects that surround him as acting and reacting upon each other, so as to produce an infinite complexity of

35 pain and pleasure; he considers man in his own nature and in his ordinary life as contemplating this with a certain quantity of immediate knowledge, with certain convictions, intuitions, and deductions, which from habit acquire the quality of intuitions; he considers him as looking upon this complex scene of ideas and sensations,

40 and finding everywhere objects that immediately excite in him sympathies which, from the necessities of his nature, are accompanied by an overbalance of enjoyment.

                    * * * * *

      I have said that poetry is the spontaneous overflow of power-
45 ful feelings: it takes its origin from emotion recollected in tranquil-

lity: the emotion is contemplated till, by a species of reaction, the tranquillity gradually disappears, and an emotion, kindred to that which was before the subject of contemplation, is gradually produced, and does itself actually exist in the mind. In this mood suc-
5   cessful composition generally begins, and in a mood similar to this it is carried on; but the emotion, of whatever kind, and in whatever degree, from various causes, is qualified by various pleasures, so that in describing any passions whatsoever, which are voluntarily described, the mind will, upon the whole, be in a state of enjoyment.
10 If Nature be thus cautious to preserve in a state of enjoyment a being so employed, the Poet ought to profit by the lesson held forth to him, and ought especially to take care, that, whatever passions he communicates to his Reader, those passions, if his Reader's mind be sound and vigorous, should always be accompanied with an over-
15 balance of pleasure. Now the music of harmonious metrical language, the sense of difficulty overcome, and the blind association of pleasure which has been previously received from works of rhyme or metre of the same or similar construction, an indistinct perception perpetually renewed of language closely resembling that of real
20 life, and yet, in the circumstance of metre, differing from it so widely—all these imperceptibly make up a complex feeling of delight, which is of the most important use in tempering the painful feeling always found intermingled with powerful descriptions of the deeper passions. This effect is always produced in pathetic and impas-
25 sioned poetry; while, in lighter compositions, the ease and gracefulness with which the Poet manages his numbers are themselves confessedly a principal source of the gratification of the Reader. All that it is *necessary* to say, however, upon this subject, may be effected by affirming, what few persons will deny, that, of two descrip-
30 tions, either of passions, manners, or characters, each of them equally well executed, the one in prose and the other in verse, the verse will be read a hundred times where the prose is read once.

Having thus explained a few of my reasons for writing in verse, and why I have chosen subjects from common life, and endeav-
35 oured to bring my language near to the real language of men, if I have been too minute in pleading my own cause, I have at the same time been treating a subject of general interest; and for this reason a few words shall be added with reference solely to these particular poems, and to some defects which will probably be found in them.
40 I am sensible that my associations must have sometimes been particular instead of general, and that, consequently, giving to things a false importance, I may have sometimes written upon unworthy subjects; but I am less apprehensive on this account, than that my language may frequently have suffered from those arbitrary con-
45 nexions of feelings and ideas with particular words and phrases,

from which no man can altogether protect himself. Hence I have no doubt, that, in some instances, feelings, even of the ludicrous, may be given to my Readers by expressions which appeared to me tender and pathetic. Such faulty expressions, were I convinced they
5   were faulty at present, and that they must necessarily continue to be so, I would willingly take all reasonable pains to correct. But it is dangerous to make these alterations on the simple authority of a few individuals, or even of certain classes of men; for where the understanding of an Author is not convinced, or his feelings altered,
10   this cannot be done without great injury to himself: for his own feelings are his stay and support; and, if he set them aside in one instance, he may be induced to repeat this act till his mind shall lose all confidence in itself, and become utterly debilitated. to this it may be added, that the critic ought never to forget that he is himself
15   exposed to the same errors as the Poet, and, perhaps, in a much greater degree: for there can be no presumption in saying of most readers, that it is not probable they will be so well acquainted with the various stages of meaning through which words have passed, or with the fickleness or stability of the relations of particular ideas to
20   each other; and, above all, since they are so much less interested in the subject, they may decide lightly and carelessly.

    Long as the Reader has been detained, I hope he will permit me to caution him against a mode of false criticism which has been applied to Poetry, in which the language closely resembles that of
25   life and nature. Such verses have been triumphed over in parodies, of which Dr. Johnson's stanza is a fair specimen:—

> I put my hat upon my head
> And walked into the Strand,
> And there I met another man
30   Whose hat was in his hand.

Immediately under these lines let us place one of the most justly admired stanzas of the 'Babes in the Wood.'

> These pretty Babes with hand in hand
> Went wandering up and down;
35   But never more they saw the Man
> Approaching from the town.

In both these stanzas the words, and the order of the words, in no respect differ from the most unimpassioned conversation. There are words in both, for example, 'the Strand,' and 'the town,' con-
40   nected with none but the most familiar ideas; yet the one stanza we admit as admirable, and the other as a fair example of the superla-

tively contemptible. Whence arises this difference? Not from the
metre, not from the language, not from the order of the words; but
the *matter* expressed in Dr. Johnson's stanza is contemptible. The
proper method of treating trivial and simple verses, to which Dr.
5   Johnson's stanza would be a fair parallelism, is not to say, this is a
bad kind of poetry, or, this is not poetry; but, this wants sense; it is
neither interesting in itself nor can *lead* to anything interesting; the
images neither originate in that sane state of feeling which arises
out of thought, nor can excite thought or feeling in the Reader. This
10   is the only sensible manner of dealing with such verses. Why trouble yourself about the species till you have previously decided upon
the genus? Why take pains to prove that an ape is not a Newton,
when it is self-evident that he is not a man?

    One request I must make of my reader, which is, that in judg-
15   ing these Poems he would decide by his own feelings genuinely,
and not by reflection upon what will probably be the judgement of
others. How common is it to hear a person say, I myself do not
object to this style of composition, or this or that expression, but, to
such and such classes of people it will appear mean or ludicrous!
20   This mode of criticism, so destructive of all sound unadulterated
judgement, is almost universal: let the Reader then abide, independently, by his own feelings, and, if he finds himself affected, let
him not suffer such conjectures to interfere with his pleasure.

    If an Author, by any single composition, has impressed us with
25   respect for his talents, it is useful to consider this as affording a pre-
sumption, that on other occasions where we have been displeased,
he, nevertheless, may not have written ill or absurdly; and further,
to give him so much credit for this one composition as may induce
us to review what has displeased us, with more care than we should
30   otherwise have bestowed upon it. This is not only an act of justice,
but, in our decisions upon poetry especially, may conduce, in a high
degree, to the improvement of our own taste; for an *accurate* taste in
poetry, and in all the other arts, as Sir Joshua Reynolds has
observed, is an *acquired* talent, which can only be produced by
35   thought and a long continued intercourse with the best models of
composition. This is mentioned, not with so ridiculous a purpose as
to prevent the most inexperienced Reader from judging for himself
(I have already said that I wish him to judge for himself), but merely to temper the rashness of decision, and to suggest, that, if Poetry
40   be a subject on which much time has not been bestowed, the judgement may be erroneous; and that, in many cases, it necessarily will
be so.

    Nothing would, I know, have so effectually contributed to fur-
ther the end which I have in view, as to have shown of what kind
45   the pleasure is, and how that pleasure is produced, which is con-

fessedly produced by metrical composition essentially different from that which I have here endeavoured to recommend: for the Reader will say that he has been pleased by such composition; and what more can be done for him? The power of any art is limited;

5 and he will suspect, that, if it be proposed to furnish him with new friends, that can be only upon condition of his abandoning his old friends. Besides, as I have said, the Reader is himself conscious of the pleasure which he has received from such composition, composition to which he has peculiarly attached the endearing name of

10 Poetry; and all men feel an habitual gratitude, and something of an honourable bigotry, for the objects which have long continued to please them: we not only wish to be pleased, but to be pleased in that particular way in which we have been accustomed to be pleased. There is in these feelings enough to resist a host of argu-

15 ments; and I should be the less able to combat them successfully, as I am willing to allow, that, in order entirely to enjoy the Poetry which I am recommending, it would be necessary to give up much of what is ordinarily enjoyed. But, would my limits have permitted me to point out how this pleasure is produced, many obstacles

20 might have been removed, and the Reader assisted in perceiving that the powers of language are not so limited as he may suppose; and that it is possible for poetry to give other enjoyments, of a purer, more lasting, and more exquisite nature. This part of the subject has not been altogether neglected, but it has not been so much my pres-

25 ent aim to prove, that the interest excited by some other kinds of poetry is less vivid, and less worthy of the nobler powers of the mind, as to offer reasons for presuming, that if my purpose were fulfilled, a species of poetry would be produced, which is genuine poetry; in its nature well adapted to interest mankind permanently,

30 and likewise important in the multiplicity and quality of its moral relations.

From what has been said, and from a perusal of the Poems, the Reader will be able clearly to perceive the object which I had in view: he will determine how far it has been attained; and, what is a

35 much more important question, whether it be worth attaining: and upon the decision of these two questions will rest my claim to the approbation of the Public.

9. SAMUEL TAYLOR COLERIDGE

Like Blake, Coleridge (1772–1834) was a man of many parts, of which poetry was one. He was a political philosopher, a very great literary critic, a religious thinker, and a man who generally illuminated whatever he turned his mind to. He and Wordsworth formed a great and famous literary friendship, but Coleridge's unfortunate (and accidental) addiction to opium caused a painful estrangement. Like Wordsworth, he wrote his major poetry relatively early on. The selections printed here celebrate the poetic power and recognize its waning. Below, Coleridge describes the genesis of the fragmentary poem, Kubla Kahn:

KUBLA KHAN
(1798)

In the summer of the year 1797, the Author, then in ill health, had retired to a lonely farm house between Porlock and Linton, on the Exmoor confines of Somerset and Devonshire. In consequence of a slight indisposition, an anodyne had been pre-scribed, from the effect of which he fell asleep in his chair at the moment that he was

5   reading the following sentence, or words of the same substance, in *Purchas's Pilgrimage:* "Here the Khan Kubla commanded a palace to be built, and a stately garden thereun-to: and thus ten miles of fertile ground were inclosed with a wall." The author contin-ued for about three hours in a profound sleep, at least of the external senses, during which time he has the most vivid confidence, that he could not have composed less

10   than from two to three hundred lines; if that indeed can be called composition in which all the images rose up before him as things, with a parallel production of the corre-spondent expressions, without any sensation or consciousness of effort. On awaking he appeared to himself to have a distinct recollection of the whole, and taking his pen, ink, and paper, instantly and eagerly wrote down the lines that are here preserved. At this

15   moment he was unfortunately called out by a person on business from Porlock, and detained by him above an hour, and on his return to his room, found, to his no small surprise and mortification, that though he still retained some vague and dim recollec-tion of the general purport of the vision, yet, with the exception of some eight or ten scattered lines and images, all the rest had passed away like the images on the surface

20   of a stream into which a stone had been cast, but, alas! without the after restoration of the latter:

9. *Samuel Taylor Coleridge*

Then all the charm
Is broken—all that phantom-world so fair
Vanishes, and a thousand circlets spread,
25   And each mis-shape[s] the other. Stay awhile,
Poor youth! who scarcely dar'st lift up thine eyes—
The stream will soon renew its smoothness, soon
The visions will return! And lo! he stays,
And soon the fragments dim of lovely forms
30   Come trembling back, unite, and now once more
The pool becomes a mirror.

[From Coleridge's *The Picture; or, the Lover's Resolution,* lines 91–100]

> Yet from the still surviving recollections in his mind, the Author has frequently purposed to finish for himself what had been originally, as it were, given to him. Αυρτον αδιον ασω [I shall sing a sweeter song tomorrow]: but the to-morrow is yet to
35   come.
> As a contrast to this vision, I have annexed a fragment of a very different character, describing with equal fidelity the dream of pain and disease.—1816

In Xanadu did Kubla Khan
A stately pleasure-dome decree:
Where Alph, the sacred river, ran
Through caverns measureless to man
5   Down to a sunless sea.
So twice five miles of fertile ground
With walls and towers were girdled round:
And there were gardens bright with sinuous rills
Where blossomed many an incense-bearing tree;
10   And here were forests ancient as the hills,
Enfolding sunny spots of greenery.

       But oh! that deep romantic chasm which slanted
       Down the green hill athwart a cedarn cover!
       A savage place! as holy and enchanted
15   As e'er beneath a waning moon was haunted
       By woman wailing for her demon-lover!
       And from this chasm, with ceaseless turmoil seething
       As if this earth in fast thick pants were breathing,
       A mighty fountain momently was forced:
20   Amid whose swift half-intermitted burst
       Huge fragments vaulted like rebounding hail,
       Or chaffy grain beneath the thresher's flail:
       And 'mid these dancing rocks at once and ever
25   It flung up momently the sacred river.

Five miles meandering with a mazy motion
Through wood and dale the sacred river ran,
Then reached the caverns measureless to man,
And sank in tumult to a lifeless ocean:
30   And 'mid this tumult Kubla heard from far
Ancestral voices prophesying war!

The shadow of the dome of pleasure
Floated midway on the waves;
Where was heard the mingled measure
35   From the fountain and the caves.
It was a miracle of rare device,
A sunny pleasure-dome with caves of ice!

A damsel with a dulcimer
In a vision once I saw:
40   It was an Abyssinian maid,
And on her dulcimer she played,
Singing of Mount Abora.
Could I revive within me
Her symphony and song,
45   To such a deep delight 'twould win me,
That with music loud and long,
I would build that dome in air,
That sunny dome! those caves of ice!
And all who heard should see them there,
50   And all should cry, Beware! Beware!
His flashing eyes, his floating hair!
Weave a circle round him thrice,
And close your eyes with holy dread,
For he on honey-dew hath fed,
55   And drunk the milk of Paradise.

DEJECTION: AN ODE

Late, late yestreen I saw the new Moon,
With the old Moon in her arms;
And I fear, I fear, my Master dear!
We shall have a deadly storm.
—*Ballad of Sir Patrick Spence*

I

Well! If the Bard was weather-wise, who made
The grand old ballad of Sir Patrick Spence,

This night, so tranquil now, will not go hence
Unroused by winds, that ply a busier trade
5   Than those which mould yon cloud in lazy flakes,
Or the dull sobbing draft, that moans and rakes
      Upon the strings of this Eolian lute,
      Which better far were mute.
   For lo! the New-moon winter-bright!
10   And overspread with phantom light,
      (With swimming phantom light o'erspread
      But rimmed and circled by a silver thread)
   I see the old Moon in her lap, foretelling
      The coming on of rain and squally blast.
15 And oh! that even now the gust were swelling,
      And the slant night-shower driving loud and fast!
Those sounds which oft have raised me, whilst they awed,
      And sent my soul abroad,
Might now perhaps their wonted impulse give,
20 Might startle this dull pain, and make it move and live!

II

A grief without a pang, void, dark, and drear,
      A stifled, drowsy, unimpassioned grief,
      Which finds no natural outlet, no relief,
        In word, or sigh, or tear—
25 O Lady! in this wan and heartless mood,
To other thoughts by yonder throstle woo'd,
      All this long eve, so balmy and serene,
Have I been gazing on the western sky,
      And its peculiar tint of yellow green:
30 And still I gaze—and with how blank an eye!
And those thin clouds above, in flakes and bars,
That give away their motion to the stars;
Those stars, that glide behind them or between,
Now sparkling, now bedimmed, but always seen:
35 Yon crescent Moon as fixed as if it grew
In its own cloudless, starless lake of blue;
I see them all so excellently fair,
I see, not feel, how beautiful they are!

III

My genial spirits fail;

40 And what can these avail
To lift the smothering weight from off my breast?
It were a vain endeavour,
Though I should gaze for ever
On that green light that lingers in the west:
45 I may not hope from outward forms to win
The passion and the life, whose fountains are within.

IV

O Lady! we receive but what we give,
And in our life alone does nature live:
Ours is her wedding-garment, ours her shroud!
50 And would we aught behold, of higher worth,
Than that inanimate cold world allowed
To the poor loveless ever-anxious crowd,
Ah! from the soul itself must issue forth,
A light, a glory, a fair luminous cloud
55 Enveloping the Earth—
And from the soul itself must there be sent
A sweet and potent voice, of its own birth,
Of all sweet sounds the life and element!

V

O pure of heart! thou need'st not ask of me
60 What this strong music in the soul may be!
What, and wherein it doth exist,
This light, this glory, this fair luminous mist,
This beautiful and beauty-making power.
Joy, virtuous Lady! Joy that ne'er was given,
65 Save to the pure, and in their purest hour,
Life, and Life's effluence, cloud at once and shower,
Joy, Lady! is the spirit and the power,

Which wedding Nature to us gives in dower,
A new Earth and new Heaven,
70 Undreamt of by the sensual and the proud—
Joy is the sweet voice, joy the luminous cloud—
We in ourselves rejoice!

And thence flows all that charms or ear or sight,
    All melodies the echoes of that voice,
75 All colours a suffusion from that light.

VI

There was a time when, though my path was rough,
    This joy within me dallied with distress,
And all misfortunes were but as the stuff
    Whence Fancy made me dreams of happiness:
80 For hope grew round me, like the twining vine,
And fruits, and foliage, not my own, seemed mine.
But now afflictions bow me down to earth:
Nor care I that they rob me of my mirth,
    But oh! each visitation
85 Suspends what nature gave me at my birth,
    My shaping spirit of Imagination.
For not to think of what I needs must feel,
    But to be still and patient, all I can;
And haply by abstruse research to steal
90   From my own nature all the natural man—
    This was my sole resource, my only plan:
Till that which suits a part infects the whole,
And now is almost grown the habit of my soul.

VII

Hence, viper thoughts, that coil around my mind,
95   Reality's dark dream!
I turn from you, and listen to the wind,
    Which long has raved unnoticed. What a scream
Of agony by torture lengthened out
That lute sent forth! Thou Wind, that ravest without,
100   Bare crag, or mountain-tairn, or blasted tree,
Or pine-grove whither woodman never clomb,
Or lonely house, long held the witches' home,
    Methinks were fitter instruments for thee,
Mad Lutanist! who in this month of showers,
105 Of dark brown gardens, and of peeping flowers,
Mak'st Devils' yule, with worse than wintry song,
The blossoms, buds, and timorous leaves among.
    Thou Actor, perfect in all tragic sounds!
Thou mighty Poet, e'en to frenzy bold!

110   What tell'st thou now about?
            'Tis of the rushing of a host in rout,
      With groans of trampled men, with smarting wounds—
At once they groan with pain, and shudder with the cold!
But hush! there is a pause of deepest silence!

115   And all that noise, as of a rushing crowd,
With groans, and tremulous shudderings—all is over—
        It tells another tale, with sounds less deep and loud!
         A tale of less affright,
         And tempered with delight,

120 As Otway's self had framed the tender lay,
         'Tis of a little child
         Upon a lonesome wild,
Not far from home, but she hath lost her way:
And now moans low in bitter grief and fear,

125 And now screams loud, and hopes to make her mother hear.

VIII

'Tis midnight, but small thoughts have I of sleep:
Full seldom may my friend such vigils keep!
Visit her, gentle Sleep! with wings of healing,
         And may this storm be but a mountain-birth,

130 May all the stars hang bright above her dwelling,
         Silent as though they watched the sleeping Earth!
         With light heart may she rise,
         Gay fancy, cheerful eyes,
        Joy lift her spirit, joy attune her voice,

135 To her may all things live, from pole to pole,
Their life the eddying of her living soul!
        O simple spirit, guided from above,
Dear Lady! friend devoutest of my choice,
Thus mayest thou ever, evermore rejoice.

—Apr. 4, 1802

10. GEORGE GORDON, LORD BYRON

George Gordon, Lord Byron (1788–1824) was in his day the most famous and celebrated of the great Romantics. His poetry ranges from tender lyrics to witty satire to long narratives. His public acts—fighting for Greek independence, swimming in the Dardanelles—captured public opinion and made him perhaps the first "celebrity" in the modern sense. His public persona *of sexual obsession and simultaneous world-weariness embodied one aspect of romanticism, though not its best.*

DARKNESS

I had a dream, which was not all a dream.
The bright sun was extinguish'd, and the stars
Did wander darkling in the eternal space,
Rayless, and pathless, and the icy earth
5   Swung blind and blackening in the moonless air;
Morn came and went—and came, and brought no day,
And men forgot their passions in the dread
Of this their desolation; and all hearts
Were chill'd into a selfish prayer for light:
10 And they did live by watchfires—and the thrones,
The palaces of crowned kings—the huts,
The habitations of all things which dwell,
Were burnt for beacons; cities were consum'd,
And men were gather'd round their blazing homes
15 To look once more into each other's face;
Happy were those who dwelt within the eye
Of the volcanos, and their mountain-torch:
A fearful hope was all the world contain'd;
Forests were set on fire—but hour by hour
20 They fell and faded—and the crackling trunks
Extinguish'd with a crash—and all was black.
The brows of men by the despairing light
Wore an unearthly aspect, as by fits
The flashes fell upon them; some lay down
25 And hid their eyes and wept; and some did rest
Their chins upon their clenched hands, and smil'd;
And others hurried to and fro, and fed
Their funeral piles with fuel, and look'd up

With mad disquietude on the dull sky,
30   The pall of a past world; and then again
With curses cast them down upon the dust,
And gnash'd their teeth and howl'd: the wild birds shriek'd
And, terrified, did flutter on the ground,
And flap their useless wings; the wildest brutes
35   Came tame and tremulous; and vipers crawl'd
And twin'd themselves among the multitude,
Hissing, but stingless—they were slain for food.
And War, which for a moment was no more,
Did glut himself again: a meal was bought
40   With blood, and each sate sullenly apart
Gorging himself in gloom: no love was left;
All earth was but one thought—and that was death
Immediate and inglorious; and the pang
Of famine fed upon all entrails—men
45   Died, and their bones were tombless as their flesh;
The meagre by the meagre were devour'd,
Even dogs assail'd their masters, all save one,
And he was faithful to a corse, and kept
The birds and beasts and famish'd men at bay,
50   Till hunger clung them, or the dropping dead
Lur'd their lank jaws; himself sought out no food,
But with a piteous and perpetual moan,
And a quick desolate cry, licking the hand
Which answer'd not with a caress—he died.
55   The crowd was famish'd by degrees; but two
Of an enormous city did survive,
And they were enemies: they met beside
The dying embers of an altar-place
Where had been heap'd a mass of holy things
60   For an unholy usage; they rak'd up,
And shivering scrap'd with their cold skeleton hands
The feeble ashes, and their feeble breath
Blew for a little life, and made a flame
Which was a mockery; then they lifted up
65   Their eyes as it grew lighter, and beheld
Each other's aspects—saw, and shriek'd, and died—
Even of their mutual hideousness they died,
Unknowing who he was upon whose brow
Famine had written Fiend. The world was void,
70   The populous and the powerful was a lump,
Seasonless, herbless, treeless, manless, lifeless—
A lump of death—a chaos of hard clay.
The rivers, lakes and ocean all stood still,

And nothing stirr'd within their silent depths;
75 Ships sailorless lay rotting on the sea,
And their masts fell down piecemeal: as they dropp'd
They slept on the abyss without a surge—
The waves were dead; the tides were in their grave,
The moon, their mistress, had expir'd before;
80 The winds were wither'd in the stagnant air,
And the clouds perish'd; Darkness had no need
Of aid from them—She was the Universe.

"SHE WALKS IN BEAUTY, LIKE THE NIGHT"

SHE walks in beauty, like the night
Of cloudless climes and starry skies,
And all that's best of dark and bright
Meets in her aspect and her eyes;
5 Thus mellow'd to that tender light
Which Heaven to gaudy day denies.

One shade the more, one ray the less,
Had half impair'd the nameless grace
Which waves in every raven tress
10 Or softly lightens o'er her face,
Where thoughts serenely sweet express
How pure, how dear their dwelling-place.

And on that cheek and o'er that brow
So soft, so calm, yet eloquent,
15 The smiles that win, the tints that glow,
But tell of days in goodness spent,—
A mind at peace with all below,
A heart whose love is innocent.

"STANZAS"

When a man hath no freedom to fight for at home,
Let him combat for that of his neighbours;
Let him think of the glories of Greece and of Rome,
And get knock'd on the head for his labours,
5   To do good to mankind is the chivalrous plan,
And is always as nobly requited;
Then battle for freedom wherever you can,
And, if not shot or hang'd, you'll get knighted.

11. PERCY BYSSHE SHELLEY

Shelley (1792–1822) was from the short-lived second generation of Romanticism. A natural rebel with a scorn for conventions, he was expelled from Oxford, eloped his way into marriage, fled England in a ménage à trois, lived in Italy in acquaintance with both Byron and Keats, and drowned in the Mediterranean in a storm at sea. Shelley's poetry tends to be highly emotional and self-dramatizing, but at times he was able to focus his scorn and produce verse that was effective as social criticism.

ODE TO THE WEST WIND
I

O wild West Wind, thou breath of Autumn's being,
Thou, from whose unseen presence the leaves dead
Are driven, like ghosts from an enchanter fleeing,

Yellow, and black, and pale, and hectic red,
5   Pestilence-stricken multitudes: O Thou,
Who chairotest to their dark wintry bed

The winged seeds, where they lie cold and low,
Each like a corpse within its grave, until
Thine azure sister of the Spring shall blow

10   Her clarion o'er the dreaming earth, and fill
(Driving sweet buds like flocks to feed in air)
With living hues and odours plain and hill:

Wild Spirit, which art moving everywhere;
Destroyer and Preserver; hear, O hear!

II

15   Thou on whose stream, 'mid the steep sky's commotion,
Loose clouds like Earth's decaying leaves are shed,
Shook from the tangled boughs of Heaven and Ocean,

Angels of rain and lightning; there are spread
On the blue surface of thine aery surge,
20   Like the bright hair uplifted from the head

Of some fierce Maenad, even from the dim verge
Of the horizon to the zenith's height,
The locks of the approaching storm. Thou Dirge

Of the dying year, to which this closing night
25   Will be the dome of a vast sepulchre,
Vaulted with all thy congregated might

Of vapors, from whose solid atmosphere
Black rain and fire and hail will burst: O hear!

III

Thou who didst waken from his summer dreams
30   The blue Mediterranean, where he lay,
Lulled by the coil of his crystalline streams,

Beside a pumice isle in Baiae's bay,
And saw in sleep old palaces and towers
Quivering within the wave's intenser day,

35   All overgrown with azure moss and flowers
So sweet, the sense faints picturing them! Thou
For whose path the Atlantic's level powers

Cleave themselves into chasms, while far below
The sea-blooms and the oozy woods which wear
40   The sapless foliage of the ocean, know

Thy voice, and suddenly grow grey with fear,
And tremble and despoil themselves: O hear!

IV

If I were a dead leaf thou mightest bear;
If I were a swift cloud to fly with thee;
45   A wave to pant beneath thy power, and share

The impulse of thy strength, only less free
Than thou, O Uncontrollable! If even
I were as in my boyhood, and could be

The comrade of thy wanderings over Heaven,
50   As then, when to outstrip thy skiey speed
Scarce seemed a vision; I would ne'er have striven

As thou with thee in prayer in my sore need.
Oh! lift me as a wave, a leaf, a cloud!
I fall upon the thorns of life! I bleed!

55   A heavy weight of hours has chained and bowed
One too like thee: tameless, and swift, and proud.

V

Make me thy lyre, even as the forest is:
What if my leaves are falling like its own!
The tumult of thy mighty harmonies

60   Will take from both a deep, autumnal tone,
Sweet though in sadness. Be thou, Spirit fierce,
My spirit! Be thou me, impetuous one!

Drive my dead thoughts over the universe
Like withered leaves to quicken a new birth!
65   And, by the incantation of this verse,

Scatter, as from an unextinguished hearth
Ashes and sparks, my words among mankind!
Be though my lips to unawakened Earth

The trumpet of a prophecy! O Wind,
70   If, Winter comes, can Spring be far behind?

ENGLAND IN 1819

An old, mad, blind, despised, and dying King;
Princes, the dregs of their dull race, who flow
Through public scorn,—mud from a muddy spring;
Rulers who neither see nor feel nor know,
5   But leechlike to their fainting country cling.
Till they drop, blind in blood, without a blow,
A people starved and stabbed in th'untilled field;
An army, which liberticide and prey
Makes as a two-edged sword to all who wield;
10   Golden and sanguine laws which tempt and slay;
Religion Christless, Godless—a book sealed;

A senate,—Time's worst statute, unrepealed—
Are graves, from which a glorious Phantom may
Burst, to illumine our tempestuous day.

OZYMANDIAS

I met a traveller from an antique land,
Who said—"two vast and trunkless legs of stone
Stand in the desert . . . near them, on the sand,
Half sunk a shattered visage lies, whose frown,
5 And wrinkled lips, and sneer of cold command,
Tell that its sculptor well those passions read
Which yet survive, stamped on these lifeless things,
The hand that mocked them, and the heart that fed;
And on the pedestal these words appear:
10 My name is Ozymandias, King of Kings,
Look on my Works ye Mighty, and despair!
Nothing beside remains. Round the decay
Of that colossal Wreck, boundless and bare
The lone and level sands stretch far away."—

MUTABILITY

The flower that smiles to-day
To-morrow dies;
All that we wish to stay
Tempts and then flies.
5 What is this world's delight?
Lightning that mocks the night,
Brief even as bright.
Virtue, how frail it is!
Friendship how rare!
10 Love, how it sells poor bliss
For proud despair!
But we, though soon they fall,
Survive their joy, and all
Which ours we call.
15 Whilst skies are blue and bright,
Whilst flowers are gay,
Whilst eyes that change ere night
Make glad the day;
Whilst yet the calm hours creep,
20 Dream thou—and from thy sleep
Then wake to weep.

12. John Keats

Keats (1795–1821) was the last of the great English Romantic poets and the first of them to die. Although he was trained as a surgeon, Keats' great ambition was to be one of the great English poets, and he bent all the resources of his life towards that end. His early work showed little promise but, as if by a heroic act of will, he succeeded in his ambition before dying of tuberculosis. Keats' great odes (the products of about six weeks of intensive work in May of 1819) are lush in diction and imagery, stately in movement, restrained in feeling, and powerful tributes to the imagination.

ODE TO MELANCHOLY

I

No, no, go not to Lethe, neither twist
    Wolfsbane, tight-rooted, for its poisonous wine;
Nor suffer thy pale forehead to be kissed
    By nightshade, ruby grape of Proserpine;
5   Make not your rosary of yew-berries,
    Nor let the beetle, nor the death-moth be
    Your mournful Psyche, nor the downy owl
A partner in your sorrow's mysteries;
    For shade to shade will come too drowsily,
10   And drown the wakeful anguish of the soul.

II

But when the melancholy fit shall fall
    Sudden from heaven like a weeping cloud,
That fosters the droop-headed flowers all,
    And hides the green hill in an April shroud;
15   Then glut thy sorrow on a morning rose,
    Or on the rainbow of the salt sand-wave,
    Or on the wealth of globed peonies;
Or if thy mistress some rich anger shows,
    Imprison her soft hand, and let her rave,
20   And feed deep, deep upon her peerless eyes.

III

She dwells with Beauty—Beauty that must die;
    And Joy, whose hand is ever at his lips
Bidding adieu; and aching Pleasure night,
    Turning to Poison while the bee-mouth sips:
25   Aye, in the very temple of Delight
    Veiled Melancholy has her sovereign shrine,
        though seen of none save him whose strenuous tongue
    Can burst Joy's grape against his palate fine;
His soul shall taste the sadness of her might,
30   And be among her cloudy trophies hung.

ODE TO A NIGHTINGALE

I

My heart aches, and a drowsy numbness pains
    My sense, as though of hemlock I had drunk,
Or emptied some dull opiate to the drains
    One minute past, and Lethe-wards had sunk:
5 'Tis not through envy of thy happy lot,
    But being too happy in thine happiness,—
      That thou, light-winged Dryad of the trees,
      In some melodious plot
Of beechen green, and shadows numberless,
10   Singest of summer in full-throated ease.

II

O, for a draught of vintage! that hath been
    Cool'd a long age in the deep-delved earth,
Tasting of Flora and the country green,
    Dance, and Provençal song, and sunburnt mirth!
15 O for a beaker full of the warm South,
    Full of the true, the blushful Hippocrene,
With beaded bubbles winking at the brim,
      And purple-stained mouth;
That I might drink, and leave the world unseen,
20   And with thee fade away into the forest dim:

III

Fade far away, dissolve, and quite forget
    What thou among the leaves hast never known,

The weariness, the fever, and the fret
    Here, where men sit and hear each other groan;
25 Where palsy shakes a few, sad, last gray hairs,
      Where youth grows pale, and spectre-thin, and dies;
        Where but to think is to be full of sorrow
And leaden-eyed despairs,
    Where Beauty cannot keep her lustrous eyes,
30   Or new Love pine at them beyond to-morrow.

IV

Away! away! for I will fly to thee,
    Not charioted by Bacchus and his pards,
But on the viewless wings of Poesy,
    Though the dull brain perplexes and retards:
35 Already with thee! tender is the night,
    And haply the Queen-Moon is on her throne,
      Cluster'd around by all her starry Fays;
        But here there is no light,
Save what from heaven is with the breezes blown
40   Through verdurous' glooms and winding mossy ways.

V

I cannot see what flowers are at my feet,
    Nor what soft incense hangs upon the boughs,
But, in embalmed darkness, guess each sweet
    Wherewith the seasonable month endows
45 The grass, the thicket, and the fruit-tree wild;
    White hawthorn, and the pastoral eglantine;
      Fast fading violets cover'd up in leaves;
        And mid-May's eldest child,
The coming musk-rose, full of dewy wine,
50 The murmurous haunt of flies on summer eves.

VI

Darkling, I listen; and, for many a time
    I have been half in love with easeful Death,
Call'd him soft names in many a mused rhyme,
    To take into the air my quiet breath;
55 Now more than ever seems it rich to die,
To cease upon the midnight with no pain,
    While thou art pouring forth thy soul abroad
      In such an ecstasy!

Still wouldst thou sing, and I have ears in vain—
60   To thy high requiem become a sod.

VII

Thou wast not born for death, immortal Bird!
        No hungry generations tread thee down;
The voice I hear this passing night was heard
        In ancient days by emperor and clown:
65 Perhaps the self-same song that found a path
        Through the sad heart of Ruth, when, sick for home,
            She stood in tears amid the alien corn;
                The same that oft-times hath
        Charm'd magic casements, opening on the foam
70 Of perilous seas, in faery lands forlorn.

VIII

Forlorn! the very word is like a bell
        To toll me back from thee to my sole self!
Adieu! the fancy cannot cheat so well
        As she is fam'd to do, deceiving elf.
75 Adieu! adieu! thy plaintive anthem fades
        Past the near meadows, over the still stream,
            Up the hill-side; and now 'tis buried deep
                In the next valley-glades:
        Was it a vision, or a waking dream?
80   Fled is that music:—Do I wake or sleep?   1819

ODE ON A GRECIAN URN

I

Thou still unravish'd bride of quietness,
        Thou foster-child of silence and slow time,
Sylvan historian, who canst thus express
        A flowery tale more sweetly than our rhyme:
5 What leaf-fring'd legend haunts about thy shape
        Of deities or mortals, or of both,
            In Tempe or the dales of Arcady?
        What men or gods are these? What maidens loth?
What mad pursuit? What struggle to escape?
10   What pipes and timbrels? What wild ecstasy?

12. John Keats

II

Heard melodies are sweet, but those unheard
   Are sweeter; therefore, ye soft pipes, play on;
Not to the sensual ear, but, more endear'd,
   Pipe to the spirit ditties of no tone:
15 Fair youth, beneath the trees, thou canst not leave
   Thy song, nor ever can those trees be bare;
    Bold lover, never, never canst thou kiss,
Though winning near the goal—yet, do not grieve;
    She cannot fade, though thou hast not thy bliss,
20   For ever wilt thou love, and she be fair!

III

Ah, happy, happy boughs! that cannot shed
   Your leaves, nor ever bid the spring adieu;
And, happy melodist, unwearied,
   For ever piping songs for ever new;
25 More happy love! more happy, happy love!
   For ever warm and still to be enjoy'd,
    For ever panting, and for ever young;
All breathing human passion far above,
   That leaves a heart high-sorrowful and cloy'd,
30   A burning forehead, and a parching tongue.

IV

Who are these coming to the sacrifice?
   To what green altar, O mysterious priest,
Lead'st thou that heifer lowing at the skies,
   And all her silken flanks with garlands drest?
35 What little town by river or sea shore,
   Or mountain-built with peaceful citadel,
    Is emptied of this folk, this pious morn?
And, little town, thy streets for evermore
   Will silent be, and not a soul to tell
40   Why thou art desolate, can e'er return.

V

O Attic shape! Fair attitude! with brede
      Of marble men and maidens overwrought,
With forest branches and the trodden weed;
      Thou, silent form, dost tease us out of thought
45 As doth eternity: Cold Pastoral!
      When old age shall this generation waste,
        Thou shalt remain, in midst of other woe
      Than ours, a friend to man, to whom thou say'st,
"Beauty is truth, truth beauty,"—that is all
50   Ye know on earth, and all ye need to know.

                               1819

ODE TO PSYCHE

O Goddess! hear these tuneless numbers, wrung
By sweet enforcement and remembrance dear,
And pardon that thy secrets should be sung
Even into thine own soft-conched ear:
5 Surely I dreamt to-day, or did I see
The winged Psyche with awaken'd eyes?
wander'd in a forest thoughtlessly,
And, on the sudden, fainting with surprise,
Saw two fair creatures, couched side by side
10 In deepest grass, beneath the whisp'ring roof
Of leaves and trembled blossoms, where there ran
      A brooklet, scarce espied:
Mid hush'd, cool-rooted flowers, fragrant-eyed,
Blue, silver-white, and budded Tyrian,
15 They lay calm-breathing, on the bedded grass;
Their arms embraced, and their pinions too;
Their lips touch'd not, but had not bade adieu,
As if disjoined by soft-handed slumber,
And ready still past kisses to outnumber
20 At tender eye-dawn of aurorean love:
      The winged boy I knew;
But who wast thou, O happy, happy dove?
      His Psyche true!

O latest born and loveliest vision far
25 Of all Olympus' faded hierarchy!
Fairer than Phoebe's sapphire-region'd star,

Or Vesper, amorous glow-worm of the sky;
Fairer than these, though temple thou hast none,
      Nor altar heap'd with flowers;
30 Nor virgin-choir to make delicious moan
        Upon the midnight hours;
No voice, no lute, no pipe, no incense sweet
From chain-swung censer teeming;
No shrine, no grove, no oracle, no heat
35 Of pale-mouth'd prophet dreaming.

O brightest! though too late for antique vows,
Too, too late for the fond believing lyre,
When holy were the haunted forest boughs,
Holy the air, the water, and the fire;
40 Yet even in these days so far retir'd
From happy pieties, thy lucent fans,
Fluttering among the faint Olympians,
I see, and sing, by my own eyes inspir'd.
So let me be thy choir, and make a moan
45   Upon the midnight hours;
Thy voice, thy lute, thy pipe, thy incense sweet
From swinged censer teeming;
Thy shrine, thy grove, thy oracle, thy heat
Of pale-mouth'd prophet dreaming.

50 Yes, I will be thy priest, and build a fane
In some untrodden region of my mind,
Where branched thoughts, new grown with pleasant pain,
Instead of pines shall murmur in the wind:
Far, far around shall those dark-cluster'd trees
55 Fledge the wild-ridged mountains steep by steep;
And there by zephyrs, streams, and birds, and bees,
The moss-lain Dryads shall be lull'd to sleep;
And in the midst of this wide quietness
A rosy sanctuary will I dress
60 With the wreath'd trellis of a working brain,
With buds, and bells, and stars without a name,
With all the gardener Fancy e'er could feign,
Who breeding flowers, will never breed the same:
And there shall be for thee all soft delight
65   That shadowy thought can win,
A bright torch, and a casement ope at night,
      To let the warm Love in!

13. RALPH WALDO EMERSON

Romanticism reached America in the 1830s, a generation later than in Europe, and its greatest voice was Emerson (1803–1882). Emerson's chief concern was to redefine the American democratic opportunity in terms different from those Americans had adapted from Benjamin Franklin. To the standard Romantic themes and emphases, he added the American sense of freedom from the limits of the past ("Why should not we have a poetry and philosophy of insight and not of tradition?"), of Special Destiny ("We have listened too long to the courtly muses of Europe"), of American possibility ("Who can set bounds to the possibilities of man?"), and of an unprecedented sense of individualism ("The individual is the world").

FROM NATURE
(1836)

A subtle chain of countless rings
The next unto the farthest brings;
The eye reads omens where it goes,
And speaks all languages the rose;
And striving to be man, the worm
Mounts through all the spires of form.

INTRODUCTION

Our age is retrospective. It builds the sepulchres of the fathers. It writes biographies, histories, and criticism. The foregoing generations beheld God and nature face to face; we, through their eyes. Why should not we also enjoy an original relation to the universe?
5   Why should not we have a poetry and philosophy of insight and not of tradition, and a religion by revelation to us, and not the history of theirs? Embosomed for a season in nature, whose floods of life stream around and through us, and invite us by the powers they supply, to action proportioned to nature, why should we grope
10 among the dry bones of the past, or put the living generation into masquerade out of its faded wardrobe? The sun shines to-day also. There is more wool and flax in the fields. There are new lands, new men, new thoughts. Let us demand our own works and laws and

worship.

Undoubtedly we have no questions to ask which are unanswerable. We must trust the perfection of the creation so far, as to believe that whatever curiosity the order of things has awakened in our minds, the order of things can satisfy. Every man's condition is a solution in hieroglyphic to those inquiries he would put. He acts it as life, before he apprehends it as truth. In like manner, nature is already, in its forms and tendencies, describing its own design. Let us interrogate the great apparition, that shines so peacefully around us. Let us inquire, to what end is nature?

All science has one aim, namely, to find a theory of nature. We have theories of races and of functions, but scarcely yet a remote approach to an idea of creation. We are now so far from the road to truth, that religious teachers dispute and hate each other, and speculative men are esteemed unsound and frivolous. But to a sound judgment, the most abstract truth is the most practical. Whenever a true theory appears, it will be its own evidence. Its test is, that it will explain all phenomena. Now many are thought not only unexplained but inexplicable; as language, sleep, madness, dreams, beasts, sex.

Philosophically considered, the universe is composed of Nature and the Soul. Strictly speaking, therefore, all that is separate from us, all which Philosophy distinguishes as the NOT ME, that is, both nature and art, all other men and my own body, must be ranked under this name, NATURE. In enumerating the values of nature and casting up their sum, I shall use the word in both senses;—in its common and in its philosophical import. In inquiries so general as our present one, the inaccuracy is not material; no confusion of thought will occur. *Nature*, in the common sense, refers to essences unchanged by man; space, the air, the river, the leaf. *Art* is applied to the mixture of his will with the same things, as in a house, a canal, a statue, a picture. But his operations taken together are so insignificant, a little chipping, baking, patching, and washing, that in an impression so grand as that of the world on the human mind, they do not vary the result.

CHAPTER 1

To go into solitude, a man needs to retire as much from his chamber as from society. I am not solitary whilst I read and write, though nobody is with me. But if a man would be alone, let him look at the stars. The rays that come from those heavenly worlds, will separate between him and what he touches. One might think the atmosphere was made transparent with this design, to give

man, in the heavenly bodies, the perpetual presence of the sublime. Seen in the streets of cities, how great they are! If the stars should appear one night in a thousand years, how would men believe and adore, and preserve for many generations the remembrance of the
5   city of God which had been shown! But every night come out these envoys of beauty, and light the universe with their admonishing smile.

The stars awaken a certain reverence, because though always present, they are inaccessible; but all natural objects make a kindred
10 impression, when the mind is open to their influence. Nature never wears a mean appearance. Neither does the wisest man extort her secret, and lose his curiosity by finding out all her perfection. Nature never became a toy to a wise spirit. The flowers, the animals, the mountains, reflected the wisdom of his best hour, as much as
15 they had delighted the simplicity of his childhood.

When we speak of nature in this manner, we have a distinct but most poetical sense in the mind. We mean the integrity of impression made by manifold natural objects. It is this which distinguishes the stick of timber of the wood-cutter, from the tree of the poet.
20 The charming landscape which I saw this morning, is indubitably made up of some twenty or thirty farms. Miller owns this field, Locke that, and Manning the woodland beyond. But none of them owns the landscape. There is a property in the horizon which no man has but he whose eye can integrate all the parts, that is, the
25 poet. This is the best part of these men's farms, yet to this their warranty deeds give no title.

To speak truly, few adult persons can see nature. Most persons do not see the sun. At least they have a very superficial seeing. The sun illuminates only the eye of the man, but shines into the eye and
30 the heart of the child. The lover of nature is he whose inward and outward senses are still truly adjusted to each other; who has retained the spirit of infancy even into the era of manhood. His intercourse with heaven and earth, becomes part of his daily food. In the presence of nature, a wild delight runs through the man, in
35 spite of real sorrows. Nature says,—he is my creature, and maugre all his impertinent griefs, he shall be glad with me. Not the sun or the summer alone, but every hour and season yields its tribute of delight; for every hour and change corresponds to and authorizes a different state of the mind, from breathless noon to grimmest mid-
40 night. Nature is a setting that fits equally well a comic or a mourning piece. In good health, the air is a cordial of incredible virtue. Crossing a bare common, in snow puddles, at twilight, under a clouded sky, without having in my thoughts any occurrence of special good fortune, I have enjoyed a perfect exhilaration. I am glad to
45 the brink of fear. In the woods too, a man casts off his years, as the

snake his slough, and at what period soever of life, is always a child.
In the woods, is perpetual youth. Within these plantations of God,
a decorum and sanctity reign, a perennial festival is dressed, and
the guest sees not how he should tire of them in a thousand years.
5   In the woods, we return to reason and faith. There I feel that nothing can befall me in life,—no disgrace, no calamity, (leaving me my
eyes,) which nature cannot repair. Standing on the bare ground,—
my head bathed by the blithe air, and uplifted into infinite space,—
all mean egotism vanishes. I become a transparent eye-ball; I am
10   nothing; I see all; the currents of the Universal Being circulate
through me; I am part or particle of God. The name of the nearest
friend sounds then foreign and accidental: to be brothers, to be
acquaintances,—master or servant, is then a trifle and a distur-
bance. I am the lover of uncontained and immortal beauty. In the
15   wilderness, I find something more dear and connate than in streets
or villages. In the tranquil landscape, and especially in the distant
line of the horizon, man beholds somewhat as beautiful as his own
nature.

The greatest delight which the fields and woods minister, is the
20   suggestion of an occult relation between man and the vegetable. I
am not alone and unacknowledged. They nod to me and I to them.
The waving of the boughs in the storm, is new to me and old. It
takes me by surprise, and yet is not unknown. Its effect is like that
of a higher thought or a better emotion coming over me, when I
25   deemed I was thinking justly or doing right.

Yet it is certain that the power to produce this delight, does not
reside in nature, but in man, or in a harmony of both. It is necessary
to use these pleasures with great temperance. For, nature is not
always tricked in holiday attire, but the same scene which yesterday
30   breathed perfume and glittered as for the frolic of the nymphs, is
overspread with melancholy today. Nature always wears the colors
of the spirit. To a man laboring under calamity, the heat of his own
fire hath sadness in it. Then, there is a kind of contempt of the landscape felt by him who has just lost by death a dear friend. The sky
35   is less grand as it shuts down over less worth in the population.

THE AMERICAN SCHOLAR

MR. PRESIDENT AND GENTLEMEN,

I greet you on the re-commencement of our literary year. Our anniversary is one of hope, and, perhaps, not enough of labor. We do not meet for games of strength or skill, for the recitation of histories, tragedies, and odes, like the ancient Greeks; for parliaments
5   of love and poesy, like the Troubadours; nor for the advancement of science, like our cotemporaries in the British and European capitals. Thus far, our holiday has been simply a friendly sign of the survival of the love of letters amongst a people too busy to give to letters any more. As such, it is precious as the sign of an indestructible instinct.
10   Perhaps the time is already come, when it ought to be, and will be, something else; when the sluggard intellect of this continent will look from under its iron lids, and fill the postponed expectation of the world with something better than the exertions of mechanical skill. Our day of dependence, our long apprenticeship to the learn-
15   ing of other lands, draws to a close. The millions, that around us are rushing into life, cannot always be fed on the sere remains of foreign harvests. Events, actions arise, that must be sung, that will sing themselves. Who can doubt, that poetry will revive and lead in a new age, as the star in the constellation Harp, which now flames in
20   our zenith, astronomers announce, shall one day be the pole-star for a thousand years?

In this hope, I accept the topic which not only usage, but the nature of our association, seem to prescribe to this day,—the AMERICAN SCHOLAR. Year by year, we come up hither to read one
25   more chapter of his biography. Let us inquire what light new days and events have thrown on his character, and his hopes.

It is one of those fables, which, out of an unknown antiquity, convey an unlooked-for wisdom, that the gods, in the beginning, divided Man into men, that he might be more helpful to himself;
30   just as the hand was divided into fingers, the better to answer its end.

The old fable covers a doctrine ever new and sublime; that there is One Man,—present to all particular men only partially, or through one faculty; and that you must take the whole society to
35   find the whole man. Man is not a farmer, or a professor, or an engineer, but he is all. Man is priest, and scholar, and statesman, and producer, and soldier. In the *divided* or social state, these functions are parcelled out to individuals, each of whom aims to do his stint of the joint work, whilst each other performs his. The fable implies,
40   that the individual, to possess himself, must sometimes return from his own labor to embrace all the other laborers. But unfortunately,

this original unit, this fountain of power, has been so distributed to multitudes, has been so minutely subdivided and peddled out, that it is spilled into drops, and cannot be gathered. The state of society is one in which the members have suffered amputation from the

5   trunk, and strut about so many walking monsters,—a good finger, a neck, a stomach, an elbow, but never a man.

       Man is thus metamorphosed into a thing, into many things. The planter, who is Man sent out into the field to gather food, is seldom cheered by any idea of the true dignity of his ministry. He sees

10   his bushel and his cart, and nothing beyond, and sinks into the farmer, instead of Man on the farm. The tradesman scarcely ever gives an ideal worth to his work, but is ridden by the routine of his craft, and the soul is subject to dollars. The priest becomes a form; the attorney, a statute-book; the mechanic, a machine; the sailor, a

15   rope of a ship.

       In this distribution of functions, the scholar is the delegated intellect. In the right state, he is, *Man Thinking*. In the degenerate state, when the victim of society, he tends to become a mere thinker, or, still worse, the parrot of other men's thinking.

20   In this view of him, as Man Thinking, the theory of his office is contained. Him nature solicits with all her placid, all her monitory pictures; him the past instructs; him the future invites. Is not, indeed, every man a student, and do not all things exist for the student's behoof? And, finally, is not the true scholar the only true mas-

25   ter? But the old oracle said, "All things have two handles: beware of the wrong one." In life, too often, the scholar errs with mankind and forfeits his privilege. Let us see him in his school, and consider him in reference to the main influences he receives.

       I. The first in time and the first in importance of the influences

30   upon the mind is that of nature. Every day, the sun; and, after sunset, night and her stars. Ever the winds blow; ever the grass grows. Every day, men and women, conversing, beholding and beholden. The scholar is he of all men whom this spectacle most engages. He must settle its value in his mind. What is nature to him? There is

35   never a beginning, there is never an end, to the inexplicable continuity of this web of God, but always circular power returning into itself. Therein it resembles his own spirit, whose beginning, whose ending, he never can find,—so entire, so boundless. Far, too, as her splendors shine, system on system shooting like rays, upward,

40   downward, without centre, without circumference,—in the mass and in the particle, nature hastens to render account of herself to the mind. Classification begins. To the young mind, every thing is individual, stands by itself. By and by, it finds how to join two things, and see in them one nature; then three, then three thousand; and so,

45   tyrannized over by its own unifying instinct, it goes on tying things

together, diminishing anomalies, discovering roots running under ground, whereby contrary and remote things cohere, and flower out from one stem. It presently learns, that, since the dawn of history, there has been a constant accumulation and classifying of facts.

5 But what is classification but the perceiving that these objects are not chaotic, and are not foreign, but have a law which is also a law of the human mind? The astronomer discovers that geometry, a pure abstraction of the human mind, is the measure of planetary motion. The chemist finds proportions and intelligible method

10 throughout matter; and science is nothing but the finding of analogy, identity, in the most remote parts. The ambitious soul sits down before each refractory fact; one after another, reduces all strange constitutions, all new powers, to their class and their law, and goes on for ever to animate the last fibre of organization, the outskirts of

15 nature, by insight.

Thus to him, to this school-boy under the bending dome of day, is suggested, that he and it proceed from one root; one is leaf and one is flower; relation, sympathy, stirring in every vein. And what is that Root? Is not that the soul of his soul?—A thought too bold,—

20 a dream too wild. Yet when this spiritual light shall have revealed the law of more earthly natures,—when he has learned to worship the soul, and to see that the natural philosophy that now is, is only the first gropings of its gigantic hand, he shall look forward to an ever expanding knowledge as to a becoming creator. He shall see,

25 that nature is the opposite of the soul, answering to it part for part. One is seal, and one is print. Its beauty is the beauty of his own mind. Its laws are the laws of his own mind. Nature then becomes to him the measure of his attainments. So much of nature as he is ignorant of, so much of his own mind does he not yet possess. And,

30 in fine, the ancient precept, "Know thyself," and the modern precept, "Study nature," become at last one maxim.

II. The next great influence into the spirit of the scholar, is, the mind of the Past,—in whatever form, whether of literature, of art, of institutions, that mind is inscribed. Books are the best type of the

35 influence of the past, and perhaps we shall get at the truth,—learn the amount of this influence more conveniently,—by considering their value alone.

The theory of books is noble. The scholar of the first age received into him the world around; brooded thereon; gave it the

40 new arrangement of his own mind, and uttered it again. It came into him, life; it went out from him, truth. It came to him, short-lived actions; it went out from him, immortal thoughts. It came to him, business; it went from him, poetry. It was dead fact; now, it is quick thought. It can stand, and it can go. It now endures, it now flies, it

45 now inspires. Precisely in proportion to the depth of mind from

which it issued, so high does it soar, so long does it sing.

Or, I might say, it depends on how far the process had gone, of transmuting life into truth. In proportion to the completeness of the distillation, so will the purity and imperishableness of the product
5 be. But none is quite perfect. As no air-pump can by any means make a perfect vacuum, so neither can any artist entirely exclude the conventional, the local, the perishable from his book, or write a book of pure thought, that shall be as efficient, in all respects, to a remote posterity, as to cotemporaries, or rather to the second age.
10 Each age, it is found, must write its own books; or rather, each generation for the next succeeding. The books of an older period will not fit this.

Yet hence arises a grave mischief. The sacredness which attaches to the act of creation,—the act of thought,—is transferred to the
15 record. The poet chanting, was felt to be a divine man: henceforth the chant is divine also. The writer was a just and wise spirit: henceforward it is settled, the book is perfect; as love of the hero corrupts into worship of his statue. Instantly, the book becomes noxious: the guide is a tyrant. The sluggish and perverted mind of the multitude,
20 slow to open to the incursions of Reason, having once so opened, having once received this book, stands upon it, and makes an outcry, if it is disparaged. Colleges are built on it. Books are written on it by thinkers, not by Man Thinking; by men of talent, that is, who start wrong, who set out from accepted dogmas, not from their own
25 sight of principles. Meek young men grow up in libraries, believing it their duty to accept the views, which Cicero, which Locke, which Bacon, have given, forgetful that Cicero, Locke, and Bacon were only young men in libraries, when they wrote these books.

Hence, instead of Man Thinking, we have the bookworm.
30 Hence, the book-learned class, who value books, as such; not as related to nature and the human constitution, but as making a sort of Third Estate with the world and the soul. Hence, the restorers of readings, the emendators, the bibliomaniacs of all degrees.

Books are the best of things, well used; abused, among the
35 worst. What is the right use? What is the one end, which all means go to effect? They are for nothing but to inspire. I had better never see a book, than to be warped by its attraction clean out of my own orbit, and made a satellite instead of a system. The one thing in the world, of value, is the active soul. This every man is entitled to; this
40 every man contains within him, although, in almost all men, obstructed, and as yet unborn. The soul active sees absolute truth; and utters truth, or creates. In this action, it is genius; not the privilege of here and there a favorite, but the sound estate of every man. In its essence, it is progressive. The book, the college, the school of
45 art, the institution of any kind, stop with some past utterance of

genius. This is good, say they—let us hold by this. They pin me down. They look backward and not forward. But genius looks forward: the eyes of man are set in his forehead, not in his hindhead: man hopes: genius creates. Whatever talents may be, if the man cre-
5 ate not, the pure efflux of the Deity is not his;—cinders and smoke there may be, but not yet flame. There are creative manners, there are creative actions, and creative words; manners, actions, words, that is, indicative of no custom or authority, but springing spontaneous from the mind's own sense of good and fair.
10   On the other part, instead of being its own seer, let it receive from another mind its truth, though it were in torrents of light, without periods of solitude, inquest, and self-recovery, and a fatal disservice is done. Genius is always sufficiently the enemy of genius by over influence. The literature of every nation bear me wit-
15 ness. The English dramatic poets have Shakspearized now for two hundred years.
    Undoubtedly there is a right way of reading, so it be sternly subordinated. Man Thinking must not be subdued by his instruments. Books are for the scholar's idle times. When he can read God
20 directly, the hour is too precious to be wasted in other men's transcripts of their readings. But when the intervals of darkness come, as come they must,—when the sun is hid, and the stars withdraw their shining,—we repair to the lamps which were kindled by their ray, to guide our steps to the East again, where the dawn is. We hear,
25 that we may speak. The Arabian proverb says, "A fig tree, looking on a fig tree, becometh fruitful."
    It is remarkable, the character of the pleasure we derive from the best books. They impress us with the conviction, that one nature wrote and the same reads. We read the verses of one of the great
30 English poets, of Chaucer, of Marvell, of Dryden, with the most modern joy,—with a pleasure, I mean, which is in great part caused by the abstraction of all *time* from their verses. There is some awe mixed with the joy of our surprise, when this poet, who lived in some past world, two or three hundred years ago, says that which
35 lies close to my own soul, that which I also had wellnigh thought and said. But for the evidence thence afforded to the philosophical doctrine of the identity of all minds, we should suppose some preëstablished harmony, some foresight of souls that were to be, and some preparation of stores for their future wants, like the fact
40 observed in insects, who lay up food before death for the young grub they shall never see.
    I would not be hurried by any love of system, by any exaggeration of instincts, to underrate the Book. We all know, that, as the human body can be nourished on any food, though it were boiled
45 grass and the broth of shoes, so the human mind can be fed by any

knowledge. And great and heroic men have existed, who had almost no other information than by the printed page. I only would say, that it needs a strong head to bear that diet. One must be an inventor to read well. As the proverb says, "He that would bring
5 home the wealth of the Indies, must carry out the wealth of the Indies." There is then creative reading as well as creative writing. When the mind is braced by labor and invention, the page of whatever book we read becomes luminous with manifold allusion. Every sentence is doubly significant, and the sense of our author is
10 as broad as the world. We then see, what is always true, that, as the seer's hour of vision is short and rare among heavy days and months, so is its record, perchance, the least part of his volume. The discerning will read, in his Plato or Shakspeare, only that least part,—only the authentic utterances of the oracle;—all the rest he
15 rejects, were it never so many times Plato's and Shakspeare's.

Of course, there is a portion of reading quite indispensable to a wise man. History and exact science he must learn by laborious reading. Colleges, in like manner, have their indispensable office,— to teach elements. But they can only highly serve us, when they aim
20 not to drill, but to create; when they gather from far every ray of various genius to their hospitable halls, and, by the concentrated fires, set the hearts of their youth on flame. Thought and knowledge are natures in which apparatus and pretension avail nothing. Gowns, and pecuniary foundations, though of towns of gold, can
25 never countervail the least sentence or syllable of wit. Forget this, and our American colleges will recede in their public importance, whilst they grow richer every year.

III. There goes in the world a notion, that the scholar should be a recluse, a valetudinarian,—as unfit for any handiwork or public
30 labor, as a penknife for an axe. The so-called "practical men" sneer at speculative men, as if, because they speculate or *see*, they could do nothing. I have heard it said that the clergy,—who are always, more universally than any other class, the scholars of their day,—are addressed as women; that the rough, spontaneous conversation of
35 men they do not hear, but only a mincing and diluted speech. They are often virtually disfranchised; and, indeed, there are advocates for their celibacy. As far as this is true of the studious classes, it is not just and wise. Action is with the scholar subordinate, but it is essential. Without it, he is not yet man. Without it, thought can
40 never ripen into truth. Whilst the world hangs before the eye as a cloud of beauty, we cannot even see its beauty. Inaction is cowardice, but there can be no scholar without the heroic mind. The preamble of thought, the transition through which it passes from the unconscious to the conscious, is action. Only so much do I know, as I have lived. Instantly we know whose words are loaded with
45 as I have lived. Instantly we know whose words are loaded with

life, and whose not.

The world,—this shadow of the soul, or *other me*, lies wide around. Its attractions are the keys which unlock my thoughts and make me acquainted with myself. I run eagerly into this resounding
5   tumult. I grasp the hands of those next me, and take my place in the ring to suffer and to work, taught by an instinct, that so shall the dumb abyss be vocal with speech. I pierce its order; I dissipate its fear; I dispose of it within the circuit of my expanding life. So much only of life as I know by experience, so much of the wilderness have
10 I vanquished and planted, or so far have I extended my being, my dominion. I do not see how any man can afford, for the sake of his nerves and his nap, to spare any action in which he can partake. It is pearls and rubies to his discourse. Drudgery, calamity, exaspera- tion, want, are instructers in eloquence and wisdom. The true schol-
15 ar grudges every opportunity of action past by, as a loss of power.

It is the raw material out of which the intellect moulds her splendid products. A strange process too, this, by which experience is converted into thought, as a mulberry leaf is converted into satin. The manufacture goes forward at all hours.

20   The actions and events of our childhood and youth, are now matters of calmest observation. They lie like fair pictures in the air. Not so with our recent actions,—with the business which we now have in hand. On this we are quite unable to speculate. Our affec- tions as yet circulate through it. We no more feel or know it, than we
25 feel the feet, or the hand, or the brain of our body. The new deed is yet a part of life,—remains for a time immersed in our unconscious life. In some contemplative hour, it detaches itself from the life like a ripe fruit, to become a thought of the mind. Instantly, it is raised, transfigured; the corruptible has put on incorruption. Henceforth it
30 is an object of beauty, however base its origin and neighborhood. Observe, too, the impossibility of antedating this act. In its grub state, it cannot fly, it cannot shine, it is a dull grub. But suddenly, without observation, the selfsame thing unfurls beautiful wings, and is an angel of wisdom. So is there no fact, no event, in our pri-
35 vate history, which shall not, sooner or later, lose its adhesive, inert form, and astonish us by soaring from our body into the empyrean. Cradle and infancy, school and playground, the fear of boys, and dogs, and ferules, the love of little maids and berries, and many another fact that once filled the whole sky, are gone already; friend
40 and relative, profession and party, town and country, nation and world, must also soar and sing.

Of course, he who has put forth his total strength in fit actions, has the richest return of wisdom. I will not shut myself out of this globe of action, and transplant an oak into a flower-pot, there to
45 hunger and pine; nor trust the revenue of some single faculty, and

exhaust one vein of thought, much like those Savoyards, who, getting their livelihood by carving shepherds, shepherdesses, and smoking Dutchmen, for all Europe, went out one day to the mountain to find stock, and discovered that they had whittled up the last
5 of their pinetrees. Authors we have, in numbers, who have written out their vein, and who, moved by a commendable prudence, sail for Greece or Palestine, follow the trapper into the prairie, or ramble round Algiers, to replenish their merchantable stock.

If it were only for a vocabulary, the scholar would be covetous
10 of action. Life is our dictionary. Years are well spent in country labors; in town,—in the insight into trades and manufactures; in frank intercourse with many men and women; in science; in art; to the one end of mastering in all their facts a language by which to illustrate and embody our perceptions. I learn immediately from
15 any speaker how much he has already lived, through the poverty or the splendor of his speech. Life lies behind us as the quarry from whence we get tiles and copestones for the masonry of to-day. This is the way to learn grammar. Colleges and books only copy the language which the field and the work-yard made.

20 But the final value of action, like that of books, and better than books, is, that it is a resource. That great principle of Undulation in nature, that shows itself in the inspiring and expiring of the breath; in desire and satiety; in the ebb and flow of the sea; in day and night; in heat and cold; and as yet more deeply ingrained in every
25 atom and every fluid, is known to us under the name of Polarity,— these "fits of easy transmission and reflection," as Newton called them, are the law of nature because they are the law of spirit.

The mind now thinks; now acts; and each fit reproduces the other. When the artist has exhausted his materials, when the fancy
30 no longer paints, when thoughts are no longer apprehended, and books are a weariness,—he has always the resource *to live*. Character is higher than intellect. Thinking is the function. Living is the functionary. The stream retreats to its source. A great soul will be strong to live, as well as strong to think. Does he lack organ or
35 medium to impart his truths? He can still fall back on this elemental force of living them. This is a total act. Thinking is a partial act. Let the grandeur of justice shine in his affairs. Let the beauty of affection cheer his lowly roof. Those "far from fame," who dwell and act with him, will feel the force of his constitution in the doings
40 and passages of the day better than it can be measured by any public and designed display. Time shall teach him, that the scholar loses no hour which the man lives. Herein he unfolds the sacred germ of his instinct, screened from influence. What is lost in seemliness is gained in strength. Not out of those, on whom systems of education
45 have exhausted their culture, comes the helpful giant to destroy the

old or to build the new, but out of unhandselled savage nature, out of terrible Druids and Berserkirs, come at last Alfred and Shakspeare.

5   I hear therefore with joy whatever is beginning to be said of the dignity and necessity of labor to every citizen. There is virtue yet in the hoe and the spade, for learned as well as for unlearned hands. And labor is everywhere welcome; always we are invited to work; only be this limitation observed, that a man shall not for the sake of wider activity sacrifice any opinion to the popular judgments and 10   modes of action.

I have now spoken of the education of the scholar by nature, by books, and by action. It remains to say somewhat of his duties.

They are such as become Man Thinking. They may all be comprised in self-trust. The office of the scholar is to cheer, to raise, and 15   to guide men by showing them facts amidst appearances. He plies the slow, unhonored, and unpaid task of observation. Flamsteed and Herschel, in their glazed observatories, may catalogue the stars with the praise of all men, and, the results being splendid and useful, honor is sure. But he, in his private observatory, cataloguing 20   obscure and nebulous stars of the human mind, which as yet no man has thought of as such,—watching days and months, sometimes, for a few facts; correcting still his old records;—must relinquish display and immediate fame. In the long period of his preparation, he must betray often an ignorance and shiftlessness in popular 25   ular arts, incurring the disdain of the able who shoulder him aside. Long he must stammer in his speech; often forego the living for the dead. Worse yet, he must accept,—how often! poverty and solitude. For the ease and pleasure of treading the old road, accepting the fashions, the education, the religion of society, he takes the cross of 30   making his own, and, of course, the self-accusation, the faint heart, the frequent uncertainty and loss of time, which are the nettles and tangling vines in the way of the self-relying and self-directed; and the state of virtual hostility in which he seems to stand to society, and especially to educated society. For all this loss and scorn, what 35   offset? He is to find consolation in exercising the highest functions of human nature. He is one, who raises himself from private considerations, and breathes and lives on public and illustrious thoughts. He is the world's eye. He is the world's heart. He is to resist the vulgar prosperity that retrogrades ever to barbarism, by 40   preserving and communicating heroic sentiments, noble biographies, melodious verse, and the conclusions of history. Whatsoever oracles the human heart, in all emergencies, in all solemn hours, has uttered as its commentary on the world of actions,—these he shall receive and impart. And whatsoever new verdict Reason from her 45   inviolable seat pronounces on the passing men and events of today,—this he shall hear and promulgate.

These being his functions, it becomes him to feel all confidence in himself, and to defer never to the popular cry. He and he only knows the world. The world of any moment is the merest appear-
5 ance. Some great decorum, some fetish of a government, some ephemeral trade, or war, or man, is cried up by half mankind and cried down by the other half, as if all depended on this particular up or down. The odds are that the whole question is not worth the poorest thought which the scholar has lost in listening to the con-
10 troversy. Let him not quit his belief that a popgun is a popgun, though the ancient and honorable of the earth affirm it to be the crack of doom. In silence, in steadiness, in severe abstraction, let him hold by himself; add observation to observation, patient of neg-lect, patient of reproach; and bide his own time,—happy enough, if
15 he can satisfy himself alone, that this day he has seen something truly. Success treads on every right step. For the instinct is sure, that prompts him to tell his brother what he thinks. He then learns, that in going down into the secrets of his own mind, he has descended into the secrets of all minds. He learns that he who has mastered
20 any law in his private thoughts, is master to that extent of all men whose language he speaks, and of all into whose language his own can be translated. The poet, in utter solitude remembering his spon-taneous thoughts and recording them, is found to have recorded that, which men in crowded cities find true for them also. The ora-
25 tor distrusts at first the fitness of his frank confessions,—his want of knowledge of the persons he addresses,—until he finds that he is the complement of his hearers;—that they drink his words because he fulfils for them their own nature; the deeper he dives into his privatest, secretest presentiment, to his wonder he finds, this is the
30 most acceptable, most public, and universally true. The people delight in it; the better part of every man feels, This is my music; this is myself.

In self-trust, all the virtues are comprehended. Free should the scholar be,—free and brave. Free even to the definition of freedom,
35 "without any hindrance that does not arise out of his own constitu-tion." Brave; for fear is a thing, which a scholar by his very function puts behind him. Fear always springs from ignorance. It is a shame to him if his tranquillity, amid dangerous times, arise from the pre-sumption, that, like children and women, his is a protected class; or
40 if he seek a temporary peace by the diversion of his thoughts from politics or vexed questions, hiding his head like an ostrich in the flowering bushes, peeping into microscopes, and turning rhymes, as a boy whistles to keep his courage up. So is the danger a danger still; so is the fear worse. Manlike let him turn and face it. Let him
45 look into its eye and search its nature, inspect its origin,—see the

whelping of this lion,—which lies no great way back; he will then find in himself a perfect comprehension of its nature and extent; he will have made his hands meet on the other side, and can henceforth defy it, and pass on superior. The world is his, who can see
5   through its pretension. What deafness, what stone-blind custom, what overgrown error you behold, is there only by sufferance,—by your sufferance. See it to be a lie, and you have already dealt it its mortal blow.

    Yes, we are the cowed,—we the trustless. It is a mischievous
10   notion that we are come late into nature; that the world was finished a long time ago. As the world was plastic and fluid in the hands of God, so it is ever to so much of his attributes as we bring to it. To ignorance and sin, it is flint. They adapt themselves to it as they may; but in proportion as a man has any thing in him divine, the fir-
15   mament flows before him and takes his signet and form. Not he is great who can alter matter, but he who can alter my state of mind. They are the kings of the world who give the color of their present thought to all nature and all art, and persuade men by the cheerful serenity of their carrying the matter, that this thing which they do,
20   is the apple which the ages have desired to pluck, now at last ripe, and inviting nations to the harvest. The great man makes the great thing. Wherever Macdonald sits, there is the head of the table. Linnæus makes botany the most alluring of studies, and wins it from the farmer and the herb-woman; Davy, chemistry; and Cuvier,
25   fossils. The day is always his, who works in it with serenity and great aims. The unstable estimates of men crowd to him whose mind is filled with a truth, as the heaped waves of the Atlantic follow the moon.

    For this self-trust, the reason is deeper than can be fathomed,—
30   darker than can be enlightened. I might not carry with me the feeling of my audience in stating my own belief. But I have already shown the ground of my hope, in adverting to the doctrine that man is one. I believe man has been wronged; he has wronged himself. He has almost lost the light, that can lead him back to his preroga-
35   tives. Men are become of no account. Men in history, men in the world of to-day are bugs, are spawn, and are called "the mass" and "the herd." In a century, in a millennium, one or two men; that is to say,—one or two approximations to the right state of every man. All the rest behold in the hero or the poet their own green and crude
40   being,—ripened; yes, and are content to be less, so *that* may attain to its full stature. What a testimony,—full of grandeur, full of pity, is borne to the demands of his own nature, by the poor clansman, the poor partisan, who rejoices in the glory of his chief. The poor and the low find some amends to their immense moral capacity, for their
45   acquiescence in a political and social inferiority. They are content to

be brushed like flies from the path of a great person, so that justice shall be done by him to that common nature which it is the dearest desire of all to see enlarged and glorified. They sun themselves in the great man's light, and feel it to be their own element. They cast
5 the dignity of man from their downtrod selves upon the shoulders of a hero, and will perish to add one drop of blood to make that great heart beat, those giant sinews combat and conquer. He lives for us, and we live in him.

Men such as they are, very naturally seek money or power; and
10 power because it is as good as money,—the "spoils," so called, "of office." And why not? for they aspire to the highest, and this, in their sleep-walking, they dream is highest. Wake them, and they shall quit the false good, and leap to the true, and leave governments to clerks and desks. This revolution is to be wrought by the
15 gradual domestication of the idea of Culture. The main enterprise of the world for splendor, for extent, is the upbuilding of a man. Here are the materials strown along the ground. The private life of one man shall be a more illustrious monarchy,—more formidable to its enemy, more sweet and serene in its influence to its friend, than any
20 kingdom in history. For a man, rightly viewed, comprehendeth the particular natures of all men. Each philosopher, each bard, each actor, has only done for me, as by a delegate, what one day I can do for myself. The books which once we valued more than the apple of the eye, we have quite exhausted. What is that but saying, that we
25 have come up with the point of view which the universal mind took through the eyes of one scribe; we have been that man, and have passed on. First, one; then, another; we drain all cisterns, and, waxing greater by all these supplies, we crave a better and more abundant food. The man has never lived that can feed us ever. The
30 human mind cannot be enshrined in a person, who shall set a barrier on any one side to this unbounded, unboundable empire. It is one central fire, which, flaming now out of the lips of Etna, lightens the capes of Sicily; and, now out of the throat of Vesuvius, illuminates the towers and vineyards of Naples. It is one light which
35 beams out of a thousand stars. It is one soul which animates all men.

But I have dwelt perhaps tediously upon this abstraction of the Scholar. I ought not to delay longer to add what I have to say, of nearer reference to the time and to this country.
40 Historically, there is thought to be a difference in the ideas which predominate over successive epochs, and there are data for marking the genius of the Classic, of the Romantic, and now of the Reflective or Philosophical age. With the views I have intimated of the oneness or the identity of the mind through all individuals, I do
45 not much dwell on these differences. In fact, I believe each individ-

ual passes through all three. The boy is a Greek; the youth, romantic; the adult, reflective. I deny not, however, that a revolution in the
leading idea may be distinctly enough traced.

5   Our age is bewailed as the age of Introversion. Must that needs
be evil? We, it seems, are critical; we are embarrassed with second
thoughts; we cannot enjoy any thing for hankering to know whereof the pleasure consists; we are lined with eyes; we see with our feet;
the time is infected with Hamlet's unhappiness,—

Sicklied o'er with the pale cast of thought.

10   Is it so bad then? Sight is the last thing to be pitied. Would we
be blind? Do we fear lest we should outsee nature and God, and
drink truth dry? I look upon the discontent of the literary class, as a
mere announcement of the fact, that they find themselves not in the
state of mind of their fathers, and regret the coming state as untried;
15   as a boy dreads the water before he has learned that he can swim. If
there is any period one would desire to be born in,—is it not the age
of Revolution; when the old and the new stand side by side, and
admit of being compared; when the energies of all men are searched
by fear and by hope; when the historic glories of the old, can be
20   compensated by the rich possibilities of the new era? This time, like
all times, is a very good one, if we but know what to do with it.

I read with joy some of the auspicious signs of the coming days,
as they glimmer already through poetry and art, through philosophy and science, through church and state.

25   One of these signs is the fact, that the same movement which
effected the elevation of what was called the lowest class in the
state, assumed in literature a very marked and as benign an aspect.
Instead of the sublime and beautiful; the near, the low, the common,
was explored and poetized. That, which had been negligently trod-
30   den under foot by those who were harnessing and provisioning
themselves for long journeys into far countries, is suddenly found
to be richer than all foreign parts. The literature of the poor, the feelings of the child, the philosophy of the street, the meaning of household life, are the topics of the time. It is a great stride. It is a sign,—
35   is it not? of new vigor, when the extremities are made active, when
currents of warm life run into the hands and the feet. I ask not for
the great, the remote, the romantic; what is doing in Italy or Arabia;
what is Greek art, or Provençal minstrelsy; I embrace the common,
I explore and sit at the feet of the familiar, the low. Give me insight
40   into to-day, and you may have the antique and future worlds. What
would we really know the meaning of? The meal in the firkin; the
milk in the pan; the ballad in the street; the news of the boat; the
glance of the eye; the form and the gait of the body;—show me the

ultimate reason of these matters; show me the sublime presence of the highest spiritual cause lurking, as always it does lurk, in these suburbs and extremities of nature; let me see every trifle bristling with the polarity that ranges it instantly on an eternal law; and the

5 shop, the plough, and the leger, referred to the like cause by which light undulates and poets sing;—and the world lies no longer a dull miscellany and lumber-room, but has form and order; there is no trifle; there is no puzzle; but one design unites and animates the farthest pinnacle and the lowest trench.

10   This idea has inspired the genius of Goldsmith, Burns, Cowper, and, in a newer time, of Goethe, Wordsworth, and Carlyle. This idea they have differently followed and with various success. In contrast with their writing, the style of Pope, of Johnson, of Gibbon, looks cold and pedantic. This writing is blood-warm. Man is surprised to

15 find that things near are not less beautiful and wondrous than things remote. The near explains the far. The drop is a small ocean. A man is related to all nature. This perception of the worth of the vulgar is fruitful in discoveries. Goethe, in this very thing the most modern of the moderns, has shown us, as none ever did, the genius

20 of the ancients.

There is one man of genius, who has done much for this philosophy of life, whose literary value has never yet been rightly estimated;—I mean Emanuel Swedenborg. The most imaginative of men, yet writing with the precision of a mathematician, he endeav-

25 ored to engraft a purely philosophical Ethics on the popular Christianity of his time. Such an attempt, of course, must have difficulty, which no genius could surmount. But he saw and showed the connection between nature and the affections of the soul. He pierced the emblematic or spiritual character of the visible, audible,

30 tangible world. Especially did his shade-loving muse hover over and interpret the lower parts of nature; he showed the mysterious bond that allies moral evil to the foul material forms, and has given in epical parables a theory of insanity, of beasts, of unclean and fearful things.

35   Another sign of our times, also marked by an analogous political movement, is, the new importance given to the single person. Every thing that tends to insulate the individual,—to surround him with barriers of natural respect, so that each man shall feel the world is his, and man shall treat with man as a sovereign state with

40 a sovereign state;—tends to true union as well as greatness. "I learned," said the melancholy Pestalozzi, "that no man in God's wide earth is either willing or able to help any other man." Help must come from the bosom alone. The scholar is that man who must take up into himself all the ability of the time, all the contributions

45 of the past, all the hopes of the future. He must be an university of

knowledges. If there be one lesson more than another, which should pierce his ear, it is, The world is nothing, the man is all; in yourself is the law of all nature, and you know not yet how a globule of sap ascends; in yourself slumbers the whole of Reason; it is for you to
5   know all, it is for you to dare all. Mr. President and Gentlemen, this confidence in the unsearched might of man belongs, by all motives, by all prophecy, by all preparation, to the American Scholar. We have listened too long to the courtly muses of Europe. The spirit of the American freeman is already suspected to be timid, imitative,
10 tame. Public and private avarice make the air we breathe thick and fat. The scholar is decent, indolent, complaisant. See already the tragic consequence. The mind of this country, taught to aim at low objects, eats upon itself. There is no work for any but the decorous and the complaisant. Young men of the fairest promise, who begin
15 life upon our shores, inflated by the mountain winds, shined upon by all the stars of God, find the earth below not in unison with these,—but are hindered from action by the disgust which the prin- ciples on which business is managed inspire, and turn drudges, or die of disgust,—some of them suicides. What is the remedy? They
20 did not yet see, and thousands of young men as hopeful now crowding to the barriers for the career, do not yet see, that, if the sin- gle man plant himself indomitably on his instincts, and there abide, the huge world will come round to him. Patience,—patience;—with the shades of all the good and great for company; and for solace, the
25 perspective of your own infinite life; and for work, the study and the communication of principles, the making those instincts preva- lent, the conversion of the world. Is it not the chief disgrace in the world, not to be an unit;—not to be reckoned one character;—not to yield that peculiar fruit which each man was created to bear, but to
30 be reckoned in the gross, in the hundred, or the thousand, of the party, the section, to which we belong; and our opinion predicted geographically, as the north, or the south? Not so, brothers and friends,—please God, ours shall not be so. We will walk on our own feet; we will work with our own hands; we will speak our own
35 minds. The study of letters shall be no longer a name for pity, for doubt, and for sensual indulgence. The dread of man and the love of man shall be a wall of defence and a wreath of joy around all. A nation of men will for the first time exist, because each believes himself inspired by the Divine Soul which also inspires all men.

14. WALT WHITMAN

Whitman (1819–1892) said of himself, "I was simmering, simmering, simmering," and then "Emerson brought me to a boil." He followed Emerson and Thoreau in developing a characteristically American form of Romanticism, a celebration of the democratic individual. His greatest poem is called "Song of Myself" and in it he celebrates that same autonomous individualism and freedom from the past.

WHEN I HEARD THE LEARN'D ASTRONOMER

When I heard the learn'd astronomer,
When the proofs, the figures, were ranged in columns before me,
When I was shown the charts and diagrams, to add, divide, and
      measure them,
5   When I sitting heard the astronomer where he lectured with much
      applause in the lecture-room,
How soon unaccountable I became tired and sick,
Till rising and gliding out I wander's off by myself,
In the mystical moist night-air, and from time to time,
10 Look'd up in perfect silence at the stars.   1867

A NOISELESS PATIENT SPIDER

A noiseless patient spider,
I mark'd where on a little promontory it stood isolated,
Mark'd how to explore the vacant vast surrounding,
It launch'd forth filament, filament, filament, out of itself,
5   Ever unreeling them, ever tirelessly speeding them.

And you O my soul where you stand,
Surrounded, detached, in measureless oceans of space,
Ceaselessly musing, venturing, throwing, seeking the spheres to
      connect them,
10 Till the bridge you will need be form'd, till the ductile anchor hold,
Till the gossamer thread you fling catch somewhere, O my soul.   1871

FROM SONG OF MYSELF (1881)

1

I celebrate myself, and sing myself,
And what I assume you shall assume,
For every atom belonging to me as good belongs to you.

    I loafe and invite my soul,
5   I lean and loafe at my ease observing a spear of summer grass.
My tongue, every atom of my blood, form'd from this soil, this air,
Born here of parents born here from parents the same, and their par-
      ents the same,
I, now thirty-seven years old in perfect health begin,
10 Hoping to cease not till death.

    Creeds and schools in abeyance,
Retiring back a while sufficed at what they are, but never forgotten,
      I harbor for good or bad, I permit to speak at every hazard,
      Nature without check with original energy.

2

15 Houses and rooms are full of perfumes, the shelves are crowded
      with perfumes,
I breathe the fragrance myself and know it and like it, The distilla-
      tion would intoxicate me also, but I shall not let it.
The atmosphere is not a perfume, it has no taste of the distillation,
20   it is odorless,
It is for my mouth forever, I am in love with it,
I will go to the bank by the wood and become undisguised and
      naked, I am mad for it to be in contact with me.
The smoke of my own breath,
25 Echoes, ripples, buzz'd whispers, love-root, silk-thread, crotch and
      vine,
My respiration and inspiration, the beating of my heart, the passing
      of blood and air through my lungs,
The sniff of green leaves and dry leaves, and of the shore and dark-
30   color'd sea-rocks, and of hay in the barn,
The sound of the belch'd words of my voice loos'd to the eddies of
      the wind,
A few light kisses, a few embraces, a reaching around of arms,
The play of shine and shade on the trees as the supple boughs wag,
35 The delight alone or in the rush of the streets, or along the fields and
      hillsides,
The feeling of health, the full-noon trill, the song of me rising from
      bed and meeting the sun.

Have you reckon'd a thousand acres much? have you reckon'd the
40   earth much?
Have you practis'd so long to learn to read?
Have you felt so proud to get at the meaning of poems?

Stop this day and night with me and you shall possess the origin of
       all poems,
45   You shall possess the good of the earth and sun, (there are millions
       of suns left,)
You shall no longer take things at second or third hand, nor look
       through the eyes of the dead, nor feed on the spectres in books,
You shall not look through my eyes either, nor take things from me,
50   You shall listen to all sides and filter them from your self.

3

I have heard what the talkers were talking, the talk of the beginning
       and the end,
But I do not talk of the beginning or the end.
There was never any more inception than there is now, Nor any
55   more youth or age than there is now, And will never be any
       more perfection than there is now, Nor any more heaven or hell
       than there is now.
Urge and urge and urge,
Always the procreant urge of the world.

60   Out of the dimness opposite equals advance, always substance and
       increase, always sex,
Always a knit of identity, always distinction, always a breed of life.
To elaborate is no avail, learn'd and unlearn'd feel that it is so.
Sure as the most certain sure, plumb in the uprights, well entretied,
65   braced in the beams,
Stout as a horse, affectionate, haughty, electrical,
I and this mystery here we stand.
Clear and sweet is my soul, and clear and sweet is all that is not my
       soul.
70   Lack one lacks both, and the unseen is proved by the seen,
Till that becomes unseen and receives proof in its turn.
Showing the best and dividing it from the worst age vexes age,
Knowing the perfect fitness and equanimity of things, while they
       discuss I am silent, and go bathe and admire myself.
75   Welcome is every organ and attribute of me, and of any man hearty
       and clean,
Not an inch nor a particle of an inch is vile, and none shall be less
       familiar than the rest.
I am satisfied—I see, dance, laugh, sing;

80 As the hugging and loving bed-fellow sleeps at my side through the
        night, and withdraws at the peep of the day with stealthy tread,
    Leaving me baskets cover'd with white towels swelling the house
        with their plenty,
    Shall I postpone my acceptation and realization and scream at my
85   eyes,
    That they turn from gazing after and down the road,
    And forthwith cipher and show me to a cent,
    Exactly the value of one and exactly the value of two, and which is
        ahead?

                            4

90 Trippers and askers surround me,
    People I meet, the effect upon me of my early life or the ward and
        city I live in, or the nation,
    The latest dates, discoveries, inventions, societies, authors old and
        new,
95 My dinner, dress, associates, looks, compliments, dues,
    The real or fancied indifference of some man or woman I love,
    The sickness of one of my folks or of myself, or ill-doing or loss or
        lack of money, or depressions or exaltations,
    Battles, the horrors of fratricidal war, the fever of doubtful news, the
100   fitful events;
    These come to me days and nights and go from me again, But they
        are not the Me myself.
    Apart from the pulling and hauling stands what I am,
    Stands amused, complacent, compassionating, idle, unitary,
105 Looks down, is erect, or bends an arm on an impalpable certain rest,
    Looking with side-curved head curious what will come next,
    Both in and out of the game and watching and wondering at it.
    Backward I see in my own days where I sweated through fog with
        linguists and contenders,
110 I have no mockings or arguments, I witness and wait.

                            5

    I believe in you my soul, the other I am must not abase itself to you,
        And you must not be abased to the other.
    Loafe with me on the grass, loose the stop from your throat,
    Not words, not music or rhyme I want, not custom or lecture, not
115   even the best,
    Only the lull I like, the hum of your valvèd voice.
    I mind how once we lay such a transparent summer morning,
    How you settled your head athwart my hips and gently turn'd over
        upon me,
120 And parted the shirt from my bosom-bone, and plunged your

tongue to my bare-stript heart,
And reach'd till you felt my beard, and reach'd till you held my feet.
Swiftly arose and spread around me the peace and knowledge that
    pass all the argument of the earth,
125 And I know that the hand of God is the promise of my own,
And I know that the spirit of God is the brother of my own,
And that all the men ever born are also my brothers, and the women
    my sisters and lovers,
And that a kelson of the creation is love,
130 And limitless are leaves stiff or drooping in the fields,
And brown ants in the little wells beneath them,
And mossy scabs of the worm fence, heap'd stones, elder, mullein
    and poke-weed.

6

A child said *What is the grass?* fetching it to me with full hands;
135 How could I answer the child? I do not know what it is any more
    than he.
I guess it must be the flag of my disposition, out of hopeful green
    stuff woven.
Or I guess it is the handkerchief of the Lord,
140 A scented gift and remembrancer designedly dropt,
Bearing the owner's name someway in the corners, that we may see
    and remark, and say *Whose?*
Or I guess the grass is itself a child, the produced babe of the vege-
    tation.
145 Or I guess it is a uniform hieroglyphic,
And it means, Sprouting alike in broad zones and narrow zones,
Growing among black folks as among white,
Kanuck, Tuckahoe, Congressman, Cuff, I give them the same, I
    receive them the same.

150 And now it seems to me the beautiful uncut hair of graves.
Tenderly will I use you curling grass,
It may be you transpire from the breasts of young men,
It may be if I had known them I would have loved them,
It may be you are from old people, or from offspring taken soon out
155   of their mothers' laps,
And here you are the mothers' laps.
This grass is very dark to be from the white heads of old mothers
Darker than the colorless beards of old men,
Dark to come from under the faint red roofs of mouths.
160 O I perceive after all so many uttering tongues,
And I perceive they do not come from the roofs of mouths for noth-
    ing.

I wish I could translate the hints about the dead young men and
165   women,
And the hints about old men and mothers, and the offspring taken
        soon out of their laps.
What do you think has become of the young and old men?
And what do you think has become of the women and children?
170 They are alive and well somewhere,
The smallest sprout shows there is really no death,
And if ever there was it led forward life, and does not wait at the
        end to arrest it,
And ceas'd the moment life appear'd.

175 All goes onward and outward, nothing collapses,
And to die is different from what any one supposed, and luckier.

7

Has any one supposed it lucky to be born?
I hasten to inform him or her it is just as lucky to die, and I know it.
I pass death with the dying and birth with the new-wash'd babe,
180   and am not contain'd between my hat and boots,
And peruse manifold objects, no two alike and every one good, The
        earth good and the stars good, and their adjuncts all good.
I am not an earth nor an adjunct of an earth,
I am the mate and companion of people, all just as immortal and
185   fathomless as myself,
(They do not know how immortal, but I know.)
Every kind for itself and its own, for me mine male and female,
For me those that have been boys and that love women,
For me the man that is proud and feels how it stings to be slighted,
190 For me the sweet-heart and the old maid, for me mothers and the
        mothers of mothers,
For me lips that have smiled, eyes that have shed tears, For me chil-
        dren and the begetters of children.
Undrape! you are not guilty to me, nor stale nor discarded,
195 I see through the broadcloth and gingham whether or no,
And am around, tenacious, acquisitive, tireless, and cannot be shak-
        en away.

8

The little one sleeps in its cradle,
I lift the gauze and took a long time, and silently brush away flies
200   with my hand.

The youngster and the red-faced girl turn aside up the bushy hill,
I peeringly view them from the top.

The suicide sprawls on the bloody floor of the bedroom,
I witness the corpse with its dabbled hair, I note where the pistol has
205   fallen.
The blab of the pave, tires of carts, sluff of boot-soles, talk of the
    promenaders,
The heavy omnibus, the driver with his interrogating thumb, the
    clank of the shod horses on the granite floor,
210 The snow-sleighs, clinking, shouted jokes, pelts of snow-balls,
The hurrahs for popular favorites, the fury of rous'd mobs,
The flap of the curtain'd litter, a sick man inside borne to the hospital,
The meeting of enemies, the sudden oath, the blows and fall,
The excited crowd, the policeman with his star quickly working his
215   passage to the centre of the crowd,
The impassive stones that receive and return so many echoes,
What groans of over-fed or half-starv'd who fall sunstruck or in fits,
What exclamations of women taken suddenly who hurry home and
    give birth to babes,
220 What living and buried speech is always vibrating here, what howls
    restrain'd by decorum,
Arrests of criminals, slights, adulterous offers made, acceptances,
    rejections with convex lips,
I mind them or the show or resonance of them—I come and I
225   depart.

9

The big doors of the country barn stand open and ready,
The dried grass of the harvest-time loads the slow-drawn wagon,
The clear light plays on the brown gray and green intertinged,
The armfuls are pack'd to the sagging mow.
230 I am there, I help, I came stretch'd atop of the load,
I felt its soft jolts, one leg reclined on the other,
I jump from the cross-beams and sieze the clover and timothy,
And roll head over heels and tangle my hair full of wisps.

10

Alone far in the wilds and mountains I hunt,
235 Wandering amazed at my own lightness and glee,
In the late afternoon choosing a safe spot to pass the night,
Kindling a fire and broiling the fresh-kill'd game,
Falling asleep on the gather'd leaves with my dog and gun by my
    side.
240 The Yankee clipper is under her sky-sails, she cuts the sparkle and
    scud,
My eyes settle the land, I bend at her prow or shout joyously from
    the deck.

The boatmen and clam-diggers arose early and stopt for me,

245 I tuck'd my trowser-ends in my boots and went and had a good time;

You should have been with us that day round the chowder-kettle.

I saw the marriage of the trapper in the open air in the far west, the bride was a red girl,

250 Her father and his friends sat near cross-legged and dumbly smoking, they had moccasins to their feet and large thick blankets hanging from their shoulders,

On a bank lounged the trapper, he was drest mostly in skins, his luxuriant beard and curls protected his neck, he held his bride

255 by the hand,

She had long eyelashes, her head was bare, her coarse straight locks descended upon her voluptuous limbs and reach'd to her feet.

The runaway slave came to my house and stopt outside,

I heard his motions crackling the twigs of the woodpile,

260 Through the swung half-door of the kitchen I saw him limpsy and weak,

And went where he sat on a log and led him in and assured him,

And brought water and fill'd a tub for his sweated body and bruis'd feet,

265 And gave him a room that enter'd from my own, and gave him some coarse clean clothes,

And remember perfectly well his revolving eyes and his awkwardness,

And remember putting plasters on the galls of his neck and ankles;

270 He staid with me a week before he was recuperated and pass'd north,

I had him sit next me at table, my fire-lock lean'd in the corner.

11

Twenty-eight young men bathe by the shore,

Twenty-eight young men and all so friendly;

275 Twenty-eight years of womanly life and all so lonesome.

She owns the fine house by the rise of the bank,

She hides handsome and richly drest aft the blinds of the window.

Which of the young men does she like the best?

Ah the homeliest of them is beautiful to her.

280 Where are you off to, lady? for I see you,

You splash in the water there, yet stay stock still in your room.

Dancing and laughing along the beach came the twenty-ninth bather,

The rest did not see her, but she saw them and loved them.

285 The beards of the young men glisten'd with wet, it ran from their
　　　　long hair,

Little streams pass'd over their bodies.

An unseen hand also pass'd over their bodies,

It descended tremblingly from their temples and ribs.

290 The young men float on their backs, their white bellies bulge to the
　　　　sun, they do not ask who seizes fast to them,

They do not know who puffs and declines with pendant and bend-
　　　　ing arch,

They do not think whom they souse with spray.

15. ABRAHAM LINCOLN

Lincoln (1809–1865) was the sixteenth president of the United States. His leadership guided the country through its greatest trauma, the Civil War, a war which Lincoln fought not for vengeance but because of necessity and out of his deep faith in the democratic ideals embodied in the Declaration of Independence and the American experiment. His political faith was balanced by a profound sense of human tragedy and a deep faith in a providential God.

THE GETTYSBURG ADDRESS

Fourscore and seven years ago our fathers brought forth on this continent a new nation, conceived in liberty, and dedicated to the proposition that all men are created equal.

Now we are engaged in a great civil war, testing whether that
5 nation, or any nation so conceived and so dedicated, can long endure. We are met on a great battle-field of that war. We have come to dedicate a portion of that field as a final resting-place for those who here gave their lives that that nation might live. It is altogether fitting and proper that we should do this.
10 But in a larger sense, we cannot dedicate—we cannot consecrate—we cannot hallow—this ground. The brave men, living and dead, who struggled here, have consecrated it far above our poor power to add or detract. The world will little note nor long remember what we say here, but it can never forget what they did here. It
15 is for us, the living, rather, to be dedicated here to the unfinished work which they who fought here have thus far so nobly advanced. It is rather for us to be here dedicated to the great task remaining before us—that from these honored dead we take increased devotion to that cause for which they gave the last full measure of devo-
20 tion; that we here highly resolve that these dead shall not have died in vain; that this nation, under God, shall have a new birth of freedom; and that government of the people, by the people, for the people, shall not perish from the earth.

SECOND INAUGURAL ADDRESS
(1865)

Fellow Countrymen:

    At this second appearing to take the oath of the presidential office, there is less occasion for an extended address than there was at the first. Then a statement, somewhat in detail, of a course to be pursued, seemed fitting and proper. Now, at the expiration of four
5   years, during which public declarations have been constantly called forth on every point and phase of the great contest which still absorbs the attention, and engrosses the energies of the nation, little that is new could be presented. The progress of our arms, upon which all else chiefly depends, is as well known to the public as to
10   myself; and it is, I trust, reasonably satisfactory and encouraging to all. With high hope for the future, no prediction in regard to it is ventured.

    On the occasion corresponding to this four years ago, all thoughts were anxiously directed to an impending civil-war. All
15   dreaded it—all sought to avert it. While the inaugural address was being delivered from this place, devoted altogether to *saving* the Union without war, insurgent agents were in the city seeking to *destroy* it without war—seeking to dissolve the Union, and divide effects, by negotiation. Both parties deprecated war; but one of them
20   would *make* war rather than let the nation survive; and the other would *accept* war rather than let it perish. And the war came.

    One eighth of the whole population were colored slaves, not distributed generally over the Union, but localized in the Southern part of it. These slaves constituted a peculiar and powerful interest.
25   All knew that this interest was, somehow, the cause of the war. To strengthen, perpetuate, and extend this interest was the object for which the insurgents would rend the Union, even by war; while the government claimed no right to do more than to restrict the territorial enlargement of it. Neither party expected for the war, the mag-
30   nitude, or the duration, which it has already attained. Neither anticipated that the *cause* of the conflict might cease with, or even before, the conflict itself should cease. Each looked for an easier triumph, and a result less fundamental and astounding. Both read the same Bible, and pray to the same God; and each invokes His aid against
35   the other. It may seem strange that any men should dare to ask a just God's assistance in wringing their bread from the sweat of other men's faces; but let us judge not that we be not judged. The prayers of both could not be answered; that of neither has been answered fully. The Almighty has his own purposes. "Woe unto the world
40   because of offences! for it must needs be that offences come; but

woe to that man by whom the offence cometh!" If we shall suppose that American Slavery is one of those offences which in the providence of God, must needs come, but which, having continued through His appointed time, He now wills to remove, and that he

45 gives to both North and South, this terrible war, as the woe due to those by whom the offence came, shall we discern therein any departure from those divine attributes which the believers in a Living God always ascribe to Him? Fondly do we hope—fervently do we pray—that this mighty scourge of war may speedily pass

50 away. Yet, if God wills that it continue, until all the wealth piled by the bond-man's two hundred and fifty years of unrequited toil shall be sunk, and every drop of blood drawn with the lash, shall be paid with another drawn with the sword, as was said three thousand years ago, so still it must be said "the judgments of the Lord, are

55 true and righteous altogether."

With malice toward none; with charity for all; with firmness in the right, as God gives us to see the right, let us strive on to finish the work we are in; to bind up the nation's wounds; to care for him who shall have born the battle, and for his widow and his orphan—

60 to do all which may achieve and cherish a just, and a lasting peace, among ourselves, and with all nations.

March 4, 1865

16. CHARLES BAUDELAIRE

Charles Baudelaire (1821–1867), translator of Edgar Allan Poe, published a single volume of poetry, Les Fleurs du Mal (The Flowers of Evil). *In these writings he expressed the Romantic myth of the artist as someone turning his back on an insensitive bourgeois society (a capital misreading of Poe); and a more profound, highly nuanced and symbolic vision of the struggle between good and evil in modern life. Baudelaire certainly sought to undercut the complacency of the modern bourgeois that reduces goodness to the routine duties of daily life.*

FROM FLOWERS OF EVIL

TO THE READER

Folly, error, sin and avarice
Occupy our minds and waste our bodies,
And we feed our polite remorse
As beggars feed their lice.

5   Our sins are stubborn, our repentance is cowardly;
We ask high prices for our vows,
And we gaily return to the muddy road,
Believing we will wash away all our spots with vile tears.

On the pillow of evil it is Thrice-Great Satan
10   Who endlessly rocks our bewitched mind,
And the rich metal of our will
Is vaporized by that wise chemist.

It is the Devil who pulls the strings that move us!
In repulsive objects we find enticing lures;
15   Each day we go down one more step toward Hell,
Without horror, through the darkness which smells rank.

Just as a lustful pauper who kisses and bites
The martyred breast of an aged whore,
We steal, as we move along, a clandestine pleasure
20   Which we squeeze hard like an old orange.

Packed tight and swarming like a million maggots,
A crowd of Demons carouse in our brains,
And, when we breathe, Death into our lungs
Descends, an invisible river, with heavy wailings.

25   If rape, poison, the knife and arson
Have not yet woven with their pleasing patterns
The banal canvas of our pitiful fate,
It is because our soul, alas, is not bold enough.

But among the jackals, panthers, bitches,
30   Monkeys, scorpions, vultures, serpents,
The monsters squealing, yelling, grunting, crawling
In the infamous menagerie of our vices

There is one uglier, more wicked and more foul than all!
Although he does not make great gestures or great cries,
35   He would gladly make the earth a shambles
And swallow the world in a yawn;

It is boredom! his eyes weeping an involuntary tear,
He dreams of gibbets as he smokes his hookah.
You know him, reader, this delicate monster,
40   —Hypocrite reader—my twin—my brother!

DESTRUCTION

Ceaselessly beside me the Demon writhes;
He swarms around me like impalpable air;
I swallow him and feel him burning my lungs
And filling them with an everlasting guilty desire.

45   At times he takes, knowing my great love for Art,
The form of the most seductive of women,
And, under specious pretexts of depression,
Accustoms my lips to infamous love charms.

Thus, far from the sight of God, he leads me,
50   Panting and crushed by fatigue, into the midst
Of the plains of Boredom, extensive and deserted,

And throws before my eyes full of confusion
Soiled clothing, opened wounds,
And the bloody apparatus of Destruction.   1861

CORRESPONDENCES

Nature is a temple, where the living
Columns sometimes breathe confusing speech;
Man walks within these groves of symbols, each
Of which regards him as a kindred thing.

5   As the long echoes, shadowy, profound,
Heard from afar, blend in a unity,
Vast as the night, as sunlight's clarity,
So perfumes, colours, sounds may correspond.

Odours there are, fresh as a baby's skin,
10   Mellow as oboes, green as meadow grass,
—Others corrupted, rich, triumphant, full,

Having dimensions infinitely vast,
Frankincense, musk, ambergris, benjamin,
Singing the senses' rapture, and the soul's.

INVITATION TO THE VOYAGE

    My sister, my child
    Imagine how sweet
To live there as lovers do!
    To kiss as we choose
5   To love and to die
In that land resembling you!
    The misty suns
    Of shifting skies
To my spirit are as dear
10   As the evasions
    Of your eyes
That shine behind their tears.

There, all is order and leisure,
Luxury, beauty, and pleasure.

15   The tables would glow
    With the lustre of years
To ornament our room.
    The rarest of blooms
    Would mingle their scents
20   With amber's vague perfume.

The ceilings, rich
The mirrors, deep—
The splendour of the East—
All whisper there
25   To the silent soul
Her sweet familiar speech.

There, all is order and leisure,
Luxury, beauty, and pleasure.

And these canals
30   Bear ships at rest,
Although in a wandering mood;
To gratify
Your least desire
They have sailed around the world.
35   The setting suns
Enrobe the fields
The canals, the entire town
With hyacinth, gold;
The world falls asleep
40   In a warmly glowing gown.

There, all is order and leisure,
Luxury, beauty, and pleasure.

17. STÉPHANE MALLARMÉ

Stéphane Mallarmé (1842-1898) was the central theorist of French Symbolism. Inspired by Baudelaire and Poe, Mallarmé envisioned and wrote a dreamlike poetry that deemphasizes concrete description and clear argument, tending instead to explore the sound and texture of language, and to evoke the subjective experience of emotional states and sense impressions. Mallarmé wrote that "to name is to destroy; to suggest is to create"; and his poems try to suggest moods and modes of experience that are always in flux. In this increasing focus on subjective experience, Mallarmé and the symbolists can be seen as an extension of Romanticism; but in his experiments with language's sonic and sensual qualities, and in his rejection of simple, direct expression, he anticipates the experiments and achievements of modernism.

SAINT

At the window ledge concealing
The ancient sandalwood gold-flaking
Of her viol dimly twinkling
Long ago with flute or mandore,

5   Stands the pallid Saint displaying
The ancient missal page unfolding
At the Magnificat outpouring
Long ago for vesper and compline:

At that monstrance glazing lightly
10   Brushed now by a harp the Angel
Fashioned in his evening flight
Just for the delicate finger

Tip which, lacking the ancient missal
Or ancient sandalwood, she poises
15   On the instrumental plumage,
Musician of silence.

Hubert Creekmore

"WILL NEW AND ALIVE THE BEAUTIFUL TODAY . . ."

Will new and alive the beautiful today
Shatter with a blow of drunken wing
This hard lake, forgotten, haunted under rime
By the transparent glacier, flights unflown!

5   A swan of long ago remembers now that he,
Magnificent but lost to hope, is doomed

For having failed to sing the realms of life
When the ennui of sterile winter gleamed.

His neck will shake off the white torment space
10   Inflicts upon the bird for his denial,
But not this horror, plumage trapped in ice.

Phantom by brilliance captive to this place,
Immobile, he assumes disdain's cold dream,
Which, in his useless exile, robes the Swan.

Patricia Terry and Maurice Z. Shroder

18. ARTHUR RIMBAUD

Arthur Rimbaud (1854–1891) was, along with Stéphane Mallarmé, one of the key figures in French Symbolism, and in his hallucinatory, frequently obscure poems, he anticipates Surrealism, both in painting and in poetry. Rimbaud's verse is frequently characterized by a confusion of the senses known as "synaesthesia," in which the impressions of one sense are described in terms of an another—for example, in seeing odors, or smelling colors. Like the other French symbolists, reality for Rimbaud is a subjective affair, a dreamlike tapestry of sense impressions.

BARBARIAN

Long after the days and the seasons, and the creatures and the countries,

The banner of bleeding meat on the silk of the seas and of the arctic flowers; (they do not exist.)

5   Delivered from the old fanfares of heroism—that still attack our heart and our head—far from the former assassins.

—Oh! the banner of bleeding meat on the silk of the seas and of the arctic flowers; (they do not exist.)

Delights!

10   Blazing coals, raining in squalls of hoarfrost,—Delights!—fires in the rain of the wind of diamonds, rain hurled down by the earthly heart eternally carbonized for us.—O world!—

(Far from the old retreats and the old flames, that are known, that are felt,)

15   Blazing coals and froths. Music, veering of whirlpools and collisions of drift ice with the stars.

O Delights, oh world, oh music! And there, the forms, the sweats, the heads of hair and the eyes, floating. And the white tears, boiling,—oh delights!—and the feminine voice borne down to the

20 bottom of the volcanoes and the arctic grottoes.

The banner . . .

THE BRIDGES

Crystalline gray skies. A strange pattern of bridges, these straight, those arched, others descending obliquely at angles to the first, and these configurations repeating themselves in the other illuminated circuits of the canal, but all so long and light that the shores, laden
5   with domes, sink and diminish. Some of these bridges are still encumbered with hovels. Others support masts, signals, frail parapets. Minor chords interweave, and flow smoothly; ropes rise from the steep banks. One detects a red jacket, perhaps other costumes and musical instruments. Are these popular tunes, fragments of manori-
10   al concerts, remnants of public anthems? The water is gray and blue, ample as an arm of the sea.

A white ray, falling from the summit of the sky, reduces to nothingness this theatrical performance.

THE DRUNKEN BOAT

As I was floating down unconcerned Rivers
I no longer felt myself steered by the haulers:
Gaudy Redskins had taken them for targets
Nailing them naked to coloured stakes.

5   I cared nothing for all my crews,
Carrying Flemish wheat or English cottons.
When, along with my haulers those uproars were done with
The Rivers let me sail downstream where I pleased.

Into the ferocious tide-rips
10   Last winter, more absorbed than the minds of children,
I ran! And the unmoored Peninsulas
Never endured more triumphant clamourings

The storm made bliss of my sea-borne awakenings.
Lighter than a cork, I danced on the waves
15   Which men call eternal rollers of victims,
For ten nights, without once missing the foolish eye of the
      harbor lights!

Sweeter than the flesh of sour apples to children,
The green water penetrated my pinewood hull
20   And washed me clean of the bluish wine-stains and the
      splashes of vomit,
Carring away both rudder and anchor.

And from that time on I bathed in the Poem
Of the Sea, star-infused and churned into milk,
25   Devouring the green azures; where, entranced in pallid flotsam,
A dreaming drowned man sometimes goes down;

Where, suddenly dyeing the bluenesses, deliriums
And slow rhythms under the gleams of the daylight,
Stronger than alcohol, vaster than music
30   Ferment the bitter rednesses of love!

I have come to know the skies splitting with lightnings, and
     the waterspouts
And the breakers and currents; I know the evening,
And Dawn rising up like a flock of doves,
35   And sometimes I have seen what men have imagined they saw!

I have seen the low-hanging sun speckled with mystic horrors.
Lighting up long violet coagulations,
Like the performers in very-antique dramas
Waves rolling back into the distances their shiverings of vene-
40   tian blinds!

I have dreamed of the green night of the dazzled snows
The kiss rising slowly to the eyes of the seas,
The circulation of undreamed-of saps,
And the yellow-blue awakenings of singing phosphorus!

45   I have followed, for whole months on end, the swells
Battering the reefs like hysterical herds of cows,
Never dreaming that the luminous feet of the Marys
Could force back the muzzles of snorting Oceans!

I have struck, do you realize, incredible Floridas
50   Where mingle with flowers the eyes of panthers
In human skins! Rainbows stretched like bridles
Under the seas' horizon, to glaucous herds!

I have seen the enormous swamps seething, traps
Where a whole leviathan rots in the reeds!
55   Downfalls of waters in the midst of the calm
And distances cataracting down into abysses!

Glaciers, suns of silver, waves of pearl, skies of red-hot coals!
Hideous wrecks at the bottom of brown gulfs
Where the giant snakes devoured by vermin

60   Fall from the twisted trees with black odours!

I should have liked to show to children those dolphins
Of the blue wave, those golden, those singing fishes.
—Foam of flowers rocked my driftings
And at times ineffable winds would lend me wings.

65   Sometimes, a martyr weary of poles and zones,
The sea whose sobs sweetened my rollings
Lifted its shadow-flowers with their yellow sucking disks
            toward me
And I hung there like a kneeling woman . . .

70   Almost an island, tossing on my beaches the brawls
And droppings of pale-eyed, clamouring birds,
And I was scudding along when across my frayed cordage
Drowned men sank backwards into sleep!

But now I, a boat lost under the hair of coves,
75   Hurled by the hurricane into the birdless ether,
I, whose wreck, dead-drunk and sodden with water, neither
            Monitor nor Hanse ships
Would have fished up;

Free, smoking, risen from violet fogs,
80   I who bored through the wall of the reddening sky
Which bears a sweetmeat good poets find delicious,
Lichens of sunlight [mixed] with azure snot,

Who ran, speckled with lunula of electricity,
A crazy plank, with black sea-horses for escort,
85   When Julys were crushing with cudgel blows
Skies of ultramarine into burning funnels;

I who trembled, to feel at fifty leagues' distance
The groans of Behemoth's rutting, and of the dense
            Maelstroms
90   Eternal spinner of blue immobilities
I long for Europe with it's aged old parapets!

I have seen archipelagos of stars! and islands
Whose delirious skies are open to sailor:
—Do you sleep, are you exiled in those bottomless nights,
95   Million golden birds, O Life Force of the future?—

18. *Arthur Rimbaud*

But, truly, I have wept too much ! The Dawns are heartbreaking.
Every moon is atrocious and every sun bitter:
Sharp love has swollen me up with heady langours.
O let my keel split! O let me sink to the bottom!

100   If there is one water in Europe I want, it is the
Black cold pool where into the scented twilight
A child squatting full of sadness, launches
A boat as fragile as a butterfly in May.

I can no more, bathed in your langours, O waves,
105   Sail in the wake of the carriers of cottons,
Nor undergo the pride of the flags and pennants,
Nor pull past the horrible eyes of the hulks.

Translated by Oliver Bernard: Arthur Rimbaud, *Collected Poems* (1962)

19. MATTHEW ARNOLD

Matthew Arnold (1822–1888) was a poet, critic, and religious con-troversialist. His melancholic poetry captures very well the romantic protest against the new industrial society ("this iron time/Of doubts, dis-putes, distractions, fears"), while his witty social criticism calls for a return to high intellectual and cultural standards. The tragedy in Arnold's life is that he could never quite believe in the Romantic world view that he saw inevitably and necessarily replacing Christianity.

DOVER BEACH

> The sea is calm tonight.
> The tide is full, the moon lies fair
> Upon the straits;—on the French coast the light
> Gleams and is gone; the cliffs of England stand,
> Glimmering and vast, out in the tranquil bay.
> Come to the window, sweet is the night-air!
> Only, from the long line of spray
> Where the sea meets the moon-blanch'd land,
> Listen! you hear the grating roar
> Of pebbles which the waves draw back, and fling,
> At their return, up the high strand,
> Begin, and cease, and then again begin,
> With tremulous cadence slow, and bring
> The eternal note of sadness in.
>
> Sophocles long ago
> Heard it on the Aegean, and it brought
> Into his mind the turbid ebb and flow
> Of human misery; we
> Find also in the sound a thought,
> Hearing it by this distant northern sea.
>
> The Sea of Faith
> Was once, too, at the full, and round earth's shore
> Lay like the folds of a bright girdle furl'd.[1]
> But now I only hear

5
10
15
20

[1]Like a gathered-up garment: the implication is that the "Sea of Faith" once comfortably surrounded all the world. The metaphor doesn't quite work: a sign, perhaps, of Victorian confusion.

25   Its melancholy, long, withdrawing roar,
        Retreating to the breath
        Of the night-wind, down the vast edges drear
        And naked shingles of the world.   [rough, pebbly beach]

        Ah, love, let us be true
30   To one another! for the world which seems
        To lie before us like a land of dreams,
        So various, so beautiful, so new,
        Hath really neither joy, nor love, nor light,
        Nor certitude, nor peace, nor help for pain;
35   And we are here as on a darkling plain
        Swept with confused alarms of struggle and flight,
        Where ignorant armies clash by night.   1851

FROM "STANZAS FROM THE GRANDE CHARTREUSE"

        For rigorous teachers seized my youth,
        And purged its faith, and trimm'd its fire,
        Show'd me the high, white star of Truth,
        There bade me gaze, and there aspire.
5   Even now their whispers pierce the gloom:
        What dost thou in this living tomb?

        Forgive me, masters of the mind!
        At whose behest I long ago
        So much unlearnt, so much resign'd—
10   I come not here to be your foe!
        I seek these anchorites, not in ruth,
        To curse and to deny your truth;

        Not as their friend, or child, I speak!
        But as, on some far northern strand,
15   Thinking of his own Gods, a Greek
        In pity and mournful awe might stand
        Before some fallen Runic stone—
        For both were faiths, and both are gone.

        Wandering between two worlds, one dead,
20   The other powerless to be born,
        With nowhere yet to rest my head,
        Like these, on earth I wait forlorn.   1855

FROM THE STUDY OF POETRY
(1880)

The future of poetry is immense, because in poetry, where it is worthy of its high destinies, our race, as time goes on, will find an ever surer and surer stay. There is not a creed which is not shaken, not an accredited dogma which is not shown to be questionable, not
5 a received tradition which does not threaten to dissolve. Our religion has materialised itself in the fact, in the supposed fact; it has attached its emotion to the fact, and now the fact is failing it. But for poetry the idea is everything; the rest is a world of illusion, of divine illusion. Poetry attaches its emotion to the idea; the idea *is* the fact.
10 The strongest part of our religion today is its unconscious poetry.

We should conceive of poetry worthily, and more highly than it has been the custom to conceive of it. We should conceive of it as capable of higher uses, and called to higher destinies, than those which in general men have assigned to it hitherto. More and more
15 mankind will discover that we have to turn to poetry to interpret life for us, to console us, to sustain us. Without poetry, our science will appear incomplete; and most of what now passes with us for religion and philosophy will be replaced by poetry.

In poetry, as a criticism of life under the conditions fixed for
20 such a criticism by the laws of poetic truth and poetic beauty, the spirit of our race will find as time goes on and as other helps fail, its consolation and stay.

20. THE VICTORIAN POETS

The conventions of Romanticism persisted into the vastly changed, rapidly industrializing, Victorian era (1837–1901) but with etiolated energy and conviction. Still, the Victorian age was the last period in which poetry was widely read and discussed by all literate people (in much the same way that movies are today). Victorian poetry is characteristically other-worldly and plaintive but quite various, nevertheless. In these selections we see Tennyson and Browning exploring in different ways the possibilities of the dramatic monologue while Bronte and Rossetti offer lyrics with more personal voices and more intimate tones.

ULYSSES
Alfred Lord Tennyson

It little profits that an idle king,
By this still hearth, among these barren crags,
Match'd with an aged wife, I mete and dole
Unequal laws unto a savage race,
5   That hoard, and sleep, and feed, and know not me.

I cannot rest from travel: I will drink
Life to the lees: All times I have enjoy'd
Greatly, have suffer'd greatly, both with those
That loved me, and alone, on shore, and when
10 Thro' scudding drifts the rainy Hyades
Vext the dim sea: I am become a name;
For always roaming with a hungry heart
Much have I seen and known; cities of men
And manners, climates, councils, governments,
15 Myself not least, but honour'd of them all;
And drunk delight of battle with my peers,
Far on the ringing plains of windy Troy.
I am a part of all that I have met;
Yet all experience is an arch wherethro'
20 Gleams that untravell'd world whose margin fades
For ever and forever when I move.

How dull it is to pause, to make an end,
To rust unburnish'd, not to shine in use!
As tho' to breathe were life! Life piled on life
25 Were all too little, and of one to me
Little remains: but every hour is saved
From that eternal silence, something more,
A bringer of new things; and vile it were
For some three suns to store and hoard myself,
30 And this gray spirit yearning in desire
To follow knowledge like a sinking star,
Beyond the utmost bound of human thought.

This is my son, mine own Telemachus,
To whom I leave the sceptre and the isle,—
35 Well-loved of me, discerning to fulfil
This labour, by slow prudence to make mild
A rugged people, and thro' soft degrees
Subdue them to the useful and the good.
Most blameless is he, centred in the sphere
40 Of common duties, decent not to fail
In offices of tenderness, and pay
Meet adoration to my household gods,
When I am gone. He works his work, I mine.

There lies the port; the vessel puffs her sail:
45 There gloom the dark, broad seas. My mariners,
Souls that have toil'd, and wrought, and thought with me—
That ever with a frolic welcome took
The thunder and the sunshine, and opposed
Free hearts, free foreheads—you and I are old;
50 Old age hath yet his honour and his toil;
Death closes all: but something ere the end,
Some work of noble note, may yet be done,
Not unbecoming men that strove with Gods.
The lights begin to twinkle from the rocks:
55 The long day wanes: the slow moon climbs: the deep
Moans round with many voices. Come, my friends,
'T is not too late to seek a newer world.
Push off, and sitting well in order smite
The sounding furrows; for my purpose holds
60 To sail beyond the sunset, and the baths
Of all the western stars, until I die.
It may be that the gulfs will wash us down:
It may be we shall touch the Happy Isles,
And see the great Achilles, whom we knew.

65 Tho' much is taken, much abides; and tho'
     We are not now that strength which in old days
     Moved earth and heaven, that which we are, we are;
     One equal temper of heroic hearts,
     Made weak by time and fate, but strong in will
70 To strive, to seek, to find, and not to yield.

THE LOTOS-EATERS
Alfred Lord Tennyson

    "COURAGE!" he said, and pointed toward the land,
    "This mounting wave will roll us shoreward soon."
    In the afternoon they came unto a land
    In which it seemed always afternoon.
5   All round the coast the languid air did swoon,
    Breathing like one that hath a weary dream.
    Full-faced above the valley stood the moon;
    And, like a downward smoke, the slender stream
    Along the cliff to fall and pause and fall did seem.

10 A land of streams! some, like a downward smoke,
    Slow-dropping veils of thinnest lawn, did go;
    And some thro' wavering lights and shadows broke,
    Rolling a slumbrous sheet of foam below.
    They saw the gleaming river seaward flow
15 From the inner land; far off, three mountain-tops,
    Three silent pinnacles of aged snow,
    Stood sunset-flush'd; and, dew'd with showery drops,
    Up-clomb the shadowy pine above the woven copse.

    The charmed sunset linger'd low adown
20 In the red West; thro' mountain clefts the dale
    Was seen far inland, and the yellow down
    Border'd with palm, and many a winding vale
    And meadow, set with slender galingale;
    A land where all things always seem'd the same!
25 And round about the keel with faces pale,
    Dark faces pale against that rosy flame,
    The mild-eyed melancholy Lotos-eaters came.

    Branches they bore of that enchanted stem,
    Laden with flower and fruit, whereof they gave
30 To each, but whoso did receive of them
    And taste, to him the gushing of the wave

Far far away did seem to mourn and rave
On alien shores; and if his fellow spake,
His voice was thin, as voices from the grave;
35   And deep-asleep he seem'd, yet all awake,
And music in his ears his beating heart did make.

They sat them down upon the yellow sand,
Between the sun and moon upon the shore;
And sweet it was to dream of Fatherland,
40   Of child, and wife, and slave; but evermore
Most weary seem'd the sea, weary the oar,
Weary the wandering fields of barren foam.
Then some one said, "We will return no more;"
And all at once they sang, "Our island home
45   Is far beyond the wave; we will no longer roam."

CHORIC SONG

I

There is sweet music here that softer falls
Than petals from blown roses on the grass,
Or night-dews on still waters between walls
Of shadowy granite, in a gleaming pass;
50   Music that gentlier on the spirit lies,
Than tir'd eyelids upon tir'd eyes;
Music that brings sweet sleep down from the blissful skies.
Here are cool mosses deep,
And thro' the moss the ivies creep,
55   And in the stream the long-leaved flowers weep,
And from the craggy ledge the poppy hangs in sleep.

II

Why are we weigh'd upon with heaviness,
And utterly consumed with sharp distress,
While all things else have rest from weariness?
60   All things have rest: why should we toil alone,
We only toil, who are the first of things,
And make perpetual moan,
Still from one sorrow to another thrown;
Nor ever fold our wings,
65   And cease from wanderings,

Nor steep our brows in slumber's holy balm;
Nor harken what the inner spirit sings,
"There is no joy but calm!"—
Why should we only toil, the roof and crown of things?

III

70 Lo! in the middle of the wood,
The folded leaf is woo'd from out the bud
With winds upon the branch, and there
Grows green and broad, and takes no care,
Sun-steep'd at noon, and in the moon
75 Nightly dew-fed; and turning yellow
Falls, and floats adown the air.
Lo! sweeten'd with the summer light,
The full-juiced apple, waxing over-mellow,
Drops in a silent autumn night.
80 All its allotted length of days
The flower ripens in its place,
Ripens and fades, and falls, and hath no toil,
Fast-rooted in the fruitful soil.

IV

Hateful is the dark-blue sky,
85 Vaulted o'er the dark-blue sea.
Death is the end of life; ah, why
Should life all labor be?
Let us alone. Time driveth onward fast,
And in a little while our lips are dumb.
90 Let us alone. What is it that will last?
All things are taken from us, and become
Portions and parcels of the dreadful past.
Let us alone. What pleasure can we have
To war with evil? Is there any peace
95 In ever climbing up the climbing wave?
All things have rest, and ripen toward the grave
In silence—ripen, fall, and cease:
Give us long rest or death, dark death, or dreamful ease.

V

How sweet it were, hearing the downward stream,
100 With half-shut eyes ever to seem
　　Falling asleep in a half-dream!
　　To dream and dream, like yonder amber light,
　　Which will not leave the myrrh-bush on the height;
　　To hear each other's whisper'd speech;
105 Eating the Lotos day by day,
　　To watch the crisping ripples on the beach,
　　And tender curving lines of creamy spray;
　　To lend our hearts and spirits wholly
　　To the influence of mild-minded melancholy;
110 To muse and brood and live again in memory,
　　With those old faces of our infancy
　　Heap'd over with a mound of grass,
　　Two handfuls of white dust, shut in an urn of brass!

VI

Dear is the memory of our wedded lives,
115 And dear the last embraces of our wives
　　And their warm tears; but all hath suffer'd change;
　　For surely now our household hearths are cold,
　　Our sons inherit us, our looks are strange,
　　And we should come like ghosts to trouble joy.
120 Or else the island princes over-bold
　　Have eat our substance, and the minstrel sings
　　Before them of the ten years' war in Troy,
　　And our great deeds, as half-forgotten things.
　　Is there confusion in the little isle?
125 Let what is broken so remain.
　　The Gods are hard to reconcile;
　　'Tis hard to settle order once again.
　　There *is* confusion worse than death,
　　Trouble on trouble, pain on pain,
130 Long labor unto aged breath,
　　Sore task to hearts worn out by many wars
　　And eyes grown dim with gazing on the pilot-stars.

VII

But, propped on beds of amaranth and moly,
How sweet—while warm airs lull us, blowing lowly—
135 With half-dropped eyelids still,
Beneath a heaven dark and holy,
To watch the long bright river drawing slowly
His waters from the purple hill—
To hear the dewy echoes calling
140 From cave to cave thro' the thick-twined vine—
To watch the emerald-color'd water falling
Thro' many a woven acanthus-wreath divine!
Only to hear and see the far-off sparkling brine,
Only to hear were sweet, stretch'd out beneath the pine.

VIII

145 The Lotos blooms below the barren peak,
The Lotos blows by every winding creek;
All day the wind breathes low with mellower tone;
Thro' every hollow cave and alley lone
Round and round the spicy downs the yellow Lotos-dust is blown.
150 We have had enough of action, and of motion we,
Roll'd to starboard, roll'd to larboard, when the surge was
seething free,
Where the wallowing monster spouted his foam-fountains in the sea.
Let us swear an oath, and keep it with an equal mind,
155 In the hollow Lotos-land to live and lie reclined
On the hills like Gods together, careless of mankind.
For they lie beside their nectar, and the bolts are hurl'd
Far below them in the valleys, and the clouds are lightly curl'd
Round their golden houses, girdled with the gleaming world;
160 Where they smile in secret, looking over wasted lands,
Blight and famine, plague and earthquake, roaring deeps and fiery
sands,
Clanging fights, and flaming towns, and sinking ships, and pray-
ing hands.
165 But they smile, they find a music centred in a doleful song
Steaming up, a lamentation and an ancient tale of wrong,
Like a tale of little meaning tho' the words are strong;
Chanted from an ill-used race of men that cleave the soil,
Sow the seed, and reap the harvest with enduring toil,
170 Storing yearly little dues of wheat, and wine and oil;
Till they perish and they suffer—some, 'tis whisper'd—down in
hell

Suffer endless anguish, others in Elysian valleys dwell,
Resting weary limbs at last on beds of asphodel.
175 Surely, surely, slumber is more sweet than toil, the shore
Than labor in the deep mid-ocean, wind and wave and oar;
O, rest ye, brother mariners, we will not wander more.

MY LAST DUCHESS
Robert Browning

That's my last Duchess painted on the wall,
Looking as if she were alive. I call
That piece a wonder, now: Frà Pandolf's hands
Worked busily a day, and there she stands.
5 Will't please you sit and look at her? I said
"Frà Pandolf" by design, for never read
Strangers like you that pictured countenance,
The depth and passion of its earnest glance,
But to myself they turned (since none puts by
10 The curtain I have drawn for you, but I)
And seemed as they would ask me, if they durst,
How such a glance came there; so, not the first
Are you to turn and ask thus. Sir, 'twas not
Her husband's presence only, called that spot
15 Of joy into the Duchess' cheek: perhaps
Frà Pandolf chanced to say, "Her mantle laps
Over my Lady's wrist too much," or "Paint
Must never hope to reproduce the faint
Half-flush that dies along her throat"; such stuff
20 Was courtesy, she thought, and cause enough
For calling up that spot of joy. She had
A heart . . . how shall I say? . . . too soon made glad,
Too easily impressed; she liked whate'er
She looked on, and her looks went everywhere.
25 Sir, 'twas all one! My favour at her breast,
The dropping of the daylight in the West,
The bough of cherries some officious fool
Broke in the orchard for her, the white mule
She rode with round the terrace—all and each
30 Would draw from her alike the approving speech,
Or blush, at least. She thanked men,—good; but thanked
Somehow . . . I know not how . . . as if she ranked
My gift of a nine-hundred-years-old name
With anybody's gift. Who'd stoop to blame
35 This sort of trifling? Even had you skill

In speech—(which I have not)—to make your will
Quite clear to such an one, and say, "Just this
Or that in you disgusts me; here you miss,
Or there exceed the mark"—and if she let
40 Herself be lessoned so, nor plainly set
Her wits to yours, forsooth, and made excuse,
—E'en then would be some stooping; and I chuse
Never to stoop. Oh, sir, she smiled, no doubt,
Whene'er I passed her; but who passed without
45 Much the same smile? This grew; I gave commands;
Then all smiles stopped together. There she stands
As if alive. Will 't please you rise? We'll meet
The company below, then. I repeat,
The Count your Master's known munificence
50 Is ample warrant that no just pretence
Of mine for dowry will be disallowed;
Though his fair daughter's self, as I avowed
At starting, is my object. Nay, we'll go
Together down, Sir! Notice Neptune, though,
55 Taming a sea-horse, thought a rarity,
Which Claus of Innsbruck cast in bronze for me.

COUNT GISMOND—AIX IN PROVENCE
Robert Browning

Christ God who savest man, save most
    Of men Count Gismond who saved me!
Count Gauthier, when he chose his post,
    Chose time and place and company
5   To suit it; when he struck at length
My honour, 't was with all his strength.
And doubtlessly, ere he could draw
    All points to one, he must have schemed!
That miserable morning saw
10   Few half so happy as I seemed,
While being dressed in queen's array
To give our tourney prize away.
I thought they loved me, did me grace
    To please themselves; 't was all their deed;
15   God makes, or fair or foul, our face;
    If showing mine so caused to bleed
My cousins' hearts, they should have dropped
A word, and straight the play had stopped.
They, too, so beauteous! Each a queen
20   By virtue of her brow and breast;
Not needing to be crowned, I mean,
    As I do. E'en when I was dressed,
Had either of them spoke, instead
Of glancing sideways with still head!
25   But no: they let me laugh, and sing
    My birthday song quite through, adjust
The last rose in my garland, fling
    A last look on the mirror, trust
My arms to each an arm of theirs,
30   And so descend the castle-stairs—
And come out on the morning troop
    Of merry friends who kissed my cheek,
And called me queen, and made me stoop
    Under the canopy—(a streak
35   That pierced it, of the outside sun,
Powdered with gold its gloom's soft dun)—
And they could let me take my state
    And foolish throne amid applause
Of all come there to celebrate
40   My queen's-day—Oh I think the cause
Of much was, they forgot no crowd

Makes up for parents in their shroud!
However that be, all eyes were bent
    Upon me, when my cousins cast
45 Theirs down; 't was time I should present
    The victor's crown, but . . . there, 't will last
No long time . . . the old mist again
Blinds me as then it did. How vain!
See! Gismond's at the gate, in talk
50   With his two boys: I can proceed.
Well, at that moment, who should stalk
    Forth boldly—to my face, indeed—
But Gauthier? and he thundered "Stay!"
And all stayed. "Bring no crowns, I say!
55 "Bring torches! Wind the penance-sheet
    "About her! Let her shun the chaste,
    "Or lay herself before their feet!
    "Shall she, whose body I embraced
    "A night long, queen it in the day?
60 "For honour's sake no crowns, I say!"
I? What I answered? As I live,
    I never fancied such a thing
As answer possible to give.
    What says the body when they spring
65 Some monstrous torture-engine's whole
Strength on it? No more says the soul.
Till out strode Gismond; then I knew
    That I was saved. I never met
His face before, but, at first view,
70   I felt quite sure that God had set
Himself to Satan; would who spend
A minute's mistrust on the end?
He strode to Gauthier, in his throat
    Gave him the lie, then struck his mouth
75 With one back-handed blow that wrote
    In blood men's verdict there. North, South,
East, West, I looked. The lie was dead,
And damned, and truth stood up instead.
This glads me most, that I enjoyed
80   The heart o' the joy, with my content
In watching Gismond unalloyed
    By any doubt of the event:
God took that on him-I was bid
Watch Gismond for my part: I did.
85 Did I not watch him while he let
    His armourer just brace his greaves,

      Rivet his hauberk, on the fret
          The while! His foot . . . my memory leaves
90 No least stamp out nor how anon
      He pulled his ringing gauntlets on.
      And e'en before the trumpet's sound
          Was finished, prone lay the false knight,
      Prone as his lie, upon the ground:
95   Gismond flew at him, used no sleight
      O' the sword, but open-breasted drove,
      Cleaving till out the truth he clove.
      Which done, he dragged him to my feet
          And said, "Here die, but end thy breath
100 "In full confession, lest thou fleet
          "From my first, to God's second death!
      "Say, hast thou lied? "And, "I have lied
      "To God and her," he said, and died.
      Then Gismond, kneeling to me, asked
105   —What safe my heart holds, though no word
      Could I repeat now, if I tasked
          My powers for ever, to a third
      Dear even as you are. Pass the rest
      Until I sank upon his breast.
110 Over my head his arm he flung
          Against the world; and scarce I felt
      His sword (that dripped by me and swung)
          A little shifted in its belt:
      For he began to say the while
115 How South our home lay many a mile.
      So, 'mid the shouting multitude
          We two walked forth to never more
      Return. My cousins have pursued
          Their life, untroubled as before
120 I vexed them. Gauthier's dwelling-place
      God lighten! May his soul find grace!
      Our elder boy has got the clear
          Great brow, tho' when his brother's black
      Full eye shows scorn, it . . . Gismond here?
125   And have you brought my tercel back?
      I was just telling Adela
      How many birds it struck since May.

PORPHYRIA'S LOVER
Robert Browning

The rain set early in to-night,
    The sullen wind was soon awake,
It tore the elm-tops down for spite,
    And did its worst to vex the lake:
5   I listen'd with heart fit to break.
When glided in Porphyria; straight
    She shut the cold out and the storm,
And kneel'd and made the cheerless grate
    Blaze up, and all the cottage warm;
10   Which done, she rose, and from her form
Withdrew the dripping cloak and shawl,
    And laid her soil'd gloves by, untied
Her hat and let the damp hair fall,
    And, last, she sat down by my side
15   And call'd me. When no voice replied,
She put my arm about her waist,
    And made her smooth white shoulder bare,
And all her yellow hair displaced,
    And, stooping, made my cheek lie there,
20   And spread, o'er all, her yellow hair,
Murmuring how she loved me—she
    Too weak, for all her heart's endeavour,
To set its struggling passion free
    From pride, and vainer ties dissever,
25   And give herself to me for ever.
But passion sometimes would prevail,
    Nor could to-night's gay feast restrain
A sudden thought of one so pale
    For love of her, and all in vain:
30   So, she was come through wind and rain.
Be sure I look'd up at her eyes
    Happy and proud; at last I knew
Porphyria worshipp'd me; surprise
    Made my heart swell, and still it grew
35   While I debated what to do.
That moment she was mine, mine, fair,
    Perfectly pure and good: I found
A thing to do, and all her hair
    In one long yellow string I wound
40   Three times her little throat around,
And strangled her. No pain felt she;

I am quite sure she felt no pain.
As a shut bud that holds a bee,
    I warily oped her lids: again
45   Laugh'd the blue eyes without a stain.
And I untighten'd next the tress
    About her neck; her cheek once more
Blush'd bright beneath my burning kiss:
    I propp'd her head up as before,
50   Only, this time my shoulder bore
Her head, which droops upon it still:
    The smiling rosy little head,
So glad it has its utmost will,
    That all it scorn'd at once is fled,
55   And I, its love, am gain'd instead!
Porphyria's love: she guess'd not how
    Her darling one wish would be heard.
And thus we sit together now,
    And all night long we have not stirr'd,
60   And yet God has not said a word!

NO COWARD SOUL IS MINE
Emily Bronte

No coward soul is mine,
No trembler in the world's storm-troubled sphere:
I see Heaven's glories shine,
And Faith shines equal, arming me from Fear.

5   O God within my breast,
Almighty, ever-present Deity!
Life, that in me has rest,
As I, undying Life, have power in Thee!.

Vain are the thousand creeds
10 That move men's hearts: unutterably vain;
Worthless as withered weeds,
Or idlest froth amid the boundless main,

To waken doubt in one
Holding so fast by Thy infinity,
15 So surely anchored on
The steadfast rock of Immortality.

With wide-embracing love
Thy Spirit animates eternal years,
Pervades and broods above,
20 Changes, sustains, dissolves, creates, and rears.

Though earth and moon were gone,
And suns and universes ceased to be,
And Thou wert left alone,
Every existence would exist in Thee.

25 There is not room for Death,
Nor atom that his might could render void:
Thou—Thou art Being and Breath,
And what Thou art may never be destroyed.

GOBLIN MARKET
Christina Rossetti

Morning and evening
Maids heard the goblins cry:
"Come buy our orchard fruits,
Come buy, come buy:
5   Apples and quinces,
Lemons and oranges,
Plump unpeck'd cherries,
Melons and raspberries,
Bloom-down-cheek'd peaches,
10   Swart-headed mulberries,
Wild free-born cranberries,
Crab-apples, dewberries,
Pine-apples, blackberries,
Apricots, strawberries;—
15   All ripe together
In summer weather,—
Morns that pass by,
Fair eves that fly;
Come buy, come buy:
20   Our grapes fresh from the vine,
Pomegranates full and fine,
Dates and sharp bullaces,
Rare pears and greengages,
Damsons and bilberries,
25   Taste them and try:
Currants and gooseberries,
Bright-fire-like barberries,
Figs to fill your mouth,
Citrons from the South,
30   Sweet to tongue and sound to eye;
Come buy, come buy."

Evening by evening
Among the brookside rushes,
Laura bow'd her head to hear,
35   Lizzie veil'd her blushes:
Crouching close together
In the cooling weather,
With clasping arms and cautioning lips,
With tingling cheeks and finger tips.
40   "Lie close," Laura said,

Pricking up her golden head:
"We must not look at goblin men,
We must not buy their fruits:
Who knows upon what soil they fed
45   Their hungry thirsty roots?"
"Come buy," call the goblins
Hobbling down the glen.
"Oh," cried Lizzie, "Laura, Laura,
You should not peep at goblin men."
50   Lizzie cover'd up her eyes,
Cover'd close lest they should look;
Laura rear'd her glossy head,
And whisper'd like the restless brook:
"Look, Lizzie, look, Lizzie,
55   Down the glen tramp little men.
One hauls a basket,
One bears a plate,
One lugs a golden dish
Of many pounds weight.
60   How fair the vine must grow
Whose grapes are so luscious;
How warm the wind must blow
Through those fruit bushes."
"No," said Lizzie, "No, no, no;
65   Their offers should not charm us,
Their evil gifts would harm us."
She thrust a dimpled finger
In each ear, shut eyes and ran:
Curious Laura chose to linger
70   Wondering at each merchant man.
One had a cat's face,
One whisk'd a tail,
One tramp'd at a rat's pace,
One crawl'd like a snail,
75   One like a wombat prowl'd obtuse and furry,
One like a ratel tumbled hurry skurry.
She heard a voice like voice of doves
Cooing all together:
They sounded kind and full of loves
80   In the pleasant weather.

Laura stretch'd her gleaming neck
Like a rush-imbedded swan,
Like a lily from the beck,
Like a moonlit poplar branch,

85 Like a vessel at the launch
   When its last restraint is gone.

   Backwards up the mossy glen
   Turn'd and troop'd the goblin men,
   With their shrill repeated cry,
90 "Come buy, come buy."
   When they reach'd where Laura was
   They stood stock still upon the moss,
   Leering at each other,
   Brother with queer brother;
95 Signalling each other,
   Brother with sly brother.
   One set his basket down,
   One rear'd his plate;
   One began to weave a crown
100 Of tendrils, leaves, and rough nuts brown
      (Men sell not such in any town);
   One heav'd the golden weight
   Of dish and fruit to offer her:
   "Come buy, come buy," was still their cry.
105 Laura stared but did not stir,
   Long'd but had no money:
   The whisk-tail'd merchant bade her taste
   In tones as smooth as honey,
   The cat-faced purr'd,
110 The rat-faced spoke a word
   Of welcome, and the snail-paced even was heard;
   One parrot-voiced and jolly
   Cried "Pretty Goblin" still for "Pretty Polly;"—
   One whistled like a bird.

115 But sweet-tooth Laura spoke in haste:
   "Good folk, I have no coin;
   To take were to purloin:
   I have no copper in my purse,
   I have no silver either,
120 And all my gold is on the furze
   That shakes in windy weather
   Above the rusty heather."
   "You have much gold upon your head,"
   They answer'd all together:
125 "Buy from us with a golden curl."
   She clipp'd a precious golden lock,
   She dropp'd a tear more rare than pearl,

Then suck'd their fruit globes fair or red:
Sweeter than honey from the rock,
130 Stronger than man-rejoicing wine,
Clearer than water flow'd that juice;
She never tasted such before,
How should it cloy with length of use?
She suck'd and suck'd and suck'd the more
135 Fruits which that unknown orchard bore;
She suck'd until her lips were sore;
Then flung the emptied rinds away
But gather'd up one kernel stone,
And knew not was it night or day
140 As she turn'd home alone.

Lizzie met her at the gate
Full of wise upbraidings:
"Dear, you should not stay so late,
Twilight is not good for maidens;
145 Should not loiter in the glen
In the haunts of goblin men.
Do you not remember Jeanie,
How she met them in the moonlight,
Took their gifts both choice and many,
150 Ate their fruits and wore their flowers
Pluck'd from bowers
Where summer ripens at all hours?
But ever in the noonlight
She pined and pined away;
155 Sought them by night and day,
Found them no more, but dwindled and grew grey;
Then fell with the first snow,
While to this day no grass will grow
Where she lies low:
160 I planted daisies there a year ago
That never blow.
You should not loiter so."
"Nay, hush," said Laura:
"Nay, hush, my sister:
165 I ate and ate my fill,
Yet my mouth waters still;
To-morrow night I will
Buy more;" and kiss'd her:
"Have done with sorrow;
170 I'll bring you plums to-morrow
Fresh on their mother twigs,

Cherries worth getting;
You cannot think what figs
My teeth have met in,
175 What melons icy-cold
Piled on a dish of gold
Too huge for me to hold,
What peaches with a velvet nap,
Pellucid grapes without one seed:
180 Odorous indeed must be the mead
Whereon they grow, and pure the wave they drink
With lilies at the brink,
And sugar-sweet their sap."

Golden head by golden head,
185 Like two pigeons in one nest
Folded in each other's wings,
They lay down in their curtain'd bed:
Like two blossoms on one stem,
Like two flakes of new-fall'n snow,
190 Like two wands of ivory
Tipp'd with gold for awful kings.
Moon and stars gaz'd in at them,
Wind sang to them lullaby,
Lumbering owls forbore to fly,
195 Not a bat flapp'd to and fro
Round their rest:
Cheek to cheek and breast to breast
Lock'd together in one nest.

Early in the morning
200 When the first cock crow'd his warning,
Neat like bees, as sweet and busy,
Laura rose with Lizzie:
Fetch'd in honey, milk'd the cows,
Air'd and set to rights the house,
205 Kneaded cakes of whitest wheat,
Cakes for dainty mouths to eat,
Next churn'd butter, whipp'd up cream,
Fed their poultry, sat and sew'd;
Talk'd as modest maidens should:
210 Lizzie with an open heart,
Laura in an absent dream,
One content, one sick in part;
One warbling for the mere bright day's delight,
One longing for the night.

215 At length slow evening came:
       They went with pitchers to the reedy brook;
       Lizzie most placid in her look,
       Laura most like a leaping flame.
       They drew the gurgling water from its deep;
220 Lizzie pluck'd purple and rich golden flags,
       Then turning homeward said: "The sunset flushes
       Those furthest loftiest crags;
       Come, Laura, not another maiden lags.
       No wilful squirrel wags,
225 The beasts and birds are fast asleep."
       But Laura loiter'd still among the rushes
       And said the bank was steep.

       And said the hour was early still
       The dew not fall'n, the wind not chill;
230 Listening ever, but not catching
       The customary cry,
       "Come buy, come buy,"
       With its iterated jingle
       Of sugar-baited words:
235 Not for all her watching
       Once discerning even one goblin
       Racing, whisking, tumbling, hobbling;
       Let alone the herds
       That used to tramp along the glen,
240 In groups or single,
       Of brisk fruit-merchant men.

       Till Lizzie urged, "O Laura, come;
       I hear the fruit-call but I dare not look:
       You should not loiter longer at this brook:
245 Come with me home.
       The stars rise, the moon bends her arc,
       Each glowworm winks her spark,
       Let us get home before the night grows dark:
       For clouds may gather
250 Though this is summer weather,
       Put out the lights and drench us through;
       Then if we lost our way what should we do?"

       Laura turn'd cold as stone
       To find her sister heard that cry alone,
255 That goblin cry,
       "Come buy our fruits, come buy."

Must she then buy no more such dainty fruit?
Must she no more such succous pasture find,
Gone deaf and blind?
260 Her tree of life droop'd from the root:
She said not one word in her heart's sore ache;
But peering thro' the dimness, nought discerning,
Trudg'd home, her pitcher dripping all the way;
So crept to bed, and lay
265 Silent till Lizzie slept;
Then sat up in a passionate yearning,
And gnash'd her teeth for baulk'd desire, and wept
As if her heart would break.

Day after day, night after night,
270 Laura kept watch in vain
In sullen silence of exceeding pain.
She never caught again the goblin cry:
"Come buy, come buy;"—
She never spied the goblin men
275 Hawking their fruits along the glen:
But when the noon wax'd bright
Her hair grew thin and grey;
She dwindled, as the fair full moon doth turn
To swift decay and burn
280 Her fire away.

One day remembering her kernel-stone
She set it by a wall that faced the south;
Dew'd it with tears, hoped for a root,
Watch'd for a waxing shoot,
285 But there came none;
It never saw the sun,
It never felt the trickling moisture run:
While with sunk eyes and faded mouth
She dream'd of melons, as a traveller sees
290 False waves in desert drouth
With shade of leaf-crown'd trees,
And burns the thirstier in the sandful breeze.

She no more swept the house,
Tended the fowls or cows,
295 Fetch'd honey, kneaded cakes of wheat,
Brought water from the brook:
But sat down listless in the chimney-nook
And would not eat.

Tender Lizzie could not bear
300 To watch her sister's cankerous care
Yet not to share.
She night and morning
Caught the goblins' cry:
"Come buy our orchard fruits,
305 Come buy, come buy;"—
Beside the brook, along the glen,
She heard the tramp of goblin men,
The yoke and stir
Poor Laura could not hear;
310 Long'd to buy fruit to comfort her,
But fear'd to pay too dear.
She thought of Jeanie in her grave,
Who should have been a bride;
But who for joys brides hope to have
315 Fell sick and died
In her gay prime,
In earliest winter time
With the first glazing rime,
With the first snow-fall of crisp winter time.

320 Till Laura dwindling
Seem'd knocking at Death's door:
Then Lizzie weigh'd no more
Better and worse;
But put a silver penny in her purse,
325 Kiss'd Laura, cross'd the heath with clumps of furze
At twilight, halted by the brook:
And for the first time in her life
Began to listen and look.

Laugh'd every goblin
330 When they spied her peeping:
Came towards her hobbling,
Flying, running, leaping,
Puffing and blowing,
Chuckling, clapping, crowing,
335 Clucking and gobbling,
Mopping and mowing,
Full of airs and graces,
Pulling wry faces,
Demure grimaces,
340 Cat-like and rat-like,
Ratel- and wombat-like,

Snail-paced in a hurry,
Parrot-voiced and whistler,
Helter skelter, hurry skurry,
345 Chattering like magpies,
Fluttering like pigeons,
Gliding like fishes,—
Hugg'd her and kiss'd her:
Squeez'd and caress'd her: ·
350 Stretch'd up their dishes,
Panniers, and plates:
"Look at our apples
Russet and dun,
Bob at our cherries,
355 Bite at our peaches,
Citrons and dates,
Grapes for the asking,
Pears red with basking
Out in the sun,
360 Plums on their twigs;
Pluck them and suck them,
Pomegranates, figs."—

"Good folk," said Lizzie,
Mindful of Jeanie:
365 "Give me much and many: —
Held out her apron,
Toss'd them her penny.
"Nay, take a seat with us,
Honour and eat with us,"
370 They answer'd grinning:
"Our feast is but beginning.
Night yet is early,
Warm and dew-pearly,
Wakeful and starry:
375 Such fruits as these
No man can carry:
Half their bloom would fly,
Half their dew would dry,
Half their flavour would pass by.
380 Sit down and feast with us,
Be welcome guest with us,
Cheer you and rest with us."—
"Thank you," said Lizzie: "But one waits
At home alone for me:
385 So without further parleying,

If you will not sell me any
Of your fruits though much and many,
Give me back my silver penny
I toss'd you for a fee."—
390 They began to scratch their pates,
No longer wagging, purring,
But visibly demurring,
Grunting and snarling.
One call'd her proud,
395 Cross-grain'd, uncivil;
Their tones wax'd loud,
Their look were evil.
Lashing their tails
They trod and hustled her,
400 Elbow'd and jostled her,
Claw'd with their nails,
Barking, mewing, hissing, mocking,
Tore her gown and soil'd her stocking,
Twitch'd her hair out by the roots,
405 Stamp'd upon her tender feet,
Held her hands and squeez'd their fruits
Against her mouth to make her eat.

White and golden Lizzie stood,
Like a lily in a flood,—
410 Like a rock of blue-vein'd stone
Lash'd by tides obstreperously,—
Like a beacon left alone
In a hoary roaring sea,
Sending up a golden fire,—
415 Like a fruit-crown'd orange-tree
White with blossoms honey-sweet
Sore beset by wasp and bee,—
Like a royal virgin town
Topp'd with gilded dome and spire
420 Close beleaguer'd by a fleet
Mad to tug her standard down.

One may lead a horse to water,
Twenty cannot make him drink.
Though the goblins cuff'd and caught her,
425 Coax'd and fought her,
Bullied and besought her,
Scratch'd her, pinch'd her black as ink,
Kick'd and knock'd her,

Maul'd and mock'd her,
430   Lizzie utter'd not a word;
Would not open lip from lip
Lest they should cram a mouthful in:
But laugh'd in heart to feel the drip
Of juice that syrupp'd all her face,
435   And lodg'd in dimples of her chin,
And streak'd her neck which quaked like curd.
At last the evil people,
Worn out by her resistance,
Flung back her penny, kick'd their fruit
440   Along whichever road they took,
Not leaving root or stone or shoot;
Some writh'd into the ground,
Some div'd into the brook
With ring and ripple,
445   Some scudded on the gale without a sound,
Some vanish'd in the distance.

In a smart, ache, tingle,
Lizzie went her way;
Knew not was it night or day;
450   Sprang up the bank, tore thro' the furze,
Threaded copse and dingle,
And heard her penny jingle
Bouncing in her purse,—
Its bounce was music to her ear.
455   She ran and ran
As if she fear'd some goblin man
Dogg'd her with gibe or curse
Or something worse:
But not one goblin scurried after,
460   Nor was she prick'd by fear;
The kind heart made her windy-paced
That urged her home quite out of breath with haste
And inward laughter.

She cried, "Laura," up the garden,
465   "Did you miss me?
Come and kiss me.
Never mind my bruises,
Hug me, kiss me, suck my juices
Squeez'd from goblin fruits for you,
470   Goblin pulp and goblin dew.
Eat me, drink me, love me;

Laura, make much of me;
For your sake I have braved the glen
And had to do with goblin merchant men."

475 Laura started from her chair,
Flung her arms up in the air,
Clutch'd her hair:
"Lizzie, Lizzie, have you tasted
For my sake the fruit forbidden?
480 Must your light like mine be hidden,
Your young life like mine be wasted,
Undone in mine undoing,
And ruin'd in my ruin,
Thirsty, canker'd, goblin-ridden?"—
485 She clung about her sister,
Kiss'd and kiss'd and kiss'd her:
Tears once again
Refresh'd her shrunken eyes,
Dropping like rain
490 After long sultry drouth;
Shaking with aguish fear, and pain,
She kiss'd and kiss'd her with a hungry mouth.

Her lips began to scorch,
That juice was wormwood to her tongue,
495 She loath'd the feast:
Writhing as one possess'd she leap'd and sung,
Rent all her robe, and wrung
Her hands in lamentable haste,
And beat her breast.
500 Her locks stream'd like the torch
Borne by a racer at full speed,
Or like the mane of horses in their flight,
Or like an eagle when she stems the light
Straight toward the sun,
505 Or like a caged thing freed,
Or like a flying flag when armies run.

Swift fire spread through her veins, knock'd at her heart,
Met the fire smouldering there
And overbore its lesser flame;
510 She gorged on bitterness without a name:
Ah! fool, to choose such part
Of soul-consuming care!
Sense fail'd in the mortal strife:

Like the watch-tower of a town
515   Which an earthquake shatters down,
Like a lightning-stricken mast,
Like a wind-uprooted tree
Spun about,
Like a foam-topp'd waterspout
520   Cast down headlong in the sea,
She fell at last;
Pleasure past and anguish past,
Is it death or is it life?

Life out of death.
525   That night long Lizzie watch'd by her,
Counted her pulse's flagging stir,
Felt for her breath,
Held water to her lips, and cool'd her face
With tears and fanning leaves:
530   But when the first birds chirp'd about their eaves,
And early reapers plodded to the place
Of golden sheaves,
And dew-wet grass
Bow'd in the morning winds so brisk to pass,
535   And new buds with new day
Open'd of cup-like lilies on the stream,
Laura awoke as from a dream,
Laugh'd in the innocent old way,
Hugg'd Lizzie but not twice or thrice;
540   Her gleaming locks show'd not one thread of grey,
Her breath was sweet as May
And light danced in her eyes.

Days, weeks, months, years
Afterwards, when both were wives
545   With children of their own;
Their mother-hearts beset with fears,
Their lives bound up in tender lives;
Laura would call the little ones
And tell them of her early prime,
550   Those pleasant days long gone
Of not-returning time:
Would talk about the haunted glen,
The wicked, quaint fruit-merchant men,
Their fruits like honey to the throat
555   But poison in the blood;
(Men sell not such in any town):

Would tell them how her sister stood
In deadly peril to do her good,
And win the fiery antidote:
560 Then joining hands to little hands
Would bid them cling together,
"For there is no friend like a sister
In calm or stormy weather;
To cheer one on the tedious way,
565 To fetch one if one goes astray,
To lift one if one totters down,
To strengthen whilst one stands."

21. EMILY DICKINSON

Dickinson (1830–1886) was the great reclusive poet in America in the second half of the nineteenth century. She industriously wrote nearly eighteen hundred poems, including nearly a thousand in the Civil War period of 1861–1865, but she never made any serious attempt to publish them. Her reasons must always remain an object of speculation. Dickinson is the poet of decaying religious certainty. For her, Nature was no longer an expressive sign of a transcendent order; her inner richness met a silent outer world. Uncomfortable with the Protestant orthodoxy of her world, Dickinson still had a strong desire to believe. But she could never for long reach that elusive state.

290

Of Bronze — and Blaze —
The North — Tonight —
So adequate — it forms —
So preconcerted with itself —
5   So distant — to alarms —
An Unconcern so sovereign
To Universe, or me —
Infects my simple spirit
With Taints of Majesty —
10   Till I take vaster attitudes —
And strut upon my stem —
Disdaining Men, and Oxygen,
For Arrogance of them —
My Splendors are Menagerie —
15   But their Competeless Show
Will entertain the Centuries
When I, am long ago,
An Island in dishonoured Grass —
Whom none but Beetles — know.   1861

21. *Emily Dickinson*

303

The Soul selects her own Society—
Then—shuts the Door—
To her divine Majority—
Present no more—
5   Unmoved—she notes the Chariots—pausing At her low Gate—
Unmoved—an Emperor be kneeling Upon her Mat—
I've known her—from an ample nation—
Choose One—
Then—close the Valves of her attention—
10 Like Stone—

313

I should have been too glad, I see —
Too lifted — for the scant degree
Of Life's penurious Round —
My little Circuit would have shamed
5   This new Circumference — have blamed —
The homelier time behind.

I should have been too saved — I see —
Too rescued — Fear too dim to me
That I could spell the Prayer
10 I knew so perfect — yesterday —
That Scalding one — Sabachthani —
Recited fluent — here —

Earth would have been too much — I see —
And Heaven — not enough for me —
15 I should have had the Joy
Without the Fear — to justify —
The Palm — without the Calvary —
So Savior — Crucify —

Defeat — whets Victory — they say —
20 The Reefs — in old Gethsemane —
Endear the Coast — beyond!
'Tis Beggars — Banquets — can define —
'Tis Parching — vitalizes Wine —
"Faith" bleats — to understand!   1862

331

I tend my flowers for thee—
Bright Absentee!
My Fuchsia's Coral Seams
Rip—while the Sower—dreams—

5   Geraniums—tint—and spot—
Low Daisies—dot—
My Cactus—splits her Beard
To show her throat—

Carnations—tip their spice—
10 And Bees—pick up—
A Hyacinth—I hid—
Puts out a Ruffled Head—

And odors fall
From flasks—so small—
15 You marvel how they held—

Globe Roses—break their satin glake—
Upon my Garden floor—
Yet—thou—not there—
I had as lief they bore
20 No Crimson—more—

Thy flower—be gay—
Her Lord—away!
It ill becometh me—
I'll dwell in Calyx—Gray—
25 How modestly—alway—
Thy Daisy—
Draped for thee!

401

What Soft — Cherubic Creatures —
These Gentlewomen are —
One would as soon assault a Plush —
Or violate a Star —
5   Such Dimity Convictions —
A Horror so refined
Of freckled Human Nature —
Of Deity — ashamed —
It's such a common — Glory —
10 A Fisherman's — Degree —
Redemption — Brittle Lady —
Be so — ashamed of Thee —   1862

501

This World is not Conclusion.
A Species stands beyond —
Invisible, as Music —
But positive, as Sound —
5   It beckons, and it baffles —
Philosophy — don't know —
And through a Riddle, at the last —
Sagacity, must go —
To guess it, puzzles scholars —
10 To gain it, Men have borne
Contempt of Generations
And Crucifixion, shown —
Faith slips — and laughs, and rallies —
Blushes, if any see —
15 Plucks at a twig of Evidence —
And asks a Vane, the way —
Much Gesture, from the Pulpit —
Strong Hallelujahs roll —
Narcotics cannot still the Tooth
20 That nibbles at the soul —   1862

668

"Nature" is what we see —
The Hill — the Afternoon —
Squirrel — Eclipse — the Bumble bee —
Nay — Nature is Heaven —
5   Nature is what we hear —
The Bobolink — the Sea —
Thunder — the Cricket —
Nay — Nature is Harmony —
Nature is what we know —
10 Yet have no art to say —
So impotent Our Wisdom is
To her Simplicity.   1863

712

Because I could not stop for Death —
He kindly stopped for me —
The Carriage held but just Ourselves —
And Immortality.
5   We slowly drove — He knew no haste
And I had put away
My labor and my leisure too,
For His Civility —
We passed the School, where Children strove
10 At Recess — in the Ring —
We passed the Fields of Gazing Grain —
We passed the Setting Sun —

Or rather — He passed Us —
The Dews drew quivering and chill —
15 For only Gossamer, my Gown —
My Tippet — only Tulle —
We paused before a House that seemed
A Swelling of the Ground —
The Roof was scarcely visible —
20 The Cornice — in the Ground —
Since then — 'tis Centuries — and yet
Feels shorter than the Day
I first surmised the Horses' Heads
Were toward Eternity —   1863

732

She rose to His Requirement—dropt
The playthings of her life
To take the honorable work
Of woman and of wife.

5   If aught she missed in her new day
Of amplitude, or awe,
Or first prospective, or the gold
In using wore away,

It lay unmentioned, as the sea
10   Develops pearl and weed,
But only to himself is known
The fathoms they abide

1551

Those — dying then,
Knew where they went —
They went to God's Right Hand —
That Hand is amputated now
5   And God cannot be found —
The abdication of Belief
Makes the Behavior small —
Better an ignis fatuus
Than no illumine at all —   1882

22. GERARD MANLEY HOPKINS

While still an undergraduate, Hopkins (1844–1889) was received into the Catholic Church by John Henry Newman. He decided to offer his great gifts to God by embracing the most rigorous life he knew, that of the Society of Jesus. He burnt his early work, and for seven years he wrote no poetry until he believed himself invited to do so by his religious superior. For the next fourteen years he wrote the greatest poetry of the Victorian Age, but after an early effort at publishing in the Jesuits' own magazine was rebuffed, his verse was read by only three or four other people. He had been dead twenty-nine years before one of them—Robert Bridges, by this time Poet Laureate—published his work. Hopkins' poetry moves in an opposite direction from Romanticism. His religious faith meant that for him Nature was a sign of the transcendent, and his poetry expresses this sacramental confidence: "The world is charged with the grandeur of God."

GOD'S GRANDEUR

The world is charged with the grandeur of God.
   It will flame out, like shining from shook foil;
   It gathers to a greatness, like the ooze of oil
Crushed. Why do men then now not reck his rod?
5   Generations have trod, have trod, have trod;
     And all is seared with trade; bleared, smeared with toil;
     And wears man's smudge and shares man's smell: the soil
Is bare now, nor can foot feel, being shod.

And for all this, nature is never spent;
10   There lives the dearest freshness deep down things;
And though the last lights off the black West went
     Oh, morning, at the brown brink eastward, springs—
Because the Holy Ghost over the bent
     World broods with warm breast and with ah! bright wings.

1877

PIED BEAUTY

Glory be to God for dappled things—
    For skies of couple-colour as a brinded cow;
      For rose-moles all in stipple upon trout that swim;
Fresh-firecoal chestnut falls; finches' wings;
5   Landscape plotted and pieced—fold, fallow, and plough;
    And all trades, their gear and tackle and trim.

All things counter, original, spare, strange;
    Whatever is fickle, freckled (who knows how?)
    With swift, slow; sweet, sour; adazzle, dim;
10 He fathers-forth whose beauty is past change:
        Praise him.

1877

AS KINGFISHERS CATCH FIRE

As kingfishers catch fire, dragonflies draw flame;
As tumbled over rim in roundy wells
Stones ring; like each tucked string tells, each hung bell's
Bow swung finds tongue to fling out broad its name;
5 Each mortal thing does one thing and the same:
Deals out that being indoors each one dwells;
Selves—goes itself; *myself* it speaks and spells,
Crying *What I do is me: for that I came.*

I say more: the just man justices;
10 Keeps grace: that keeps all his goings graces;
Acts in God's eye what in God's eye he is—
Christ—for Christ plays in ten thousand places,
Lovely in limbs, and lovely in eyes not his
To the Father through the features of men's faces.

1881

23. THOMAS HARDY

Thomas Hardy (1840–1928) was an English novelist and poet, born in Dorsetshire, which would serve as the model for the Wessex of his many novels, including Far from the Madding Crowd *(1876),* The Return of the Native *(1879),* Tess of the D'Urbervilles *(1897) and* Jude the Obscure *(1897). After* Jude, *Hardy abandoned fiction writing, and turned exclusively to poetry, of which he became a prolific writer until the end of his life.*

Hardy's world view is bleak; both his poems and novels tend to focus on protagonists who stand powerless against a cruel—or worse, indifferent—universe governed by an almost mechanical chance. He was very aware of his position "between" two worlds, the fading world of the nineteenth century and the intimidating, impersonal world of twentieth century modernity; his great poem "The Darkling Thrush" (1900) bids farewell to the nineteenth century and looks forward, with some anxiety, to the new world being born.

HAP

If but some vengeful god would call to me
From up the sky, and laugh: 'Thou suffering thing,
Know that thy sorrow is my ecstasy,
That thy love's loss is my hate's profiting!'

5   Then would I bear it, clench myself, and die,
Steeled by the sense of ire unmerited;
Half-eased in that a Powerfuller than I
Had willed and meted me the tears I shed.

But not so. How arrives it joy lies slain,
10   And why unblooms the best hope ever sown?
—Crass Casualty obstructs the sun and rain,
And dicing Time for gladness casts a moan. . . .
These purblind Doomsters had as readily strown
Blisses about my pilgrimage as pain.   1866

NEUTRAL TONES

We stood by a pond that winter day,
And the sun was white, as though chidden of God,
And a few leaves lay on the starving sod;
    —They had fallen from an ash, and were gray.

5   Your eyes on me were as eyes that rove
Over tedious riddles of years ago;
And some words played between us to and fro
    On which lost the more by our love.

The smile on your mouth was the deadest thing
10   Alive enough to have strength to die;
And a grin of bitterness swept thereby
    Like an ominous bird a-wing. . . .

Since then, keen lessons that love deceives,
And wrings with wrong, have shaped to me
15   Your face, and the God-curst sun, and a tree,
    And a pond edged with grayish leaves.   1864

THE DARKLING THRUSH

I leant upon a coppice gate
    When Frost was spectre-gray,
And Winter's dregs made desolate
    The weakening eye of day.
5   The tangled bine-stems scored the sky
    Like strings of broken lyres,
And all mankind that haunted nigh
    Had sought their household fires.

The land's sharp features seemed to be
10   The Century's corpse outleant,
His crypt the cloudy canopy,
    The wind his death-lament.
The ancient pulse of germ and birth
    Was shrunken hard and dry,
15   And every spirit upon earth
    Seemed fervourless as I.

At once a voice arose among
    The bleak twigs overhead
In a full-hearted evensong

20   Of joy illimited;
An aged thrush, frail, gaunt, and small,
        In blast-beruffied plume,
Had chosen thus to fling his soul
        Upon the growing gloom.

25   So little cause for carolings
        Of such ecstatic sound
Was written on terrestrial things
        Afar or nigh around,
That I could think there trembled through
30   His happy good-night air
Some blessed Hope, whereof he knew
        And I was unaware.   31 December 1900

24. FYODOR DOSTOYEVSKY

Dostoyevsky (1821–1881) began his writing career as a liberal humanist and Romantic, and this impulse led him into political activities for which he was arrested in 1848 and sentenced to death. The sentence was altered to imprisonment in Siberia, followed by a period of exile. During those ten years Dostoyevsky underwent a deep religious conversion to the person of Christ as mediated through the Orthodox Church. After his exile, he continued his writing career but from a changed perspective. A small legacy enabled him to travel in Western Europe in 1862–1863 and there he perceived that the West was embracing nihilism by abandoning its religious roots and ignoring life's spiritual dimension. Fearing the effect of such Western ideas on Russia, Dostoyevsky devoted his work to showing the spiritual emptiness of both the Enlightenment and Romantic world views. Notes from the Underground *was the first of such warnings, and it anticipates the later and longer novels such as* The Devils *and* The Brothers Karamazov *both in its themes and in its dialectical structure.*

NOTES FROM THE UNDERGROUND

PART I: UNDERGROUND

I

I am a sick man. . . . I am a spiteful man. I am an unattractive man. I believe my liver is diseased. However, I know nothing at all about my disease, and do not know for certain what ails me. I don't consult a doctor for it, and never have, though I have a respect for
5   medicine and doctors. Besides, I am extremely superstitious, sufficiently so to respect medicine, anyway (I am well-educated enough not to be superstitious, but I am superstitious). No, I refuse to consult a doctor from spite. That you probably will not understand. Well, I understand it, though. Of course, I can't explain who it is
10   precisely that I am mortifying in this case by my spite: I am perfectly well aware that I cannot "pay out" the doctors by not consulting them; I know better than anyone that by all this I am only injuring myself and no one else. But still, if I don't consult a doctor it is from spite. My liver is bad, well—let it get worse!
15   I have been going on like that for a long time—twenty years.

Now I am forty. I used to be in the government service, but am no
longer. I was a spiteful official. I was rude and took pleasure in
being so. I did not take bribes, you see, so I was bound to find a recompense in that, at least. (A poor jest, but I will not scratch it out. I
5   wrote it thinking it would sound very witty; but now that I have
seen myself that I only wanted to show off in a despicable way, I
will not scratch it out on purpose!)

When petitioners used to come for information to the table at
which I sat, I used to grind my teeth at them, and felt intense enjoy-
10   ment when I succeeded in making anybody unhappy. I almost did
succeed. For the most part they were all timid people—of course,
they were petitioners. But of the uppish ones there was one officer
in particular I could not endure. He simply would not be humble,
and clanked his sword in a disgusting way. I carried on a feud with
15   him for eighteen months over that sword. At last I got the better of
him. He left off clanking it. That happened in my youth, though.

But do you know, gentlemen, what was the chief point about
my spite? Why, the whole point, the real sting of it lay in the fact
that continually, even in the moment of the acutest spleen, I was
20   inwardly conscious with shame that I was not only not a spiteful
but not even an embittered man, that I was simply scaring sparrows
at random and amusing myself by it. I might foam at the mouth, but
bring me a doll to play with, give me a cup of tea with sugar in it,
and maybe I should be appeased. I might even be genuinely
25   touched, though probably I should grind my teeth at myself afterwards and lie awake at night with shame for months after. That was
my way.

I was lying when I said just now that I was a spiteful official. I
was lying from spite. I was simply amusing myself with the peti-
30   tioners and with the officer, and in reality I never could become
spiteful. I was conscious every moment in myself of many, very
many elements absolutely opposite to that. I felt them positively
swarming in me, these opposite elements. I knew that they had
been swarming in me all my life and craving some outlet from me,
35   but I would not let them, would not let them, purposely would not
let them come out. They tormented me till I was ashamed: they
drove me to convulsions and—sickened me, at last, how they sickened me! Now, are not you fancying, gentlemen, that I am expressing remorse for something now, that I am asking your forgiveness
40   for something? I am sure you are fancying that . . . However, I
assure you I do not care if you are. . . .

It was not only that I could not become spiteful, I did not know
how to become anything; neither spiteful nor kind, neither a rascal
nor an honest man, neither a hero nor an insect. Now, I am living
45   out my life in my corner, taunting myself with the spiteful and use-

less consolation that an intelligent man cannot become anything
seriously, and it is only the fool who becomes anything. Yes, a man
in the nineteenth century must and morally ought to be pre-eminently a characterless creature; a man of character, an active man is
5   pre-eminently a limited creature. That is my conviction of forty
years. I am forty years old now, and you know forty years is a whole
lifetime; you know it is extreme old age. To live longer than forty
years is bad manners, is vulgar, immoral. Who does live beyond
forty? Answer that, sincerely and honestly. I will tell you who do:
10   fools and worthless fellows. I tell all old men that to their face, all
these venerable old men, all these silver-haired and reverend sen-
iors! I tell the whole world that to its face! I have a right to say so,
for I shall go on living to sixty myself. To seventy! To
eighty! . . . Stay, let me take breath . . .
15   You imagine no doubt, gentlemen, that I want to amuse you.
You are mistaken in that, too. I am by no means such a mirthful person as you imagine, or as you may imagine; however, irritated by
all this babble (and I feel that you are irritated) you think fit to ask
me who I am—then my answer is, I am a collegiate assessor. I was
20   in the service that I might have something to eat (and solely for that
reason), and when last year a distant relation left me six thousand
roubles in his will I immediately retired from the service and settled
down in my corner. I used to live in this corner before, but now I
have settled down in it. My room is a wretched, horrid one in the
25   outskirts of the town. My servant is an old countrywoman, ill-
natured from stupidity, and, moreover, there is always a nasty smell
about her. I am told that the Petersburg climate is bad for me, and
that with my small means it is very expensive to live in Petersburg.
I know all that better than all these sage and experienced counsel-
30   lors and monitors. . . . But I am remaining in Petersburg; I am not
going away from Petersburg! I am not going away because . . . ech!
Why, it is absolutely no matter whether I am going away or not
going away.
      But what can a decent man speak of with most pleasure?
35   Answer: Of himself.
      Well, so I will talk about myself.

II

      I want now to tell you, gentlemen, whether you care to hear it
or not, why I could not even become an insect. I tell you solemnly,
that I have many times tried to become an insect. But I was not
40   equal even to that. I swear, gentlemen, that to be too conscious is an
illness—a real thorough-going illness. For man's everyday needs, it
would have been quite enough to have the ordinary human con-

sciousness, that is, half or a quarter of the amount which falls to the lot of a cultivated man of our unhappy nineteenth century, especially one who has the fatal ill-luck to inhabit Petersburg, the most theoretical and intentional town on the whole terrestrial globe. (There are intentional and unintentional towns.) It would have been quite enough, for instance, to have the consciousness by which all so-called direct persons and men of action live. I bet you think I am writing all this from affectation, to be witty at the expense of men of action; and what is more, that from ill-bred affectation, I am clanking a sword like my officer. But, gentlemen, whoever can pride himself on his diseases and even swagger over them?

Though, after all, everyone does do that; people do pride themselves on their diseases, and I do, may be, more than anyone. We will not dispute it; my contention was absurd. But yet I am firmly persuaded that a great deal of consciousness, every sort of consciousness, in fact, is a disease. I stick to that. Let us leave that, too, for a minute. Tell me this: why does it happen that at the very, yes, at the very moments when I am most capable of feeling every refinement of all that is "sublime and beautiful," as they used to say at one time, it would, as though of design, happen to me not only to feel but to do such ugly things, such that . . . Well, in short, actions that all, perhaps, commit; but which, as though purposely, occurred to me at the very time when I was most conscious that they ought not to be committed. The more conscious I was of goodness and of all that was "sublime and beautiful," the more deeply I sank into my mire and the more ready I was to sink in it altogether. But the chief point was that all this was, as it were, not accidental in me, but as though it were bound to be so. It was as though it were my most normal condition, and not in the least disease or depravity, so that at last all desire in me to struggle against this depravity passed. It ended by my almost believing (perhaps actually believing) that this was perhaps my normal condition. But at first, in the beginning, what agonies I endured in that struggle! I did not believe it was the same with other people, and all my life I hid this fact about myself as a secret. I was ashamed (even now, perhaps, I am ashamed): I got to the point of feeling a sort of secret abnormal, despicable enjoyment in returning home to my corner on some disgusting Petersburg night, acutely conscious that that day I had committed a loathsome action again, that what was done could never be undone, and secretly, inwardly gnawing, gnawing at myself for it, tearing and consuming myself till at last the bitterness turned into a sort of shameful accursed sweetness, and at last—into positive real enjoyment! Yes, into enjoyment, into enjoyment! I insist upon that. I have spoken of this because I keep wanting to know for a fact whether other people feel such enjoyment? I will explain; the enjoyment was

just from the too intense consciousness of one's own degradation; it was from feeling oneself that one had reached the last barrier, that it was horrible, but that it could not be otherwise; that there was no escape for you; that you never could become a different man; that
5   even if time and faith were still left you to change into something different you would most likely not wish to change; or if you did wish to, even then you would do nothing; because perhaps in reality there was nothing for you to change into.

    And the worst of it was, and the root of it all, that it was all in
10 accord with the normal fundamental laws of over-acute consciousness, and with the inertia that was the direct result of those laws, and that consequently one was not only unable to change but could do absolutely nothing. Thus it would follow, as the result of acute consciousness, that one is not to blame in being a scoundrel; as
15 though that were any consolation to the scoundrel once he has come to realise that he actually is a scoundrel. But enough. . . . Ech, I have talked a lot of nonsense, but what have I explained? How is enjoyment in this to be explained? But I will explain it. I will get to the bottom of it! That is why I have taken up my pen. . . .

20   I, for instance, have a great deal of *amour propre.* I am as suspicious and prone to take offence as a humpback or a dwarf. But upon my word I sometimes have had moments when if I had happened to be slapped in the face I should, perhaps, have been positively glad of it. I say, in earnest, that I should probably have been able to
25 discover even in that a peculiar sort of enjoyment—the enjoyment, of course, of despair; but in despair there are the most intense enjoyments, especially when one is very acutely conscious of the hopelessness of one's position. And when one is slapped in the face— why then the consciousness of being rubbed into a pulp would pos-
30 itively overwhelm one. The worst of it is, look at it which way one will, it still turns out that I was always the most to blame in everything. And what is most humiliating of all, to blame for no fault of my own but, so to say, through the laws of nature. In the first place, to blame because I am cleverer than any of the people surrounding
35 me. (I have always considered myself cleverer than any of the people surrounding me, and sometimes, would you believe it, have been positively ashamed of it. At any rate, I have all my life, as it were, turned my eyes away and never could look people straight in the face.) To blame, finally, because even if I had had magnanimity,
40 I should only have had more suffering from the sense of its uselessness. I should certainly have never been able to do anything from being magnanimous—neither to forgive, for my assailant would perhaps have slapped me from the laws of nature, and one cannot forgive the laws of nature; nor to forget, for even if it were owing to
45 the laws of nature, it is insulting all the same. Finally, even if I had

wanted to be anything but magnanimous, had desired on the contrary to revenge myself on my assailant, I could not have revenged
myself on any one for anything because I should certainly never
have made up my mind to do anything, even if I had been able to.
5   Why should I not have made up my mind? About that in particular
I want to say a few words.

III

With people who know how to revenge themselves and to
stand up for themselves in general, how is it done? Why, when they
are possessed, let us suppose, by the feeling of revenge, then for the
10   time there is nothing else but that feeling left in their whole being.
Such a gentleman simply dashes straight for his object like an infuriated bull with its horns down, and nothing but a wall will stop
him. (By the way: facing the wall, such, gentlemen—that is, the
"direct" persons and men of action—are genuinely nonplussed. For
15   them a wall is not an evasion, as for us people who think and. consequently do nothing; it is not an excuse for turning aside, an excuse
for which we are always very glad, though we scarcely believe in it
ourselves, as a rule. No, they are nonplussed in all sincerity. The
wall has for them something tranquillising, morally soothing,
20   final—maybe even something mysterious . . . but of the wall later.)
Well, such a direct person I regard as the real normal man, as
his tender mother nature wished to see him when she graciously
brought him into being on the earth. I envy such a man till I am
green in the face. He is stupid. I am not disputing that, but perhaps
25   the normal man should be stupid, how do you know? Perhaps it is
very beautiful, in fact. And I am the more persuaded of that suspicion, if one can call it so, by the fact that if you take, for instance, the
antithesis of the normal man, that is, the man of acute consciousness, who has come, of course, not out of the lap of nature but out
30   of a retort (this is almost mysticism, gentlemen, but I suspect this,
too), this retort-made man is sometimes so nonplussed in the presence of his antithesis that with all his exaggerated consciousness he
genuinely thinks of himself as a mouse and not a man. It may be an
acutely conscious mouse, yet it is a mouse, while the other is a man,
35   and therefore, et cætera, et cætera. And the worst of it is, he himself,
his very own self, looks on himself as a mouse; no one asks him to
do so; and that is an important point. Now let us look at this mouse
in action. Let us suppose, for instance, that it feels insulted, too (and
it almost always does feel insulted), and wants to revenge itself, too.
40   There may even be a greater accumulation of spite in it than in
l'homme de la nature et de la vérité. The base and nasty desire to vent
that spite on its assailant rankles perhaps even more nastily in it

than in *l'homme de la nature et de la vérité*. For through his innate stupidity the latter looks upon his revenge as justice pure and simple;
while in consequence of his acute consciousness the mouse does not
believe in the justice of it. To come at last to the deed itself, to the
5   very act of revenge. Apart from the one fundamental nastiness the
luckless mouse succeeds in creating around it so many other nasti-
nesses in the form of doubts and questions, adds to the one question
so many unsettled questions that there inevitably works up around
it a sort of fatal brew, a stinking mess, made up of its doubts, emo-
10 tions, and of the contempt spat upon it by the direct men of action
who stand solemnly about it as judges and arbitrators, laughing at
it till their healthy sides ache. Of course the only thing left for it is
to dismiss all that with a wave of its paw, and, with a smile of
assumed contempt in which it does not even itself believe, creep
15 ignominiously into its mouse-hole. There in its nasty, stinking,
underground home our insulted, crushed and ridiculed mouse
promptly becomes absorbed in cold, malignant and, above all, everlasting spite. For forty years together it will remember its injury
down to the smallest, most ignominious details, and every time will
20 add, of itself, details still more ignominious, spitefully teasing and
tormenting itself with its own imagination. It will itself be ashamed
of its imaginings, but yet it will recall it all, it will go over and over
every detail, it will invent unheard of things against itself, pretending that those things might happen, and will forgive nothing.
25 Maybe it will begin to revenge itself, too, but, as it were, piecemeal,
in trivial ways, from behind the stove, incognito, without believing
either in its own right to vengeance, or in the success of its revenge,
knowing that from all its efforts at revenge it will suffer a hundred
times more than he on whom it revenges itself, while he, I daresay,
30 will not even scratch himself. On its deathbed it will recall it all over
again, with interest accumulated over all the years and . . .

But it is just in that cold, abominable half despair, half belief, in
that conscious burying oneself alive for grief in the underworld for
forty years, in that acutely recognised and yet partly doubtful hope-
35 lessness of one's position, in that hell of unsatisfied desires turned
inward, in that fever of oscillations, of resolutions determined for
ever and repented of again a minute later—that the savour of that
strange enjoyment of which I have spoken lies. It is so subtle, so difficult of analysis, that persons who are a little limited, or even sim-
40 ply persons of strong nerves, will not understand a single atom of
it. "Possibly," you will add on your own account with a grin, "people will not understand it either who have never received a slap in
the face," and in that way you will politely hint to me that I, too,
perhaps, have had the experience of a slap in the face in my life, and
45 so I speak as one who knows. I bet that you are thinking that. But

set your minds at rest, gentlemen, I have not received a slap in the
face, though it is absolutely a matter of indifference to me what you
may think about it. Possibly, I even regret, myself, that I have given
so few slaps in the face during my life. But enough . . . not another
5   word on that subject of such extreme interest to you.

I will continue calmly concerning persons with strong nerves
who do not understand a certain refinement of enjoyment. Though
in certain circumstances these gentlemen bellow their loudest like
bulls, though this, let us suppose, does them the greatest credit, yet,
10   as I have said already, confronted with the impossible they subside
at once. The impossible means the stone wall! What stone wall?
Why, of course, the laws of nature, the deductions of natural science, mathematics. As soon as they prove to you, for instance, that
you are descended from a monkey, then it is no use scowling, accept
15   it for a fact. When they prove to you that in reality one drop of your
own fat must be dearer to you than a hundred thousand of your fellow-creatures, and that this conclusion is the final solution of all so-
called virtues and duties and all such prejudices and fancies, then
you have just to accept it, there is no help for it, for twice two is a
20   law of mathematics. Just try refuting it.

"Upon my word, they will shout at you, it is no use protesting:
it is a case of twice two makes four! Nature does not ask your permission, she has nothing to do with your wishes, and whether you
like her laws or dislike them, you are bound to accept her as she is,
25   and consequently all her conclusions. A wall, you see, is a wall . . .
and so on, and so on."

Merciful Heavens! but what do I care for the laws of nature and
arithmetic, when, for some reason I dislike those laws and the fact
that twice two makes four? Of course I cannot break through the
30   wall by battering my head against it if I really have not the strength
to knock it down, but I am not going to be reconciled to it simply
because it is a stone wall and I have not the strength.

As though such a stone wall really were a consolation, and really did contain some word of conciliation, simply because it is as true
35   as twice two makes four. Oh, absurdity of absurdities! How much
better it is to understand it all, to recognise it all, all the impossibil-
ities and the stone wall; not to be reconciled to one of those impos-
sibilities and stone walls if it disgusts you to be reconciled to it; by
the way of the most inevitable, logical combinations to reach the
40   most revolting conclusions on the everlasting theme, that even for
the stone wall you are yourself somehow to blame, though again it
is as clear as day you are not to blame in the least, and therefore
grinding your teeth in silent impotence to sink into luxurious inertia, brooding on the fact that there is no one even for you to feel vin-
45   dictive against, that you have not, and perhaps never will have, an

object for your spite, that it is a sleight of hand, a bit of juggling, a cardsharper's trick, that it is simply a mess, no knowing what and no knowing who, but in spite of all these uncertainties and jugglings, still there is an ache in you, and the more you do not know,
5   the worse the ache.

IV

"Ha, ha, ha! You will be finding enjoyment in toothache next," you cry, with a laugh.

"Well, even in toothache there is enjoyment," I answer. I had toothache for a whole month and I know there is. In that case, of
10   course, people are not spiteful in silence, but moan; but they are not candid moans, they are malignant moans, and the malignancy is the whole point. The enjoyment of the sufferer finds expression in those moans; if he did not feel enjoyment in them he would not moan. It is a good example, gentlemen, and I will develop it. Those moans
15   express in the first place all the aimlessness of your pain, which is so humiliating to your consciousness; the whole legal system of nature on which you spit disdainfully, of course, but from which you suffer all the same while she does not. They express the consciousness that you have no enemy to punish, but that you have
20   pain; the consciousness that in spite of all possible Wagenheims you are in complete slavery to your teeth; that if someone wishes it, your teeth will leave off aching, and if he does not, they will go on aching another three months; and that finally if you are still contumacious and still protest, all that is left you for your own gratification is to
25   thrash yourself or beat your wall with your fist as hard as you can, and absolutely nothing more. Well, these mortal insults, these jeers on the part of someone unknown, end at last in an enjoyment which sometimes reaches the highest degree of voluptuousness. I ask you, gentlemen, listen sometimes to the moans of an educated man of
30   the nineteenth century suffering from toothache, on the second or third day of the attack, when he is beginning to moan, not as he moaned on the first day, that is, not simply because he has toothache, not just as any coarse peasant, but as a man affected by progress and European civilisation, a man who is "divorced from
35   the soil and the national elements," as they express it now-a-days. His moans become nasty, disgustingly malignant, and go on for whole days and nights. And of course he knows himself that he is doing himself no sort of good with his moans; he knows better than anyone that he is only lacerating and harassing himself and others
40   for nothing; he knows that even the audience before whom he is making his efforts, and his whole family, listen to him with loathing, do not put a ha'porth of faith in him, and inwardly understand that

he might moan differently, more simply, without trills and flourish-
es, and that he is only amusing himself like that from ill-humour,
from malignancy. Well, in all these recognitions and disgraces it is
that there lies a voluptuous pleasure. As though he would say: "I
5   am worrying you, I am lacerating your hearts, I am keeping everyone in the house awake. Well, stay awake then, you, too, feel every
minute that I have toothache. I am not a hero to you now, as I tried
to seem before, but simply a nasty person, an impostor. Well, so be
it, then! I am very glad that you see through me. It is nasty for you
10 to hear my despicable moans: well, let it be nasty; here I will let you
have a nastier flourish in a minute. . . ." You do not understand even
now, gentlemen? No, it seems our development and our consciousness must go further to understand all the intricacies of this pleasure. You laugh? Delighted. My jests, gentlemen, are of course in bad
15 taste, jerky, involved, lacking self-confidence. But of course that is
because I do not respect myself. Can a man of perception respect
himself at all?

V

Come, can a man who attempts to find enjoyment in the very
feeling of his own degradation possibly have a spark of respect for
20 himself? I am not saying this now from any mawkish kind of
remorse. And, indeed, I could never endure saying, "Forgive me,
Papa, I won't do it again," not because I am incapable of saying
that—on the contrary, perhaps just because I have been too capable
of it, and in what a way, too. As though of design I used to get into
25 trouble in cases when I was not to blame in any way. That was the
nastiest part of it. At the same time I was genuinely touched and
penitent, I used to shed tears and, of course, deceived myself,
though I was not acting in the least and there was a sick feeling in
my heart at the time. . . . For that one could not blame even the laws
30 of nature, though the laws of nature have continually all my life
offended me more than anything. It is loathsome to remember it all,
but it was loathsome even then. Of course, a minute or so later I
would realise wrathfully that it was all a lie, a revolting lie, an
affected lie, that is, all this penitence, this emotion, these vows of
35 reform. You will ask why did I worry myself with such antics:
answer, because it was very dull to sit with one's hands folded, and
so one began cutting capers. That is really it. Observe yourselves
more carefully, gentlemen, then you will understand that it is so. I
invented adventures for myself and made up a life, so as at least to
40 live in some way. How many times it has happened to me—well, for
instance, to take offence simply on purpose, for nothing; and one
knows oneself, of course, that one is offended at nothing; that one is

putting it on, but yet one brings oneself at last to the point of being really offended. All my life I have had an impulse to play such pranks, so that in the end I could not control it in myself. Another time, twice, in fact, I tried hard to be in love. I suffered, too, gentle-
5 men, I assure you. In the depth of my heart there was no faith in my suffering, only a faint stir of mockery, but yet I did suffer, and in the real, orthodox way; I was jealous, beside myself . . . and it was all from *ennui*, gentlemen, all from *ennui*; inertia overcame me. You know the direct, legitimate fruit of consciousness is inertia, that is,
10 conscious sitting-with-the-hands-folded. I have referred to this already. I repeat, I repeat with emphasis: all "direct" persons and men of action are active just because they are stupid and limited. How explain that? I will tell you: in consequence of their limitation they take immediate and secondary causes for primary ones, and in
15 that way persuade themselves more quickly and easily than other people do that they have found an infallible foundation for their activity, and their minds are at ease and you know that is the chief thing. To begin to act, you know, you must first have your mind completely at ease and no trace of doubt left in it. Why, how am I,
20 for example to set my mind at rest? Where are the primary causes on which I am to build? Where are my foundations? Where am I to get them from? I exercise myself in reflection, and consequently with me every primary cause at once draws after itself another still more primary, and so on to infinity. That is just the essence of every
25 sort of consciousness and reflection. It must be a case of the laws of nature again. What is the result of it in the end? Why, just the same. Remember I spoke just now of vengeance. (I am sure you did not take it in.) I said that a man revenges himself because he sees justice in it. Therefore he has found a primary cause, that is, justice. And so
30 he is at rest on all sides, and consequently he carries out his revenge calmly and successfully, being persuaded that he is doing a just and honest thing. But I see no justice in it, I find no sort of virtue in it either, and consequently if I attempt to revenge myself, it is only out of spite. Spite, of course, might overcome everything, all my doubts,
35 and so might serve quite successfully in place of a primary cause, precisely because it is not a cause. But what is to be done if I have not even spite (I began with that just now, you know). In conse- quence again of those accursed laws of consciousness, anger in me is subject to chemical disintegration. You look into it, the object flies
40 off into air, your reasons evaporate, the criminal is not to be found, the wrong becomes not a wrong but a phantom, something like the toothache, for which no one is to blame, and consequently there is only the same outlet left again—that is, to beat the wall as hard as you can. So you give it up with a wave of the hand because you
45 have not found a fundamental cause. And try letting yourself be

carried away by your feelings, blindly, without reflection, without a primary cause, repelling consciousness at least for a time; hate or love, if only not to sit with your hands folded. The day after tomorrow, at the latest, you will begin despising yourself for having
5 knowingly deceived yourself. Result: a soap-bubble and inertia. Oh, gentlemen, do you know, perhaps I consider myself an intelligent man, only because all my life I have been able neither to begin nor to finish anything. Granted I am a babbler, a harmless vexatious babbler, like all of us. But what is to be done if the direct and sole
10 vocation of every intelligent man is babble, that is, the intentional pouring of water through a sieve?

VI

Oh, if I had done nothing simply from laziness! Heavens, how I should have respected myself, then. I should have respected myself because I should at least have been capable of being lazy;
15 there would at least have been one quality, as it were, positive in me, in which I could have believed myself. Question: What is he? Answer: A sluggard; how very pleasant it would have been to hear that of oneself! It would mean that I was positively defined, it would mean that there was something to say about me.
20 "Sluggard"—why, it is a calling and vocation, it is a career. Do not jest, it is so. I should then be a member of the best club by right, and should find my occupation in continually respecting myself. I knew a gentleman who prided himself all his life on being a connoisseur of Lafitte. He considered this as his positive virtue, and never
25 doubted himself. He died, not simply with a tranquil, but with a triumphant conscience, and he was quite right, too. Then I should have chosen a career for myself, I should have been a sluggard and a glutton, not a simple one, but, for instance, one with sympathies for everything sublime and beautiful. How do you like that? I have
30 long had visions of it. That "sublime and beautiful" weighs heavily on my mind at forty. But that is at forty; then—oh, then it would have been different! I should have found for myself a form of activity in keeping with it, to be precise, drinking to the health of everything "sublime and beautiful." I should have snatched at every
35 opportunity to drop a tear into my glass and then to drain it to all that is "sublime and beautiful." I should then have turned everything into the sublime and the beautiful; in the nastiest, unquestionable trash, I should have sought out the sublime and the beautiful. I should have exuded tears like a wet sponge. An artist, for
40 instance, paints a picture worthy of Gay. At once I drink to the health of the artist who painted the picture worthy of Gay, because I love all that is "sublime and beautiful." An author has written *As*

you will: at once I drink to the health of "anyone you will" because I love all that is "sublime and beautiful."

    I should claim respect for doing so. I should persecute anyone who would not show me respect. I should live at ease, I should die
5   with dignity, why, it is charming, perfectly charming! And what a good round belly I should have grown, what a treble chin I should have established, what a ruby nose I should have coloured for myself, so that everyone would have said, looking at me: "Here is an asset! Here is something real and solid!" And, say what you like,
10   it is very agreeable to hear such remarks about oneself in this negative age.

VII

    But these are all golden dreams. Oh, tell me, who was it first announced, who was it first proclaimed, that man only does nasty things because he does not know his own interests; and that if he
15   were enlightened, if his eyes were opened to his real normal interests, man would at once cease to do nasty things, would at once become good and noble because, being enlightened and understanding his real advantage, he would see his own advantage in the good and nothing else, and we all know that not one man can, con-
20   sciously, act against his own interests, consequently, so to say, through necessity, he would begin doing good? Oh, the babe! Oh, the pure, innocent child! Why, in the first place, when in all these thousands of years has there been a time when man has acted only from his own interest? What is to be done with the millions of facts
25   that bear witness that men, *consciously,* that is fully understanding their real interests, have left them in the background and have rushed headlong on another path, to meet peril and danger, compelled to this course by nobody and by nothing, but, as it were, simply disliking the beaten track, and have obstinately, wilfully, struck
30   out another difficult, absurd way, seeking it almost in the darkness. So, I suppose, this obstinacy and perversity were pleasanter to them than any advantage. . . . Advantage! What is advantage? And will you take it upon yourself to define with perfect accuracy in what the advantage of man consists? And what if it so, happens that a
35   man's advantage, *sometimes,* not only may, but even must, consist in his desiring in certain cases what is harmful to himself and not advantageous. And if so, if there can be such a case, the whole principle falls into dust. What do you think—are there such cases? You laugh; laugh away, gentlemen, but only answer me: have man's
40   advantages been reckoned up with perfect certainty? Are there not some which not only have not been included but cannot possibly be included under any classification? You see, you gentlemen have, to

the best of my knowledge, taken your whole register of human
advantages from the averages of statistical figures and politico-eco-
nomical formulas. Your advantages are prosperity, wealth, freedom,
peace—and so on, and so on. So that the man who should, for
5 instance, go openly and knowingly in opposition to all that list
would, to your thinking, and indeed mine, too, of course, be an
obscurantist or an absolute madman: would not he? But, you know,
this is what is surprising: why does it so happen that all these stat-
isticians, sages and lovers of humanity, when they reckon up
10 human advantages invariably leave out one? They don't even take
it into their reckoning in the form in which it should be taken, and
the whole reckoning depends upon that. It would be no greater
matter, they would simply have to take it, this advantage, and add
it to the list. But the trouble is, that this strange advantage does not
15 fall under any classification and is not in place in any list. I have a
friend for instance . . . Ech! gentlemen, but of course he is your
friend, too; and indeed there is no one, no one to whom he is not a
friend! When he prepares for any undertaking this gentleman
immediately explains to you, elegantly and clearly, exactly how he
20 must act in accordance with the laws of reason and truth. What is
more, he will talk to you with excitement and passion of the true
normal interests of man; with irony he will upbraid the short sight-
ed fools who do not understand their own interests, nor the true significance of virtue; and, within a quarter of an hour, without any
25 sudden outside provocation, but simply through something inside
him which is stronger than all his interests, he will go off on quite a
different tack—that is, act in direct opposition to what he has just
been saying about himself, in opposition to the laws of reason, in
opposition to his own advantage, in fact in opposition to every-
30 thing . . . I warn you that my friend is a compound personality and
therefore it is difficult to blame him as an individual. The fact is,
gentlemen, it seems there must really exist something that is dearer
to almost every man than his greatest advantages, or (not to be
illogical) there is a most advantageous advantage (the very one
35 omitted of which we spoke just now) which is more important and
more advantageous than all other advantages, for the sake of which
a man if necessary is ready to act in opposition to all laws; that is, in
opposition to reason, honour, peace, prosperity—in fact, in opposition to all those excellent and useful things if only he can attain that
40 fundamental, most advantageous advantage which is dearer to him
than all. "Yes, but it's advantage all the same," you will retort. But
excuse me, I'll make the point clear, and it is not a case of playing
upon words. What matters is, that this advantage is remarkable
from the very fact that it breaks down all our classifications, and
45 continually shatters every system constructed by lovers of mankind

for the benefit of mankind. In fact, it upsets everything. But before I mention this advantage to you, I want to compromise myself personally, and therefore I boldly declare that all these fine systems, all these theories for explaining to mankind their real normal interests,

5 in order that inevitably striving to pursue these interests they may at once become good and noble—are, in my opinion, so far, mere logical exercises! Yes, logical exercises. Why, to maintain this theory of the regeneration of mankind by means of the pursuit of his own advantage is to my mind almost the same thing . . . as to affirm, for

10 instance, following Buckle, that through civilisation mankind becomes softer, and consequently less bloodthirsty and less fitted for warfare. Logically it does seem to follow from his arguments. But man has such a predilection for systems and abstract deductions that he is ready to distort the truth intentionally, he is ready to

15 deny the evidence of his senses only to justify his logic. I take this example because it is the most glaring instance of it. Only took about you: blood is being spilt in streams, and in the merriest way, as though it were champagne. Take the whole of the nineteenth century in which Buckle lived. Take Napoleon—the Great and also the

20 present one. Take North America—the eternal union. Take the farce of Schleswig-Holstein. . . . And what is it that civilisation softens in us? The only gain of civilisation for mankind is the greater capacity for variety of sensations—and absolutely nothing more. And through the development of this manysidedness man may come to

25 finding enjoyment in bloodshed. In fact, this has already happened to him. Have you noticed that it is the most civilised gentlemen who have been the subtlest slaughterers, to whom the Attilas and Stenka Razins could not hold a candle, and if they are not so conspicuous as the Attilas and Stenka Razins it is simply because they are so

30 often met with, are so ordinary and have become so familiar to us. In any case civilisation has made mankind if not more bloodthirsty, at least more vilely, more loathsomely bloodthirsty. In old days he saw justice in bloodshed and with his conscience at peace exterminated those he thought proper. Now we do think bloodshed abom-

35 inable and yet we engage in this abomination, and with more energy than ever. Which is worse? Decide that for yourselves. They say that Cleopatra (excuse an instance from Roman history) was fond of sticking gold pins into her slave-girls' breasts and derived gratification from their screams and writhings. You will say that that was in

40 the comparatively barbarous times; that these are barbarous times too, because also, comparatively speaking, pins are stuck in even now; that though man has now learned to see more clearly than in barbarous ages, he is still far from having learnt to act as reason and science would dictate. But yet you are fully convinced that he will

45 be sure to learn when he gets rid of certain old bad habits, and when

common sense and science have completely reeducated human
nature and turned it in a normal direction. You are confident that
then man will cease from *intentional* error and will, so to say, be
compelled not to want to set his will against his normal interests.
5   That is not all; then, you say, science itself will teach man (though to
my mind it's a superfluous luxury) that he never has really had any
caprice or will of his own, and that he himself is something of the
nature of a piano-key or the stop of an organ, and that there are,
besides, things called the laws of nature; so that everything he does
10   is not done by his willing it, but is done of itself, by the laws of
nature. Consequently we have only to discover these laws of nature,
and man will no longer have to answer for his actions and life will
become exceedingly easy for him. All human actions will then, of
course, be tabulated according to these laws, mathematically, like
15   tables of logarithms up to 108,000, and entered in an index; or, better still, there would be published certain edifying works of the
nature of encyclopædic lexicons, in which everything will be so
clearly calculated and explained that there will be no more incidents
or adventures in the world.
20   Then—this is all what you say—new economic relations will be
established, all ready-made and worked out with mathematical
exactitude, so that every possible question will vanish in the twinkling of an eye, simply because every possible answer to it will be
provided. Then the "Palace of Crystal" will be built. Then . . . In fact,
25   those will be halcyon days. Of course there is no guaranteeing (this
is my comment) that it will not be, for instance, frightfully dull then
(for what will one have to do when everything will be calculated
and tabulated), but on the other hand everything will be extraordinarily rational. Of course boredom may lead you to anything. It is
30   boredom sets one sticking golden pins into people, but all that
would not matter. What is bad (this is my comment again) is that I
dare say people will be thankful for the gold pins then. Man is stupid, you know, phenomenally stupid; or rather he is not at all stupid, but he is so ungrateful that you could not find another like him
35   in all creation. I, for instance, would not be in the least surprised if
all of a sudden, *à propos* of nothing, in the midst of general prosperity a gentleman with an ignoble, or rather with a reactionary and
ironical, countenance were to arise and, putting his arms akimbo,
say to us all: "I say, gentleman, hadn't we better kick over the whole
40   show and scatter rationalism to the winds, simply to send these logarithms to the devil, and to enable us to live once more at our own
sweet foolish will!" That again would not matter, but what is
annoying is that he would be sure to find followers—such is the
nature of man. And all that for the most foolish reason, which, one
45   would think, was hardly worth mentioning: that is, that man every-

where and at all times, whoever he may be, has preferred to act as
he chose and not in the least as his reason and advantage dictated.
And one may choose what is contrary to one's own interests, and
sometimes one *positively ought* (that is my idea). One's own free
5 unfettered choice, one's own caprice, however wild it may be, one's
own fancy worked up at times to frenzy— is that very "most advantageous advantage" which we have overlooked, which comes
under no classification and against which all systems and theories
are continually being shattered to atoms. And how do these
10 wiseacres know that man wants a normal, a virtuous choice? What
has made them conceive that man must want a rationally advantageous choice? What man wants is simply *independent* choice, whatever that independence may cost and wherever it may lead. And
choice, of course, the devil only knows what choice.

VIII

15   "Ha! ha! ha! But you know there is no such thing as choice in
reality, say what you like," you will interpose with a chuckle.
"Science has succeeded in so far analysing man that we know
already that choice and what is called freedom of will is nothing
else than—"
20   Stay, gentlemen, I meant to begin with that myself I confess, I
was rather frightened. I was just going to say that the devil only
knows what choice depends on, and that perhaps that was a very
good thing, but I remembered the teaching of science . . . and pulled
myself up. And here you have begun upon it. Indeed, if there real-
25 ly is some day discovered a formula for all our desires and
caprices—that is, an explanation of what they depend upon, by
what laws they arise, how they develop, what they are aiming at in
one case and in another and so on, that is a real mathematical formula—then, most likely, man will at once cease to feel desire,
30 indeed, he will be certain to. For who would want to choose by
rule? Besides, he will at once be transformed from a human being
into an organ-stop or something of the sort; for what is a man without desires, without free will and without choice, if not a stop in an
organ? What do you think? Let us reckon the chances—can such a
35 thing happen or not?
       "H'm!" you decide. "Our choice is usually mistaken from a
false view of our advantage. We sometimes choose absolute nonsense because in our foolishness we see in that nonsense the easiest
means for attaining a supposed advantage. But when all that is
40 explained and worked out on paper (which is perfectly possible, for
it is contemptible and senseless to suppose that some laws of nature
man will never understand), then certainly so-called desires will no

longer exist. For if a desire should come into conflict with reason we shall then reason and not desire, because it will be impossible retaining our reason to be *senseless* in our desires, and in that way knowingly act against reason and desire to injure ourselves. And as
5   all choice and reasoning can be really calculated—because there will some day be discovered the laws of our so-called free will—so, joking apart, there may one day be something like a table constructed of them, so that we really shall choose in accordance with it. If, for instance, some day they calculate and prove to me that I made a
10 long nose at someone because I could not help making a long nose at him and that I had to do it in that particular way, what *freedom is* left me, especially if I am a learned man and have taken my degree somewhere? Then I should be able to calculate my whole life for thirty years beforehand. In short, if this could be arranged there
15 would be nothing left for us to do; anyway, we should have to understand that. And, in fact, we ought unwearyingly to repeat to ourselves that at such and such a time and in such and such circumstances nature does not ask our leave; that we have got to take her as she is and not fashion her to suit our fancy, and if we really
20 aspire to formulas and tables of rules, and well, even . . . to the chemical retort, there's no help for it, we must accept the retort too, or else it will be accepted without our consent. . . ."

Yes, but here I come to a stop! Gentlemen, you must excuse me for being over-philosophical; it's the result of forty years under-
25 ground! Allow me to indulge my fancy You see, gentlemen, reason is an excellent thing, there's no disputing that, but reason is nothing but reason and satisfies only the rational side of man's nature, while will is a manifestation of the whole life, that is, of the whole human life including reason and all the impulses. And although our life, in
30 this manifestation of it, is often worthless, yet it is life and not simply extracting square roots. Here I, for instance, quite naturally want to live, in order to satisfy all my capacities for life, and not simply my capacity for reasoning, that is, not simply one twentieth of my capacity for life. What does reason know? Reason only knows
35 what it has succeeded in learning (some things, perhaps, it will never learn; this is a poor comfort, but why not say so frankly?) and human nature acts as a whole, with everything that is in it, consciously or unconsciously, and, even it if goes wrong, it lives. I suspect, gentlemen, that you are looking at me with compassion; you
40 tell me again that an enlightened and developed man, such, in short, as the future man will be, cannot consciously desire anything disadvantageous to himself, that that can be proved mathematically. I thoroughly agree, it can—by mathematics. But I repeat for the hundredth time, there is one case, one only, when man may con-
45 sciously, purposely, desire what is injurious to himself, what is stu-

pid, very stupid—simply in order to have the right to desire for himself even what is very stupid and not to be bound by an obligation to desire only what is sensible. Of course, this very stupid thing, this caprice of ours, may be in reality, gentlemen, more

5 advantageous for us than anything else on earth, especially in certain cases. And in particular it may be more advantageous than any advantage even when it does us obvious harm, and contradicts the soundest conclusions of our reason concerning our advantage—for in any circumstances it preserves for us what is most precious and

10 most important—that is, our personality, our individuality. Some, you see, maintain that this really is the most precious thing for mankind; choice can, of course, if it chooses, be in agreement with reason; and especially if this be not abused but kept within bounds. It is profitable and sometimes even praiseworthy. But very often,

15 and even most often, choice is utterly and stubbornly opposed to reason . . . and . . . and . . . do you know that that, too, is profitable, sometimes even praiseworthy? Gentlemen, let us suppose that man is not stupid. (Indeed one cannot refuse to suppose that, if only from the one consideration, that, if man is stupid, then who is

20 wise?) But if he is not stupid, he is monstrously ungrateful! Phenomenally ungrateful. In fact, I believe that the best definition of man is the ungrateful biped. But that is not all, that is not his worst defect; his worst defect is his perpetual moral obliquity, perpetual—from the days of the Flood to the Schleswig-Holstein peri-

25 od. Moral obliquity and consequently lack of good sense; for it has long been accepted that lack of good sense is due to no other cause than moral obliquity. Put it to the test and cast your eyes upon the history of mankind. What will you see? Is it a grand spectacle? Grand, if you like. Take the Colossus of Rhodes, for instance, that's

30 worth something. With good reason Mr. Anaevsky testifies of it that some say that it is the work of man's hands, while others maintain that it has been created by nature herself. Is it many-coloured? May be it is many-coloured, too: if one takes the dress uniforms, military and civilian, of all peoples in all ages—that alone is worth some-

35 thing, and if you take the undress uniforms you will never get to the end of it; no historian would be equal to the job. Is it monotonous? May be it's monotonous too: it's fighting and fighting; they are fighting now, they fought first and they fought last—you will admit, that it is almost too monotonous. In short, one may say any-

40 thing about the history of the world—anything that might enter the most disordered imagination. The only thing one can't say is that it's rational. The very word sticks in one's throat. And, indeed, this is the odd thing that is continually happening: there are continually turning up in life moral and rational persons, sages and lovers of

45 humanity who make it their object to live all their lives as morally

and rationally as possible, to be, so to speak, a light to their neighbours simply in order to show them that it is possible to live morally and rationally in this world. And yet we all know that those very
people sooner or later have been false to themselves, playing some
5   queer trick, often a most unseemly one. Now I ask you: what can be
expected of man since he is a being endowed with strange qualities?
Shower upon him every earthly blessing, drown him in a sea of
happiness, so that nothing but bubbles of bliss can be seen on the
surface; give him economic prosperity, such that he should have
10   nothing else to do but sleep, eat cakes and busy himself with the
continuation of his species, and even then out of sheer ingratitude,
sheer spite, man would play you some nasty trick. He would even
risk his cakes and would deliberately desire the most fatal rubbish,
the most uneconomical absurdity, simply to introduce into all this
15   positive good sense his fatal fantastic element. It is just his fantastic
dreams, his vulgar folly that he will desire to retain, simply in order
to prove to himself—as though that were so necessary—that men
still are men and not the keys of a piano, which the laws of nature
threaten to control so completely that soon one will be able to desire
20   nothing but by the calendar. And that is not all: even if man really
were nothing but a piano-key, even if this were proved to him by
natural science and mathematics, even then he would not become
reasonable, but would purposely do something perverse out of simple ingratitude, simply to gain his point. And if he does not find
25   means he will contrive destruction and chaos, will contrive sufferings of all sorts, only to gain his point! He will launch a curse upon
the world, and as only man can curse (it is his privilege, the primary
distinction between him and other animals), may be by his curse
alone he will attain his object—that is, convince himself that he is a
30   man and not a piano-key! If you say that all this, too, can be calculated and tabulated—chaos and darkness and curses, so that the
mere possibility of calculating it all beforehand would stop it all,
and reason would reassert itself, then man would purposely go
mad in order to be rid of reason and gain his point! I believe in it, I
35   answer for it, for the whole work of man really seems to consist in
nothing but proving to himself every minute that he is a man and
not a piano-key! It may be at the cost of his skin, it may be by can-
nibalism! And this being so, can one help being tempted to rejoice
that it has not yet come off, and that desire still depends on some-
40   thing we don't know?

       You will scream at me (that is, if you condescend to do so) that
no one is touching my free will, that all they are concerned with is
that my will should of itself, of its own free will, coincide with my
own normal interests, with the laws of nature and arithmetic.
45   Good heavens, gentlemen, what sort of free will is left when we

come to tabulation and arithmetic, when it will all be a case of twice
two make four? Twice two makes four without my will. As if free
will meant that!

IX

Gentlemen, I am joking, and I know myself that my jokes are
5   not brilliant, but you know one can't take everything as a joke. I am,
perhaps, jesting against the grain. Gentlemen, I am tormented by
questions; answer them for me. You, for instance, want to cure men
of their old habits and reform their will in accordance with science
and good sense. But how do you know, not only that it is possible,
10 but also that it is *desirable* to reform man in that way? And what
leads you to the conclusion that man's inclinations *need* reforming?
In short, how do you know that such a reformation will be a benefit to man? And to go to the root of the matter, why are you so positively convinced that not to act against his real normal interests
15 guaranteed by the conclusions of reason and arithmetic is certainly
always advantageous for man and must always be a law for
mankind? So far, you know, this is only your supposition. It may be
the law of logic, but not the law of humanity. You think, gentlemen,
perhaps that I am mad? Allow me to defend myself. I agree that
20 man is pre-eminently a creative animal, predestined to strive consciously for an object and to engage in engineering—that is, incessantly and eternally to make new roads, *wherever they may lead.* But
the reason why he wants sometimes to go off at a tangent may just
be that he is *predestined* to make the road, and perhaps, too, that
25 however stupid the "direct" practical man may be, the thought
sometimes will occur to him that the road almost always does lead
somewhere, and that the destination it leads to is less important than
the process of making it, and that the chief thing is to save the well-
conducted child from despising engineering, and so giving way to
30 the fatal idleness, which, as we all know, is the mother of all the
vices. Man likes to make roads and to create, that is a fact beyond
dispute. But why has he such a passionate love for destruction and
chaos also? Tell me that! But on that point I want to say a couple of
words myself. May it not be that he loves chaos and destruction
35 (there can be no disputing that he does sometimes love it) because
he is instinctively afraid of attaining his object and completing the
edifice he is constructing? Who knows, perhaps he only loves that
edifice from a distance, and is by no means in love with it at close
quarters; perhaps he only loves building it and does not want to live
40 in it, but will leave it, when completed, for the use of *les animaux
domestiques*—such as the ants, the sheep, and so on. Now the ants
have quite a different taste. They have a marvellous edifice of that

pattern which endures for ever—the ant-heap.

With the ant-heap the respectable race of ants began and with the ant-heap they will probably end, which does the greatest credit to their perseverance and good sense. But man is a frivolous and
5 incongruous creature, and perhaps, like a chess player, loves the process of the game, not the end of it. And who knows (there is no saying with certainty), perhaps the only goal on earth to which mankind is striving lies in this incessant process of attaining, in other words, in life itself, and not in the thing to be attained, which
10 must always be expressed as a formula, as positive as twice two makes four, and such positiveness is not life, gentlemen, but is the beginning of death. Anyway, man has always been afraid of this mathematical certainty, and I am afraid of it now. Granted that man does nothing but seek that mathematical certainty, he traverses
15 oceans, sacrifices his life in the quest, but to succeed, really to find it, he dreads, I assure you. He feels that when he has found it there will be nothing for him to look for. When workmen have finished their work they do at least receive their pay, they go to the tavern, then they are taken to the police-station—and there is occupation
20 for a week. But where can man go? Anyway, one can observe a certain awkwardness about him when he has attained such objects. He loves the process of attaining, but does not quite like to have attained, and that, of course, is very absurd. In fact, man is a comical creature; there seems to be a kind of jest in it all. But yet mathe-
25 matical certainty is after all, something insufferable. Twice two makes four seems to me simply a piece of insolence. Twice two makes four is a pert coxcomb who stands with arms akimbo barring your path and spitting. I admit that twice two makes four is an excellent thing, but if we are to give everything its due, twice two
30 makes five is sometimes a very charming thing too.

And why are you so firmly, so triumphantly, convinced that only the normal and the positive—in other words, only what is conducive to welfare—is for the advantage of man? Is not reason in error as regards advantage? Does not man, perhaps, love something
35 besides well-being? Perhaps he is just as fond of suffering? Perhaps suffering is just as great a benefit to him as well-being? Man is sometimes extraordinarily, passionately, in love with suffering, and that is a fact. There is no need to appeal to universal history to prove that; only ask yourself, if you are a man and have lived at all. As far
40 as my personal opinion is concerned, to care only for well-being seems to me positively ill- bred. Whether it's good or bad, it is sometimes very pleasant, too, to smash things. I hold no brief for suffering nor for well-being either. I am standing for . . . my caprice, and for its being guaranteed to me when necessary. Suffering would
45 be out of place in vaudevilles, for instance; I know that. In the

"Palace of Crystal" it is unthinkable; suffering means doubt, nega-
tion, and what would be the good of a "palace of crystal" if there
could be any doubt about it? And yet I think man will never
renounce real suffering, that is, destruction and chaos. Why, suffer-
5   ing is the sole origin of consciousness. Though I did lay it down at
the beginning that consciousness is the greatest misfortune for man,
yet I know man prizes it and would not give it up for any satisfaction. Consciousness, for instance, is infinitely superior to twice two
makes four. Once you have mathematical certainty there is nothing
10   left to do or to understand. There will be nothing left but to bottle
up your five senses and plunge into contemplation. While if you
stick to consciousness, even though the same result is attained, you
can at least flog yourself at times, and that will, at any rate, liven
you up. Reactionary as it is, corporal punishment is better than
15   nothing.

X

You believe in a palace of crystal that can never be destroyed—
a palace at which one will not be able to put out one's tongue or
make a long nose on the sly. And perhaps that is just why I am
afraid of this edifice, that it is of crystal and can never be destroyed
20   and that one cannot put one's tongue out at it even on the sly.
You see, if it were not a palace, but a hen-house, I might creep
into it to avoid getting wet, and yet I would not call the hen-house
a palace out of gratitude to it for keeping me dry. You laugh and say
that in such circumstances a hen-house is as good as a mansion. Yes,
25   I answer, if one had to live simply to keep out of the rain.
But what is to be done if I have taken it into my head that that
is not the only object in life, and that if one must live one had better
live in a mansion? That is my choice, my desire. You will only eradicate it when you have changed my preference. Well, do change it,
30   allure me with something else, give me another ideal. But meanwhile I will not take a hen-house for a mansion. The palace of crystal may be an idle dream, it may be that it is inconsistent with the
laws of nature and that I have invented it only through my own stupidity, through the old-fashioned irrational habits of my generation.
35   But what does it matter to me that it is inconsistent? That makes no
difference since it exists in my desires, or rather exists as long as my
desires exist. Perhaps you are laughing again? Laugh away; I will
put up with any mockery rather than pretend that I am satisfied
when I am hungry, I know, anyway, that I will not be put off with a
40   compromise, with a recurring zero, simply because it is consistent
with the laws of nature and actually exists. I will not accept as the
crown of my desires a block of buildings with tenements for the

poor on a lease of a thousand years, and perhaps with a sign-board
of a dentist hanging out. Destroy my desires, eradicate my ideals,
show me something better, and I will follow you. You will say, perhaps, that it is not worth your trouble; but in that case I can give you
5 the same answer. We are discussing things seriously; but if you
won't deign to give me your attention, I will drop your acquaintance. I can retreat into my underground hole.

But while I am alive and have desires I would rather my hand
were withered off than bring one brick to such a building! Don't
10 remind me that I have just rejected the palace of crystal for the sole
reason that one cannot put out one's tongue at it. I did not say
because I am so fond of putting my tongue out. Perhaps the thing I
resented was, that of all your edifices there has not been one at
which one could not put out one's tongue. On the contrary, I would
15 let my tongue be cut off out of gratitude if things could be so
arranged that I should lose all desire to put it out. It is not my fault
that things cannot be so arranged, and that one must be satisfied
with model flats. Then why am I made with such desires? Can I
have been constructed simply in order to come to the conclusion
20 that all my construction is a cheat? Can this be my whole purpose?
I do not believe it.

But do you know what: I am convinced that we underground
folk ought to be kept on a curb. Though we may sit forty years
underground without speaking, when we do come out into the light
25 of day and break out, talk and talk and talk. . . .

XI

The long and the short of it is, gentlemen, that it is better to do
nothing! Better conscious inertia! And so hurrah for underground!
Though I have said that I envy the normal man to the last drop of
my bile, yet I should not care to be in his place such as he is now
30 (though I shall not cease envying him). No, no; anyway the underground life is more advantageous, There, at any rate, one can . . . Oh,
but even now I am lying! I am lying because I know myself that it
is not underground that is better, but something different, quite different, for which I am thirsting, but which I cannot find! Damn
35 underground![*]

[*]According to Dostoyevsky, the "swine of a censor" mutilated this passage
by taking out words that more directly indicated what it is Underground
Man is thirsting for—faith in Christ (mediated to him *in potentia* by Liza in
Part II, an offering of grace through love which he rejects). Apparently, the
censor thought Dostoyevsky was being ironic. In later printings
Dostoyevsky allowed the passage to stand, however, because he saw that
the imagery and allusions point the reader in the right direction.

I will tell you another thing that would be better, and that is, If I myself believed in anything of what I have just written. I swear to you, gentlemen, there is not one thing, not one word of what I have written that I really believe. That is, I believe it, perhaps, but at the same time I feel and suspect that I am lying like a cobbler.

"Then why have you written all this?" you will say to me. "I ought to put you underground for forty years without anything to do and then come to you in your cellar, to find out what stage you have reached! How can a man be left with nothing to do for forty years?"

"Isn't that shameful, isn't that humiliating?" you will say, perhaps, wagging your heads contemptuously. "You thirst for life and try to settle the problems of life by a logical tangle. And how persistent, how insolent are your sallies, and at the same time what a scare you are in! You talk nonsense and are pleased with it; you say impudent things and are in continual alarm and apologising for them. You declare that you are afraid of nothing and at the same time try to ingratiate yourself in our good opinion. You declare that you are gnashing your teeth and at the same time you try to be witty so as to amuse us. You know that your witticisms are not witty, but you are evidently well satisfied with their literary value. You may, perhaps, have really suffered, but you have no respect for your own suffering. You may have sincerity, but you have no modesty; out of the pettiest vanity you expose your sincerity to publicity and ignominy. You doubtlessly mean to say something, but hide your last word through fear, because you have not the resolution to utter it, and only have a cowardly impudence. You boast of consciousness, but you are not sure of your ground, for though your mind works, yet your heart is darkened and corrupt, and you cannot have a full, genuine consciousness without a pure heart. And how intrusive you are, how you insist and grimace! Lies, lies, lies!"

Of course I have myself made up all the things you say. That, too, is from underground. I have been for forty years listening to you through a crack under the floor. I have invented them myself, there was nothing else I could invent. It is no wonder that I have learned it by heart and it has taken a literary form. . . .

But can you really be so credulous as to think that I will print all this and give it to you to read too? And another problem: why do I call you "gentlemen," why do I address you as though you really were my readers? Such confessions as I intend to make are never printed nor given to other people to read. Anyway, I am not strong-minded enough for that, and I don't see why I should be. But you see a fancy has occurred to me and I want to realise it at all costs. Let me explain.

Every man has reminiscences which he would not tell to everyone, but only to his friends. He has other matters in his mind which he would not reveal even to his friends, but only to himself, and that in secret. But there are other things which a man is afraid to tell even to himself, and every decent man has a number of such things

5   stored away in his mind. The more decent he is, the greater the number of such things in his mind. Anyway, I have only lately determined to remember some of my early adventures. Till now I have always avoided them, even with a certain uneasiness. Now, when I am not only recalling them, but have actually decided to

10 write an account of them, I want to try the experiment whether one can, even with oneself, be perfectly open and not take fright at the whole truth. I will observe, in parenthesis, that Heine says that a true autobiography is almost an impossibility, and that man is bound to lie about himself. He considers that Rousseau certainly

15 told lies about himself in his confessions, and even intentionally lied, out of vanity. I am convinced that Heine is right; I quite understand how sometimes one may, out of sheer vanity, attribute regular crimes to oneself, and indeed I can very well conceive that kind of vanity. But Heine judged of people who made their confessions

20 to the public. I write only for myself, and I wish to declare once and for all that if I write as though I were addressing readers, that is simply because it is easier for me to write in that form. It is a form, an empty form—I shall never have readers. I have made this plain already . . .

25   I don't wish to be hampered by any restrictions in the compilation of my notes. I shall not attempt any system or method. I will jot things down as I remember them.

    But here, perhaps, someone will catch at the word and ask me: if you really don't reckon on readers, why do you make such com-

30 pacts with yourself—and on paper too—that is, that you won't attempt any system or method, that you jot things down as you remember them, and so on, and so on? Why are you explaining? Why do you apologise?

    Well, there it is, I answer.

35   There is a whole psychology in all this, though. Perhaps it is simply that I am a coward. And perhaps that I purposely imagine an audience before me in order that I may be more dignified while I write. There are perhaps thousands of reasons. Again, what is my object precisely in writing? If it is not for the benefit of the public

40 why should I not simply recall these incidents in my own mind without putting them on paper?

    Quite so; but yet it is more imposing on paper. There is something more impressive in it; I shall be better able to criticise myself and improve my style. Besides, I shall perhaps obtain actual relief

45 from writing. Today, for instance, I am particularly oppressed by

one memory of a distant past. It came back vividly to my mind a
few days ago, and has remained haunting me like an annoying tune
that one cannot get rid of. And yet I must get rid of it somehow. I
have hundreds of such reminiscences; but at times some one stands
5   out from the hundred and oppresses me. For some reason I believe
that if I write it down I should get rid of it. Why not try?

Besides, I am bored, and I never have anything to do. Writing
will be a sort of work. They say work makes man kind-hearted and
honest. Well, here is a chance for me, anyway.

10   Snow is falling today, yellow and dingy. It fell yesterday, too,
and a few days ago. I fancy it is the wet snow that has reminded me
of that incident which I cannot shake off now. And so let it be a story
à propos of the falling snow.

PART II: À PROPOS OF THE WET SNOW

When from dark error's subjugation
15   My words of passionate exhortation
      Had wrenched thy fainting spirit free;
And writhing prone in thine affliction
Thou didst recall with malediction
      The vice that had encompassed thee:
20   And when thy slumbering conscience, fretting
      By recollection's torturing flame,
Thou didst reveal the hideous setting
      Of thy life's current ere I came:
When suddenly I saw thee sicken,
25   And weeping, hide thine anguished face,
Revolted, maddened, horror-stricken,
    At memories of foul disgrace.
              NEKRASSOV
            (translated by Juliet Soskice).

I

At that time I was only twenty-four. My life was even then
gloomy, ill-regulated, and as solitary as that of a savage. I made
30   friends with no one and positively avoided talking, and buried
myself more and more in my hole. At work in the office I never
looked at anyone, and was perfectly well aware that my compan-

ions looked upon me, not only as a queer fellow, but even looked upon me—I always fancied this—with a sort of loathing. I sometimes wondered why it was that nobody except me fancied that he was looked upon with aversion? One of the clerks had a most repul-
5 sive, pock-marked face, which looked positively villainous. I believe I should not have dared to look at anyone with such an unsightly countenance. Another had such a very dirty old uniform that there was an unpleasant odour in his proximity. Yet not one of these gentlemen showed the slightest self-consciousness—either
10 about their clothes or their countenance or their character in any way. Neither of them ever imagined that they were looked at with repulsion; if they had imagined it they would not have minded—so long as their superiors did not look at them in that way. It is clear to me now that, owing to my unbounded vanity and to the high stan-
15 dard I set for myself, I often looked at myself with furious discontent, which verged on loathing, and so I inwardly attributed the same feeling to everyone. I hated my face, for instance: I thought it disgusting, and even suspected that there was something base in my expression, and so every day when I turned up at the office I
20 tried to behave as independently as possible, and to assume a lofty expression, so that I might not be suspected of being abject. "My face may be ugly," I thought, "but let it be lofty, expressive, and, above all, *extremely* intelligent." But I was positively and painfully certain that it was impossible for my countenance ever to express
25 those qualities. And what was worst of all, I thought it actually stupid looking, and I would have been quite satisfied if I could have looked intelligent. In fact, I would even have put up with looking base if, at the same time, my face could have been thought strikingly intelligent.
30   Of course, I hated my fellow clerks one and all, and I despised them all, yet at the same time I was, as it were, afraid of them. In fact, it happened at times that I thought more highly of them than of myself. It somehow happened quite suddenly that I alternated between despising them and thinking them superior to myself. A
35 cultivated and decent man cannot be vain without setting a fearfully high standard for himself, and without despising and almost hating himself at certain moments. But whether I despised them or thought them superior I dropped my eyes almost every time I met anyone. I even made experiments whether I could face so and so's
40 looking at me, and I was always the first to drop my eyes. This worried me to distraction. I had a sickly dread, too, of being ridiculous, and so had a slavish passion for the conventional in everything external. I loved to fall into the common rut, and had a whole-hearted terror of any kind of eccentricity in myself. But how could I live
45 up to it? I was morbidly sensitive as a man of our age should be.

They were all stupid, and as like one another as so many sheep. Perhaps I was the only one in the office who fancied that I was a coward and a slave, and I fancied it just because I was more highly developed. But it was not only that I fancied it, it really was so. I was a coward and a slave. I say this without the slightest embarrassment. Every decent man of our age must be a coward and a slave. That is his normal condition. Of that I am firmly persuaded. He is made and constructed to that very end. And not only at the present time owing to some casual circumstances, but always, at all times, a decent man is bound to be a coward and a slave. It is the law of nature for all decent people all over the earth. If anyone of them happens to be valiant about something, he need not be comforted nor carried away by that; he would show the white feather just the same before something else. That is how it invariably and inevitably ends. Only donkeys and mules are valiant, and they only till they are pushed up to the wall. It is not worth while to pay attention to them for they really are of no consequence.

Another circumstance, too, worried me in those days: that there was no one like me and I was unlike anyone else. "I am alone and they are *everyone*," I thought—and pondered.

From that it is evident that I was still a youngster.

The very opposite sometimes happened. It was loathsome sometimes to go to the office; things reached such a point that I often came home ill. But all at once, *à propos* of nothing, there would come a phase of scepticism and indifference (everything happened in phases to me), and I would laugh myself at my intolerance and fastidiousness, I would reproach myself with being *romantic*. At one time I was unwilling to speak to anyone, while at other times I would not only talk, but go to the length of contemplating making friends with them. All my fastidiousness would suddenly, for no rhyme or reason, vanish. Who knows, perhaps I never had really had it, and it had simply been affected, and got out of books. I have not decided that question even now. Once I quite made friends with them, visited their homes, played preference, drank vodka, talked of promotions. . . . But here let me make a digression.

We Russians, speaking generally, have never had those foolish transcendental "romantics"—German, and still more French—on whom nothing produces any effect; if there were an earthquake, if all France perished at the barricades, they would still be the same, they would not even have the decency to affect a change, but would still go on singing their transcendental songs to the hour of their death, because they are fools. We, in Russia, have no fools; that is well known. That is what distinguishes us from foreign lands. Consequently these transcendental natures are not found amongst us in their pure form. The idea that they are is due to our "realistic"

journalists and critics of that day, always on the look out for
Kostanzhoglos and Uncle Pyotr Ivanitchs and foolishly accepting
them as our ideal; they have slandered our romantics, taking them
for the same transcendental sort as in Germany or France. On the
5 contrary, the characteristics of our "romantics" are absolutely and
directly opposed to the transcendental European type, and no
European standard can be applied to them. (Allow me to make use
of this word "romantic"—an old-fashioned and much respected
word which has done good service and is familiar to all.) The char-
10 acteristics of our romantic are to understand everything, *to see everything and to see it often incomparably more clearly than our most realistic
minds see it*; to refuse to accept anyone or anything, but at the same
time not to despise anything; to give way, to yield, from policy;
never to lose sight of a useful practical object (such as rent-free
15 quarters at the government expense, pensions, decorations), to keep
their eye on that object through all the enthusiasms and volumes of
lyrical poems, and at the same time to preserve "the sublime and
the beautiful" inviolate within them to the hour of their death, and
to preserve themselves also, incidentally, like some precious jewel
20 wrapped in cotton wool if only for the benefit of "the sublime and
the beautiful." Our "romantic" is a man of great breadth and the
greatest rogue of all our rogues, I assure you. . . . I can assure you
from experience, indeed. Of course, that is, if he is intelligent. But
what am I saying! The romantic is always intelligent, and I only
25 meant to observe that although we have had foolish romantics they
don't count, and they were only so because in the flower of their
youth they degenerated into Germans, and to preserve their precious jewel more comfortably, settled somewhere out there—by
preference in Weimar or the Black Forest.
30   I, for instance, genuinely despised my official work and did not
openly abuse it simply because I was in it myself and got a salary
for it. Anyway, take note, I did not openly abuse it. Our romantic
would rather go out of his mind—a thing, however, which very
rarely happens—than take to open abuse, unless he had some other
35 career in view; and he is never, kicked out. At most, they would take
him to the lunatic asylum as "the King of Spain" if he should go
very mad. But it is only the thin, fair people who go out of their
minds in Russia. Innumerable "romantics" attain later in life to considerable rank in the service. Their many-sidedness is remarkable!
40 And what a faculty they have for the most contradictory sensations!
I was comforted by this thought even in those days, and I am of the
same opinion now. That is why there are so many "broad natures"
among us who never lose their ideal even in the depths of degradation; and though they never stir a finger for their ideal, though they
45 are arrant thieves and knaves, yet they tearfully cherish their first

ideal and are extraordinarily honest at heart. Yes, it is only among us that the most incorrigible rogue can be absolutely and loftily honest at heart without in the least ceasing to be a rogue. I repeat, our romantics, frequently, become such accomplished rascals (I use
5   the term "rascals" affectionately), suddenly display such a sense of reality and practical knowledge that their bewildered superiors and the public generally can only ejaculate in amazement.

Their many-sidedness is really amazing, and goodness knows what it may develop into later on, and what the future has in store
10   for us. It is not a poor material! I do not say this from any foolish or boastful patriotism. But I feel sure that you are again imagining that I am joking. Or perhaps it's just the contrary and you are convinced that I really think so. Anyway, gentlemen, I shall welcome both views as an honour and a special favour. And do forgive my digres-
15   sion.

I did not, of course, maintain friendly relations with my com-rades and soon was at loggerheads with them, and in my youth and inexperience I even gave up bowing to them, as though I had cut off all relations. That, however, only happened to me once. As a rule, I
20   was always alone.

In the first place I spent most of my time at home, reading. I tried to stifle all that was continually seething within me by means of external impressions. And the only external means I had was reading. Reading, of course, was a great help—exciting me, giving
25   me pleasure and pain. But at times it bored me fearfully. One longed for movement in spite of everything, and I plunged all at once into dark, underground, loathsome vice of the pettiest kind. My wretched passions were acute, smarting, from my continual, sickly irritability. I had hysterical impulses, with tears and convulsions. I
30   had no resource except reading, that is, there was nothing in my surroundings which I could respect and which attracted me. I was overwhelmed with depression, too; I had an hysterical craving for incongruity and for contrast, and so I took to vice. I have not said all this to justify myself. . . . But, no! I am lying. I did want to justify
35   myself. I make that little observation for my own benefit, gentle-men. I don't want to lie. I vowed to myself I would not.

And so, furtively, timidly, in solitude, at night, I indulged in filthy vice, with a feeling of shame which never deserted me, even at the most loathsome moments, and which at such moments near-
40   ly made me curse. Already even then I had my underground world in my soul. I was fearfully afraid of being seen, of being met, of being recognised. I visited various obscure haunts.

One night as I was passing a tavern I saw through a lighted window some gentlemen fighting with billiard cues, and saw one of
45   them thrown out of the window. At other times I should have felt

very much disgusted, but I was in such a mood at the time, that I actually envied the gentleman thrown out of the window—and I envied him so much that I even went into the tavern and into the billiard-room. "Perhaps," I thought, "I'll have a fight, too, and
5   they'll throw me out of the window."

    I was not drunk—but what is one to do—depression will drive a man to such a pitch of hysteria? But nothing happened. It seemed that I was not even equal to being thrown out of the window and I went away without having my fight.
10   An officer put me in my place from the first moment.

    I was standing by the billiard-table and in my ignorance blocking up the way, and he wanted to pass; he took me by the shoulders and without a word—without a warning or explanation—moved me from where I was standing to another spot and passed by as
15   though he had not noticed me. I could have forgiven blows, but I could not forgive his having moved me without noticing me.

    Devil knows what I would have given for a real regular quarrel—a more decent, a more *literary* one, so to speak. I had been treated like a fly. This officer was over six foot, while I was a spindly lit-
20   tle fellow. But the quarrel was in my hands. I had only to protest and I certainly would have been thrown out of the window. But I changed my mind and preferred to beat a resentful retreat.

    I went out of the tavern straight home, confused and troubled, and the next night I went out again with the same lewd intentions,
25   still more furtively, abjectly and miserably than before, as it were, with tears in my eyes—but still I did go out again. Don't imagine, though, it was cowardice made me slink away from the officer; I never have been a coward at heart, though I have always been a coward in action. Don't be in a hurry to laugh—I assure you I can
30   explain it all.

    Oh, if only that officer had been one of the sort who would consent to fight a duel! But no, he was one of those gentlemen (alas, long extinct!) who preferred fighting with cues or, like Gogol's Lieutenant Pirogov, appealing to the police. They did not fight duels
35   and would have thought a duel with a civilian like me an utterly unseemly procedure in any case—and they looked upon the duel altogether as something impossible, something free-thinking and French. But they were quite ready to bully, especially when they were over six foot.
40   I did not slink away through cowardice, but through an unbounded vanity. I was afraid not of his six foot, not of getting a sound thrashing and being thrown out of the window; I should have had physical courage enough, I assure you; but I had not the moral courage. What I was afraid of was that everyone present,
45   from the insolent marker down to the lowest little stinking, pimply

clerk in a greasy collar, would jeer at me and fail to understand
when I began to protest and to address them in literary language.
For of the point of honour—not of honour, but of the point of honour (*point d'honneur*)—one cannot speak among us except in literary
5   language. You can't allude to the "point of honour" in ordinary language. I was fully convinced (the sense of reality, in spite of all my
romanticism!) that they would all simply split their sides with
laughter, and that the officer would not simply beat me, that is,
without insulting me, but would certainly prod me in the back with
10 his knee, kick me round the billiard table, and only then perhaps
have pity and drop me out of the window.

Of course, this trivial incident could not with me end in that. I
often met that officer afterwards in the street and noticed him very
carefully. I am not quite sure whether he recognised me, I imagine
15 not; I judge from certain signs. But I—I stared at him with spite and
hatred and so it went on . . . for several years! My resentment grew
even deeper with years. At first I began making stealthy inquiries
about this officer. It was difficult for me to do so, for I knew no one.
But one day I heard someone shout his surname in the street as I
20 was following him at a distance, as though I were tied to him—and
so I learnt his surname. Another time I followed him to his flat, and
for ten kopecks learned from the porter where he lived, on which
storey, whether he lived alone or with others, and so on—in fact,
everything one could learn from a porter. One morning, though I
25 had never tried my hand with the pen, it suddenly occurred to me
to write a satire on this officer in the form of a novel which would
unmask his villainy. I wrote the novel with relish. I did unmask his
villainy, I even exaggerated it; at first I so altered his surname that
it could easily be recognised, but on second thoughts I changed it,
30 and sent the story to the *Otetchestvenniya Zapiski*. But at that time
such attacks went not the fashion and my story was not printed.
That was a great vexation to me.

Sometimes I was positively choked with resentment. At last I
determined to challenge my enemy to a duel. I composed a splen-
35 did, charming letter to him, imploring him to apologise to me, and
hinting rather plainly at a duel in case of refusal. The letter was so
composed that if the officer had had the least understanding of the
sublime and the beautiful he would certainly have flung himself on
my neck and have offered me his friendship. And how fine that
40 would have been! How we should have got on together! "He could
have shielded me with his higher rank, while I could have
improved his mind with my culture, and, well . . . my ideas, and all
sorts of things might have happened." Only fancy, this was two
years after his insult to me, and my challenge would have been a
45 ridiculous anachronism, in spite of all the ingenuity of my letter in

disguising and explaining away the anachronism. But, thank God (to this day I thank the Almighty with tears in my eyes) I did not send the letter to him. Cold shivers run down my back when I think of what might have happened if I had sent it.

5   And all at once I revenged myself in the simplest way, by a stroke of genius! A brilliant thought suddenly dawned upon me. Sometimes on holidays I used to stroll along the sunny side of the Nevsky about four o'clock in the afternoon. Though it was hardly a stroll so much as a series of innumerable miseries, humiliations and

10 resentments; but no doubt that was just what I wanted. I used to wriggle along in a most unseemly fashion, like an eel, continually moving aside to make way for generals, for officers, of the guards and the hussars, or for ladies. At such minutes there used to be a convulsive twinge at my heart, and I used to feel hot all down my

15 back at the mere thought of the wretchedness of my attire, of the wretchedness and abjectness of my little scurrying figure. This was a regular martyrdom, a continual, intolerable humiliation at the thought, which passed into an incessant and direct sensation, that I was a mere fly in the eyes of all this world, a nasty, disgusting fly—

20 more intelligent, more highly developed, more refined in feeling than any of them, of course—but a fly that was continually making way for everyone, insulted and injured by everyone. Why I inflict-ed this torture upon myself, why I went to the Nevsky, I don't know. I felt simply drawn there at every possible opportunity.

25   Already then I began to experience a rush of the enjoyment of which I spoke in the first chapter. After my affair with the officer I felt even more drawn there than before: it was on the Nevsky that I met him most frequently, there I could admire him. He, too, went there chiefly on holidays. He, too, turned out of his path for gener-

30 als and persons of high rank, and he too, wriggled between them like an eel; but people, like me, or even better dressed than me, he simply walked over; he made straight for them as though there was nothing but empty space before him, and never, under any circum-stances, turned aside. I gloated over my resentment watching him

35 and . . . always resentfully made way for him. It exasperated me that even in the street I could not be on an even footing with him.

"Why must you invariably be the first to move aside?" I kept asking myself in hysterical rage, waking up sometimes at three o'clock in the morning. "Why is it you and not he? There's no regu-

40 lation about it there's no written law. Let the making way be equal as it usually is when refined people meet; he moves half-way and you move half-way; you pass with mutual respect."

But that never happened, and I always moved aside, while he did not even notice my making way for him. And lo and behold a

45 bright idea dawned upon me! "What," I thought, "if I meet him and

don't move on one side? What if I don't move aside on purpose, even if I knock up against him? How would that be?" This audacious idea took such a hold on me that it gave me no peace. I was dreaming of it continually, horribly, and I purposely went more fre-
5   quently to the Nevsky in order to picture more vividly how I should do it when I did do it. I was delighted. This intention seemed to me more and more practical and possible.

"Of course I shall not really push him," I thought, already more good-natured in my joy. "I will simply not turn aside, will run up
10   against him, not very violently, but just shouldering each other— just as much as decency permits. I will push against him just as much as he pushes against me." At last I made up my mind completely. But my preparations took a great deal of time. To begin with, when I carried out my plan I should need to be looking rather
15   more decent, and so I had to think of my get-up. "In case of emergency, if, for instance, there were any sort of public scandal (and the public there is of the *most recherché:* the Countess walks there; Prince D. walks there; all the literary world is there), I must be well dressed; that inspires respect and of itself puts us on an equal foot-
20   ing in the eyes of the society."

With this object I asked for some of my salary in advance, and bought at Tchurkin's a pair of black gloves and a decent hat. Black gloves seemed to me both more dignified and *bon ton* than the lemon-coloured ones which I had contemplated at first. "The colour
25   is too gaudy, it looks as though one were trying to be conspicuous," and I did not take the lemon-coloured ones. I had got ready long beforehand a good shirt, with white bone studs; my overcoat was the only thing that held me back. The coat in itself was a very good one, it kept me warm; but it was wadded and it had a raccoon col-
30   lar which was the height of vulgarity. I had to change the collar at any sacrifice, and to have a beaver one like an officer's. For this purpose I began visiting the Gostiny Dvor and after several attempts I pitched upon a piece of cheap German beaver. Though these German beavers soon grow shabby and look wretched, yet at first
35   they look exceedingly well, and I only needed it for the occasion. I asked the price; even so, it was too expensive. After thinking it over thoroughly I decided to sell my raccoon collar. The rest of the money—a considerable sum for me, I decided to borrow from Anton Antonitch Syetotchkin, my immediate superior, an unas-
40   suming person, though grave and judicious. He never lent money to anyone, but I had, on entering the service, been specially recommended to him by an important personage who had got me my berth. I was horribly worried. To borrow from Anton Antonitch seemed to me monstrous and shameful. I did not sleep for two or
45   three nights. Indeed, I did not sleep well at that time, I was in a

fever; I had a vague sinking at my heart or else a sudden throbbing, throbbing, throbbing! Anton Antonitch was surprised at first, then he frowned, then he reflected, and did after all lend me the money, receiving from me a written authorisation to take from my salary a
5   fortnight later the sum that he had lent me.

In this way everything was at last ready. The handsome beaver replaced the mean-looking raccoon, and I began by degrees to get to work. It would never have done to act offhand, at random; the plan had to be carried out skilfully, by degrees. But I must confess that
10   after many efforts I began to despair: we simply could not run into each other. I made every preparation, I was quite determined—it seemed as though we should run into one another directly—and before I knew what I was doing I had stepped aside for him again and he had passed without noticing me. I even prayed as I
15   approached him that God would grant me determination. One time I had made up my mind thoroughly, but it ended in my stumbling and falling at his feet because at the very last instant when I was six inches from him my courage failed me. He very calmly stepped over me, while I flew on one side like a ball. That night I was ill
20   again, feverish and delirious.

And suddenly it ended most happily. The night before I had made up my mind not to carry out my fatal plan and to abandon it all, and with that object I went to the Nevsky for the last time, just to see how I would abandon it all. Suddenly, three paces from my
25   enemy, I unexpectedly made up my mind—I closed my eyes, and we ran full tilt, shoulder to shoulder, against one another! I did not budge an inch and passed him on a perfectly equal footing! He did not even look round and pretended not to notice it; but he was only pretending, I am convinced of that. I am convinced of that to this
30   day! Of course, I got the worst of it—he was stronger, but that was not the point. The point was that I had attained my object, I had kept up my dignity, I had not yielded a step, and had put myself publicly on an equal social footing with him. I returned home feeling that I was fully avenged for everything. I was delighted. I was
35   triumphant and sang Italian arias. Of course, I will not describe to you what happened to me three days later; if you have read my first chapter you can guess for yourself. The officer was afterwards transferred; I have not seen him now for fourteen years. What is the dear fellow doing now? Whom is he walking over?

II

40   But the period of my dissipation would end and I always felt very sick afterwards. It was followed by remorse—I tried to drive it away; I felt too sick. By degrees, however, I grew used to that too. I

grew used to everything, or rather I voluntarily resigned myself to enduring it. But I had a means of escape that reconciled every-thing—that was to find refuge in "the sublime and the beautiful," in dreams, of course. I was a terrible dreamer, I would dream for three months on end, tucked away in my corner, and you may believe me that at those moments I had no resemblance to the gentleman who, in the perturbation of his chicken heart, put a collar of German beaver on his great-coat. I suddenly became a hero. I would not have admitted my six-foot lieutenant even if he had called on me. I could not even picture him before me then. What were my dreams and how I could satisfy myself with them—it is hard to say now, but at the time I was satisfied with them. Though, indeed, even now, I am to some extent satisfied with them. Dreams were particularly sweet and vivid after a spell of dissipation; they came with remorse and with tears, with curses and transports. There were moments of such positive intoxication, of such happiness, that there was not the faintest trace of irony within me, on my honour. I had faith, hope, love. I believed blindly at such times that by some miracle, by some external circumstance, all this would suddenly open out, expand; that suddenly a vista of suitable activity—beneficent, good, and, above all, *ready made* (what sort of activity I had no idea, but the great thing was that it should be all ready for me)—would rise up before me—and I should come out into the light of day, almost rid-ing a white horse and crowned with laurel. Anything but the fore-most place I could not conceive for myself, and for that very reason I quite contentedly occupied the lowest in reality. Either to be a hero or to grovel in the mud—there was nothing between. That was my ruin, for when I was in the mud I comforted myself with the thought that at other times I was a hero, and the hero was a cloak for the mud: for an ordinary man it was shameful to defile himself, but a hero was too lofty to be utterly defiled, and so he might defile himself. It is worth noting that these attacks of the "sublime and the beautiful" visited me even during the period of dissipation and just at the times when I was touching the bottom. They came in separate spurts, as though reminding me of themselves, but did not banish the dissipation by their appearance. On the contrary, they seemed to add a zest to it by contrast, and were only sufficiently present to serve as an appetising sauce. That sauce was made up of contradic-tions and sufferings, of agonising inward analysis, and all these pangs and pin-pricks gave a certain piquancy, even a significance to my dissipation—in fact, completely answered the purpose of an appetising sauce. There was a certain depth of meaning in it. And I could hardly have resigned myself to the simple, vulgar, direct debauchery of a clerk and have endured all the filthiness of it. What could have allured me about it then and have drawn me at night into the street? No, I had a lofty way of getting out of it all.

And what loving-kindness, oh Lord, what loving-kindness I felt at times in those dreams of mine! in those "flights into the sublime and the beautiful"; though it was fantastic love, though it was never applied to anything human in reality, yet there was so much of this love that one did not feel afterwards even the impulse to apply it in reality; that would have been superfluous. Everything, however, passed satisfactorily by a lazy and fascinating transition into the sphere of art, that is, into the beautiful forms of life, lying ready, largely stolen from the poets and novelists and adapted to all sorts of needs and uses. I, for instance, was triumphant over everyone; everyone, of course, was in dust and ashes, and was forced spontaneously to recognise my superiority, and I forgave them all. I was a poet and a grand gentleman, I fell in love; I came in for countless millions and immediately devoted them to humanity, and at the same time I confessed before all the people my shameful deeds, which, of course, were not merely shameful, but had in them much that was "sublime and beautiful" something in the Manfred style. Everyone would kiss me and weep (what idiots they would be if they did not), while I should go barefoot and hungry preaching new ideas and fighting a victorious Austerlitz against the obscurantists. Then the band would play a march, an amnesty would be declared, the Pope would agree to retire from Rome to Brazil; then there would be a ball for the whole of Italy at the Villa Borghese on the shores of Lake Como, Lake Como being for that purpose transferred to the neighbourhood of Rome; then would come a scene in the bushes, and so on, and so on—as though you did not know all about it? You will say that it is vulgar and contemptible to drag all this into public after all the tears and transports which I have myself confessed. But why is it contemptible? Can you imagine that I am ashamed of it all, and that it was stupider than anything in your life, gentlemen? And I can assure you that some of these fancies were by no means badly composed. . . . It did not all happen on the shores of Lake Como. And yet you are right—it really is vulgar and contemptible. And most contemptible of all it is that now I am attempting to justify myself to you. And even more contemptible than that is my making this remark now. But that's enough, or there will be no end to it; each step will be more contemptible than the last. . . .

I could never stand more than three months of dreaming at a time without feeling an irresistible desire to plunge into society. To plunge into society meant to visit my superior at the office, Anton Antonitch Syetotchkin. He was the only permanent acquaintance I have had in my life, and I wonder at the fact myself now. But I only went to see him when that phase came over me, and when my dreams had reached such a point of bliss that it became essential at

once to embrace my fellows and all mankind; and for that purpose
I needed, at least, one human being, actually existing. I had to call
on Anton Antonitch, however, on Tuesday—his at-home day; so I
had always to time my passionate desire to embrace humanity so
5   that it might fall on a Tuesday.

     This Anton Antonitch lived on the fourth storey in a house in
Five Corners, in four low-pitched rooms, one smaller than the other,
of a particularly frugal and sallow appearance. He had two daughters and their aunt, who used to pour out the tea. Of the daughters
10   one was thirteen and another fourteen, they both had snub noses,
and I was awfully shy of them because they were always whisper-
ing and giggling together. The master of the house usually sat in his
study on a leather couch in front of the table with some grey-head-
ed gentleman, usually a colleague from our office or some other
15   department. I never saw more than two or three visitors there,
always the same. They talked about the excise duty; about business
in the senate, about salaries, about promotions, about His
Excellency, and the best means of pleasing him, and so on. I had the
patience to sit like a fool beside these people for four hours at a
20   stretch, listening to them without knowing what to say to them or
venturing to say a word. I became stupefied, several times I felt
myself perspiring, I was overcome by a sort of paralysis; but this
was pleasant and good for me. On returning home I deferred for a
time my desire to embrace all mankind.

25   I had however one other acquaintance of a sort, Simonov, who
was an old schoolfellow. I had a number of schoolfellows, indeed,
in Petersburg, but I did not associate with them and had even given
up nodding to them in the street. I believe I had transferred into the
department I was in simply to avoid their company and to cut off
30   all connection with my hateful childhood. Curses on that school
and all those terrible years of penal servitude! In short, I parted
from my schoolfellows as soon as I got out into the world. There
were two or three left to whom I nodded in the street. One of them
was Simonov, who had in no way been distinguished at school, was
35   of a quiet and equable disposition; but I discovered in him a certain
independence of character and even honesty. I don't even suppose
that he was particularly stupid. I had at one time spent some rather
soulful moments with him, but these had not lasted long and had
somehow been suddenly clouded over. He was evidently uncom-
40   fortable at these reminiscences, and was, I fancy, always afraid that
I might take up the same tone again. I suspected that he had an
aversion for me, but still I went on going to see him, not being quite
certain of it.

     And so on one occasion, unable to endure my solitude and
45   knowing that as it was Thursday Anton Antonitch's door would be

closed, I thought of Simonov. Climbing up to his fourth storey I was thinking that the man disliked me and that it was a mistake to go and see him. But as it always happened that such reflections impelled me, as though purposely, to put myself into a false posi-
5   tion, I went in. It was almost a year since I had last seen Simonov.

III

I found two of my old schoolfellows with him. They seemed to be discussing an important matter. All of them took scarcely any notice of my entrance, which was strange, for I had not met them for years. Evidently they looked upon me as something on the level of
10   a common fly. I had not been treated like that even at school, though they all hated me. I knew, of course, that they must despise me now for my lack of success in the service, and for my having let myself sink so low, going about badly dressed and so on—which seemed to them a sign of my incapacity and insignificance. But I had not
15   expected such contempt. Simonov was positively surprised at my turning up. Even in old days he had always seemed surprised at my coming. All this disconcerted me: I sat down, feeling rather miserable, and began listening to what they were saying.
They were engaged in warm and earnest conversation about a
20   farewell dinner which they wanted to arrange for the next day to a comrade of theirs called Zverkov, an officer in the army, who was going away to a distant province. This Zverkov had been all the time at school with me too. I had begun to hate him particularly in the upper forms. In the lower forms he had simply been a pretty,
25   playful boy whom everybody liked. I had hated him, however, even in the lower forms, just because he was a pretty and playful boy. He was always bad at his lessons and got worse and worse as he went on; however, he left with a good certificate, as he had powerful interests. During his last year at school he came in for an estate of
30   two hundred serfs, and as almost all of us were poor he took up a swaggering tone among us. He was vulgar in the extreme, but at the same time he was a good-natured fellow, even in his swaggering. In spite of superficial, fantastic and sham notions of honour and dignity, all but very few of us positively grovelled before Zverkov, and
35   the more so the more he swaggered. And it was not from any interested motive that they grovelled, but simply because he had been favoured by the gifts of nature. Moreover, it was, as it were, an accepted idea among us that Zverkov was a specialist in regard to tact and the social graces. This last fact particularly infuriated me. I
40   hated the abrupt self-confident tone of his voice, his admiration of his own witticisms, which were often frightfully stupid, though he was bold in his language; I hated his handsome, but stupid face (for

which I would, however, have gladly exchanged my intelligent one), and the free-and-easy military manners in fashion in the "forties." I hated the way in which he used to talk of his future conquests of women (he did not venture to begin his attack upon 5 women until he had the epaulettes of an officer, and was looking forward to them with impatience), and boasted of the duels he would constantly be fighting. I remember how I, invariably so taciturn, suddenly fastened upon Zverkov, when one day talking at a leisure moment with his schoolfellows of his future relations with 10 the fair sex, and growing as sportive as a puppy in the sun, he all at once declared that he would not leave a single village girl on his estate unnoticed, that that was his *droit de seigneur*, and that if the peasants dared to protest he would have them all flogged and double the tax on them, the bearded rascals. Our servile rabble applaud-15 ed, but I attacked him, not from compassion for the girls and their fathers, but simply because they were applauding such an insect. I got the better of him on that occasion, but though Zverkov was stupid he was lively and impudent, and so laughed it off, and in such a way that my victory was not really complete; the laugh was on his 20 side. He got the better of me on several occasions afterwards, but without malice, jestingly, casually. I remained angrily and contemptuously silent and would not answer him. When we left school he made advances to me; I did not rebuff them, for I was flattered, but we soon parted and quite naturally. Afterwards I heard of his bar-25 rack-room success as a lieutenant, and of the fast life he was leading. Then there came other rumours—of his successes in the service. By then he had taken to cutting me in the street, and I suspected that he was afraid of compromising himself by greeting a personage as insignificant as me. I saw him once in the theatre, in the third tier of 30 boxes. By then he was wearing shoulder-straps. He was twisting and twirling about, ingratiating himself with the daughters of an ancient General. In three years he had gone off considerably, though he was still rather handsome and adroit. One could see that by the time he was thirty he would be corpulent. So it was to this Zverkov 35 that my schoolfellows were going to give a dinner on his departure. They had kept up with him for those three years, though privately they did not consider themselves on an equal footing with him, I am convinced of that.

Of Simonov's two visitors, one was Ferfitchkin, a Russianised 40 German—a little fellow with the face of a monkey, a blockhead who was always deriding everyone, a very bitter enemy of mine from our days in the lower forms—a vulgar, impudent, swaggering fellow, who affected a most sensitive feeling of personal honour, though, of course, he was a wretched little coward at heart. He was 45 one of those worshippers of Zverkov who made up to the latter

from interested motives, and often borrowed money from him. Simonov's other visitor, Trudolyubov, was a person in no way remarkable—a tall young fellow, in the army, with a cold face, fairly honest, though he worshipped success of every sort, and was
5 only capable of thinking of promotion. He was some sort of distant relation of Zverkov's, and this, foolish as it seems, gave him a certain importance among us. He always thought me of no consequence whatever; his behaviour to me, though not quite courteous, was tolerable.

10 "Well, with seven roubles each," said Trudolyubov, "twenty-one roubles between the three of us, we ought to be able to get a good dinner. Zverkov, of course, won't pay."

"Of course not, since we are inviting him," Simonov decided.

"Can you imagine," Ferfitchkin interrupted hotly and conceit-
15 edly, like some insolent flunkey boasting of his master the General's decorations, "Can you imagine that Zverkov will let us pay alone? He will accept from delicacy, but he will order half a dozen bottles of champagne."

"Do we want half a dozen for the four of us?" observed
20 Trudolyubov, taking notice only of the half dozen.

"So the three of us, with Zverkov for the fourth, twenty-one roubles, at the Hôtel de Paris at five o'clock tomorrow," Simonov, who had been asked to make the arrangements, concluded finally.

"How twenty-one roubles?" I asked in some agitation, with a
25 show-of being offended; "if you count me it will not be twenty-one, but twenty-eight roubles."

It seemed to me that to invite myself so suddenly and unexpectedly would be positively graceful, and that they would all be conquered at once and would look at me with respect.

30 "Do you want to join, too?" Simonov observed, with no appearance of pleasure, seeming to avoid looking at me. He knew me through and through.

It infuriated me that he knew me so thoroughly.

"Why not? I am an old schoolfellow of his, too, I believe, and I
35 must own I feel hurt that you have left me out," I said, boiling over again.

"And where were we to find you?" Ferfitchkin put in roughly.

"You never were on good terms with Zverkov," Trudolyubov added, frowning.

40 But I had already clutched at the idea and would not give it up.

"It seems to me that no one has a right to form an opinion upon that," I retorted in a shaking voice, as though something tremendous had happened. "Perhaps that is just my reason for wishing it now, that I have not always been on good terms with him."

45 "Oh, there's no making you out . . . with these refinements,"

Trudolyubov jeered.

"We'll put your name down," Simonov decided, addressing me. "Tomorrow at five-o'clock at the Hôtel de Paris."

"What about the money?" Ferfitchkin began in an undertone, indicating me to Simonov, but he broke off, for even Simonov was embarrassed.

"That will do," said Trudolyubov, getting up. "If he wants to come so much, let him."

"But it's a private thing, between us friends," Ferfitchkin said crossly, as he, too, picked up his hat. "It's not an official gathering."

"We do not want at all, perhaps . . ."

They went away. Ferfitchkin did not greet me in any way as he went out, Trudolyubov barely nodded. Simonov, with whom I was left *tête-à-tête*, was in a state of vexation and perplexity, and looked at me queerly. He did not sit down and did not ask me to.

"H'm . . . yes . . . tomorrow, then. Will you pay your subscription now? I must ask so as to know," he muttered in embarrassment.

I flushed crimson, as I did so I remembered that I had owed Simonov fifteen roubles for ages—which I had, indeed, never forgotten, though I had not paid it.

"You will understand, Simonov, that I could have no idea when I came here. . . . I am very much vexed that I have forgotten. . . ."

"All right, all right, that doesn't matter. You can pay tomorrow after the dinner. I simply wanted to know . . . Please don't. . . ."

He broke off and began pacing the room still more vexed. As he walked he began to stamp with his heels.

"Am I keeping you?" I asked, after two minutes of silence.

"Oh!" he said, starting, "that is—to be truthful—yes. I have to go and see someone . . . not far from here," he added in an apologetic voice, somewhat abashed.

"My goodness, why didn't you say so?" I cried, seizing my cap, with an astonishingly free-and-easy air, which was the last thing I should have expected of myself.

"It's close by . . . not two paces away," Simonov repeated, accompanying me to the front door with a fussy air which did not suit him at all. "So five o'clock, punctually, tomorrow," he called down the stairs after me. He was very glad to get rid of me. I was in a fury.

"What possessed me, what possessed me to force myself upon them?" I wondered, grinding my teeth as I strode along the street, "for a scoundrel, a pig like that Zverkov! Of course I had better not go; of course, I must just snap my fingers at them. I am not bound in any way. I'll send Simonov a note by tomorrow's post. . . ."

But what made me furious was that I knew for certain that I

should go, that I should make a point of going; and the more tactless, the more unseemly my going would be, the more certainly I
would go.

And there was a positive obstacle to my going: I had no money.
5   All I had was nine roubles, I had to give seven of that to my servant,
Apollon, for his monthly wages. That was all I paid him—he had to
keep himself.

Not to pay him was impossible, considering his character. But
I will talk about that fellow, about that plague of mine, another time.
10   However, I knew I should go and should not pay him his
wages.

That night I had the most hideous dreams. No wonder; all the
evening I had been oppressed by memories of my miserable days at
school, and I could not shake them off. I was sent to the school by
15   distant relations, upon whom I was dependent and of whom I have
heard nothing since—they sent me there a forlorn, silent boy,
already crushed by their reproaches, already troubled by doubt,
and looking with savage distrust at everyone. My schoolfellows
met me with spiteful and merciless jibes because I was not like any
20   of them. But I could not endure their taunts; I could not give in to
them with the ignoble readiness with which they gave in to one
another. I hated them from the first, and shut myself away from
everyone in timid, wounded and disproportionate pride. Their
coarseness revolted me. They laughed cynically at my face, at my
25   clumsy figure; and yet what stupid faces they had themselves. In
our school the boys' faces seemed in a special way to degenerate
and grow stupider. How many fine-looking boys came to us! In a
few years they became repulsive. Even at sixteen I wondered at
them morosely; even then I was struck by the pettiness of their
30   thoughts, the stupidity of their pursuits, their games, their conver-
sations. They had no understanding of such essential things, they
took no interest in such striking, impressive subjects, that I could
not help considering them inferior to myself. It was not wounded
vanity that drove me to it, and for God's sake do not thrust upon me
35   your hackneyed remarks, repeated to nausea, that "I was only a
dreamer," while they even then had an understanding of life. They
understood nothing, they had no idea of real life, and I swear that
that was what made me most indignant with them. On the contrary,
the most obvious, striking reality they accepted with fantastic stu-
40   pidity and even at that time were accustomed to respect success.
Everything that was just, but oppressed and looked down upon,
they laughed at heartlessly and shamefully. They took rank for
intelligence; even at sixteen they were already talking about a snug
berth. Of course, a great deal of it was due to their stupidity, to the
45   bad examples with which they had always been surrounded in their

childhood and boyhood. They were monstrously depraved. Of course a great deal of that, too, was superficial and an assumption of cynicism; of course there were glimpses of youth and freshness even in their depravity; but even that freshness was not attractive,
5 and showed itself in a certain rakishness. I hated them horribly, though perhaps I was worse than any of them. They repaid me in the same way, and did not conceal their aversion for me. But by then I did not desire their affection: on the contrary, I continually longed for their humiliation. To escape from their derision I purposely
10 began to make all the progress I could with my studies and forced my way to the very top. This impressed them. Moreover, they all began by degrees to grasp that I had already read books none of them could read, and understood things (not forming part of our school curriculum) of which they had not even heard. They took a
15 savage and sarcastic view of it, but were morally impressed, especially as the teachers began to notice me on those grounds. The mockery ceased, but the hostility remained, and cold and strained relations became permanent between us. In the end I could not put up with it: with years a craving for society, for friends, developed in
20 me. I attempted to get on friendly terms with some of my schoolfellows; but somehow or other my intimacy with them was always strained and soon ended of itself. Once, indeed, I did have a friend. But I was already a tyrant at heart; I wanted to exercise unbounded sway over him; I tried to instil into him a contempt for his sur-
25 roundings; I required of him a disdainful and complete break with those surroundings. I frightened him with my passionate affection; I reduced him to tears, to hysterics. He was a simple and devoted soul; but when he devoted himself to me entirely I began to hate him immediately and repulsed him—as though all I needed him for
30 was to win a victory over him, to subjugate him and nothing else. But I could not subjugate all of them; my friend was not at all like them either, he was, in fact, a rare exception. The first thing I did on leaving school was to give up the special job for which I had been destined so as to break all ties, to curse my past and shake the dust
35 from off my feet. . . . And goodness knows why, after all that, I should go trudging off to Simonov's!

Early next morning I roused myself and jumped out of bed with excitement, as though it were all about to happen at once. But I believed that some radical change in my life was coming, and
40 would inevitably come that day. Owing to its rarity, perhaps, any external event, however trivial, always made me feel as though some radical change in my life were at hand. I went to the office, however, as usual, but sneaked away home two hours earlier to get ready. The great thing, I thought, is not to be the first to arrive, or
45 they will think I am overjoyed at coming. But there were thousands

of such great points to consider, and they all agitated and overwhelmed me. I polished my boots a second time with my own
hands; nothing in the world would have induced Apollon to clean
them twice a day, as he considered that it was more than his duties
5   required of him. I stole the brushes to clean them from the passage,
being careful he should not detect it, for fear of his contempt. Then
I minutely examined my clothes and thought that everything
looked old, worn and threadbare. I had let myself get too slovenly.
My uniform, perhaps, was tidy, but I could not go out to dinner in
10   my uniform. The worst of it was that on the knee of my trousers was
a big yellow stain. I had a foreboding that that stain would deprive
me of nine-tenths of my personal dignity. I knew, too, that it was
very poor to think so. "But this is no time for thinking: now I am in
for the real thing," I thought, and my heart sank. I knew, too, per-
15   fectly well even then, that I was monstrously exaggerating the facts.
But how could I help it? I could not control myself and was already
shaking with fever. With despair I pictured to myself how coldly
and disdainfully that "scoundrel" Zverkov would meet me; with
what dull-witted, invincible contempt the blockhead Trudolyubov
20   would look at me; with what impudent rudeness the insect
Ferfitchkin would snigger at me in order to curry favour with
Zverkov; how completely Simonov would take it all in, and how he
would despise me for the abjectness of my vanity and lack of spirit—and, worst of all, how paltry, *unliterary*, commonplace it would
25   all be. Of course, the best thing would be not to go at all. But that
was most impossible of all: if I feel impelled to do anything, I seem
to be pitchforked into it. I should have jeered at myself ever afterwards: "So you funked it, you funked it, you funked the *real thing!*"
On the contrary, I passionately longed to show all that "rabble" that
30   I was by no means such a spiritless creature as I seemed to myself.
What is more, even in the acutest paroxysm of this cowardly fever,
I dreamed of getting the upper hand, of dominating them, carrying
them away, making them like me—if only for my "elevation of
thought and unmistakable wit." They would abandon Zverkov, he
35   would sit on one side, silent and ashamed, while I should crush
him. Then, perhaps, we would be reconciled and drink to our everlasting friendship; but what was most bitter and humiliating for me
was that I knew even then, knew fully and for certain, that I needed nothing of all this really, that I did not really want to crush, to
subdue, to attract them, and that I did not care a straw really for the
result, even if I did achieve it. Oh, how I prayed for the day to pass
quickly! In unutterable anguish I went to the window, opened the
40   movable pane and looked out into the troubled darkness of the
thickly falling wet snow. At last my wretched little clock hissed out
five. I seized my hat and, trying not to look at Apollon, who had

been all day expecting his month's wages, but in his foolishness was unwilling to be the first to speak about it, I slipped between him and the door and, jumping into a high-class sledge, on which I spent my last half rouble, I drove up in grand style to the Hôtel de
5   Paris.

IV

I had been certain the day before that I should be the first to arrive. But it was not a question of being the first to arrive. Not only were they not there, but I had difficulty in finding our room. The table was not laid even. What did it mean? After a good many ques-
10   tions I elicited from the waiters that the dinner had been ordered not for five, but for six o'clock. This was confirmed at the buffet too. I felt really ashamed to go on questioning them. It was only twenty-five minutes past five. If they changed the dinner hour they ought at least to have let me know—that is what the post is for, and
15   not to have put me in an absurd position in my own eyes and . . . and even before the waiters. I sat down; the servant began laying the table; I felt even more humiliated when he was present. Towards six o'clock they brought in candles, though there were lamps burning in the room. It had not occurred to the waiter, how-
20   ever, to bring them in at once when I arrived. In the next room two gloomy, angry-looking persons were eating their dinners in silence at two different tables. There was a great deal of noise, even shouting, in a room further away; one could hear the laughter of a crowd of people, and nasty little shrieks in French: there were ladies at the
25   dinner. It was sickening, in fact. I rarely passed more unpleasant moments, so much so that when they did arrive all together punctually at six I was overjoyed to see them, as though they were my deliverers, and even forgot that it was incumbent upon me to show resentment.
30   Zverkov walked in at the head of them; evidently he was the leading spirit. He and all of them were laughing; but, seeing me, Zverkov drew himself up a little, walked up to me deliberately with a slight, rather jaunty bend from the waist. He shook hands with me in a friendly, but not overfriendly, fashion, with a sort of circum-
35   spect courtesy like that of a General, as though in giving me his hand he were warding off something. I had imagined, on the contrary, that on coming in he would at once break into his habitual thin, shrill laugh and fall to making his insipid jokes and witticisms. I had been preparing for them ever since the previous day, but I had
40   not expected such condescension, such high-official courtesy. So, then, he felt himself ineffably superior to me in every respect! If he only meant to insult me by that high-official tone, it would not mat-

ter, I thought—I could pay him back for it one way or another. But what if, in reality, without the least desire to be offensive, that sheepshead had a notion in earnest that he was superior to me and could only look at me in a patronising way? The very supposition
5   made me gasp.

"I was surprised to hear of your desire to join us," he began, lisping and drawling, which was something new. "You and I seem to have seen nothing of one another. You fight shy of us. You shouldn't. We are not such terrible people as you think. Well, any-
10   way, I am glad to renew our acquaintance."

And he turned carelessly to put down his hat on the window.

"Have you been waiting long?" Trudolyubov inquired.

"I arrived at five o'clock as you told me yesterday," I answered aloud, with an irritability that threatened an explosion.
15   "Didn't you let him know that we had changed the hour?" said Trudolyubov to Simonov.

"No, I didn't. I forgot," the latter replied, with no sign of regret, and without even apologising to me he went off to order the *hors d'oeuvre*.
20   "So you've been here a whole hour? Oh, poor fellow!" Zverkov cried ironically, for to his notions this was bound to be extremely funny. That rascal Ferfitchkin followed with his nasty little snigger like a puppy yapping. My position struck him, too, as exquisitely ludicrous and embarrassing.
25   "It isn't funny at all!" I cried to Ferfitchkin, more and more irritated. "It wasn't my fault, but other people's. They neglected to let me know. It was . . . it was . . . it was simply absurd."

"It's not only absurd, but something else as well," muttered Trudolyubov, naïvely taking my part. "You are not hard enough
30   upon it. It was simply rudeness—unintentional, of course. And how could Simonov . . . h'm!"

"If a trick like that had been played on me," observed Ferfitchkin, "I should . . ."

"But you should have ordered something for yourself,"
35   Zverkov interrupted, "or simply asked for dinner without waiting for us."

"You will allow that I might have done that without your permission," I rapped out. "If I waited, it was. . . ."

"Let us sit down, gentlemen," cried Simonov, coming in.
40   "Everything is ready; I can answer for the champagne; it is capitally frozen. . . . You see, I did not know your address, where was I to look for you?" he suddenly turned to me, but again he seemed to avoid looking at me. Evidently he had something against me. It must have been what happened yesterday.
45   All sat down; I did the same. It was a round table. Trudolyubov

was on my left, Simonov on my right, Zverkov was sitting opposite, Ferfitchkin next to him, between him and Trudolyubov.

"Tell me, are you . . . in a government office?" Zverkov went on attending to me. Seeing that I was embarrassed he seriously
5   thought that he ought to be friendly to me, and, so to speak, cheer me up.

"Does he want me to throw a bottle at his head?" I thought, in a fury. In my novel surroundings I was unnaturally ready to be irritated.

10   "In the N—— office," I answered jerkily, with my eyes on my plate.

"And ha-ave you a go-od berth? I say, what ma-a-de you leave your original job?"

"What ma-a-de me was that I wanted to leave my original job,"
15   I drawled more than he, hardly able to control myself. Ferfitchkin went off into a guffaw. Simonov looked at me ironically. Trudolyubov left off eating and began looking at me with curiosity.

Zverkov winced, but he tried not to notice it.

"And the remuneration?"
20   "What remuneration?"

"I mean, your sa-a-lary?"

"Why are you cross-examining me?" However, I told him at once what my salary was. I turned horribly red.

"It is not very handsome," Zverkov observed majestically.
25   "Yes, you can't afford to dine at cafés on that," Ferfitchkin added insolently.

"To my thinking it's very poor," Trudolyubov observed gravely.

"And how thin you have grown! How you have changed!"
30   added Zverkov, with a shade of venom in his voice, scanning me and my attire with a sort of insolent compassion.

"Oh, spare his blushes," cried Ferfitchkin, sniggering.

"My dear sir, allow me to tell you I am not blushing," I broke out at last; "do you hear? I am dining here, at this café, at my own
35   expense, not at other people's—note that, Mr. Ferfitchkin."

"Wha-at? Isn't every one here dining at his own expense? You would seem to be . . ." Ferfitchkin flew out at me, turning as red as a lobster, and looking me in the face with fury

"Tha-at," I answered, feeling I had gone too far, "and I imagine
40   it would be better to talk of something more intelligent."

"You intend to show off your intelligence, I suppose?"

"Don't disturb yourself, that would be quite out of place here."

"Why are you clacking away like that, my good sir, eh? Have you gone out of your wits in your office?"
45   "Enough, gentlemen, enough!" Zverkov cried, authoritatively.

"How stupid it is!" muttered Simonov.

"It really is stupid. We have met here, a company of friends, for a farewell dinner to a comrade and you carry on an altercation," said Trubolyubov, rudely addressing himself to me alone. "You invited yourself to join us, so don't disturb the general harmony."

"Enough, enough!" cried Zverkov. "Give over, gentlemen, it's out of place. Better let me tell you how I nearly got married the day before yesterday. . . ."

And then followed a burlesque narrative of how this gentleman had almost been married two days before. There was not a word about the marriage, however, but the story was adorned with generals, colonels and kammer-junkers, while Zverkov almost took the lead among them. It was greeted with approving laughter; Ferfitchkin positively squealed.

No one paid any attention to me, and I sat crushed and humiliated.

"Good Heavens, these are not the people for me!" I thought. "And what a fool I have made of myself before them! I let Ferfitchkin go too far, though. The brutes imagine they are doing me an honour in letting me sit down with them. They don't understand that it's an honour to them and not to me! I've grown thinner! My clothes! Oh, damn my trousers! Zverkov noticed the yellow stain on the knee as soon as he came in. . . . But what's the use! I must get up at once, this very minute, take my hat and simply go without a word . . . with contempt! And tomorrow I can send a challenge. The scoundrels! As though I cared about the seven roubles. They may think. . . . Damn it! I don't care about the seven roubles. I'll go this minute!"

Of course I remained. I drank sherry and Lafitte by the glassful in my discomfiture. Being unaccustomed to it, I was quickly affected. My annoyance increased as the wine went to my head. I longed all at once to insult them all in a most flagrant manner and then go away. To seize the moment and show what I could do, so that they would say, "He's clever, though he is absurd," and . . . and . . . in fact, damn them all!

I scanned them all insolently with my drowsy eyes. But they seemed to have forgotten me altogether. They were noisy, vociferous, cheerful. Zverkov was talking all the time. I began listening. Zverkov was talking of some exuberant lady whom he had at last led on to declaring her love (of course, he was lying like a horse), and how he had been helped in this affair by an intimate friend of his, a Prince Kolya, an officer in the hussars, who had three thousand serfs.

"And yet this Kolya, who has three thousand serfs, has not put in an appearance here tonight to see you off," I cut in suddenly.

For one minute every one was silent. "You are drunk already." Trudolyubov deigned to notice me at last, glancing contemptuously in my direction. Zverkov, without a word, examined me as though I were an insect. I dropped my eyes. Simonov made haste to

5   fill up the glasses with champagne.

Trudolyubov raised his glass, as did everyone else but me.

"Your health and good luck on the journey!" he cried to Zverkov. "To old times, to our future, hurrah!"

They all tossed off their glasses, and crowded round Zverkov

10   to kiss him. I did not move; my full glass stood untouched before me.

"Why, aren't you going to drink it?" roared Trudolyubov, losing patience and turning menacingly to me.

"I want to make a speech separately, on my own

15   account . . . and then I'll drink it, Mr. Trudolyubov."

"Spiteful brute!" muttered Simonov. I drew myself up in my chair and feverishly seized my glass, prepared for something extraordinary, though I did not know myself precisely what I was going to say

20   "*Silence!*" cried Ferfitchkin. "Now for a display of wit!"

Zverkov waited very gravely, knowing what was coming.

"Mr. Lieutenant Zverkov," I began, "let me tell you that I hate phrases, phrasemongers and men in corsets . . . that's the first point, and there is a second one to follow it."

25   There was a general stir.

"The second point is: I hate ribaldry and ribald talkers. Especially ribald talkers! The third point: I love justice, truth and honesty." I went on almost mechanically, for I was beginning to shiver with horror myself and had no idea how I came to be talking

30   like this. "I love thought, Monsieur Zverkov; I love true comradeship, on an equal footing and not . . . H'm . . . I love . . . But, however, why not? I will drink your health, too, Mr. Zverkov. Seduce the Circassian girls, shoot the enemies of the fatherland and . . . and . . . to your health, Monsieur Zverkov!"

35   Zverkov got up from his seat, bowed to me and said:

"I am very much obliged to you." He was frightfully offended and turned pale.

"Damn the fellow!" roared Trudolyubov, bringing his fist down on the table.

40   "Well, he wants a punch in the face for that," squealed Ferfitchkin.

"We ought to turn him out," muttered Simonov.

"Not a word, gentlemen, not a movement!" cried Zverkov solemnly, checking the general indignation. "I thank you all, but I

45   can show him for myself how much value I attach to his words."

"Mr. Ferfitchkin, you will give me satisfaction tomorrow for your words just now!" I said aloud, turning with dignity to Ferfitchkin.

"A duel, you mean? Certainly," he answered. But probably I
5 was so ridiculous as I challenged him and it was so out of keeping with my appearance that everyone including Ferfitchkin was prostrate with laughter.

"Yes, let him alone, of course! He is quite drunk," Trodulyubov said with disgust.

10 "I shall never forgive myself for letting him join us," Simonov muttered again.

"Now is the time to throw a bottle at their heads," I thought to myself. I picked up the bottle . . . and filled my glass. . . . "No, I'd better sit on to the end, " I went on thinking; "you would be
15 pleased, my friends, if I went away. Nothing will induce me to go. I'll go on sitting here and drinking to the end, on purpose, as a sign that I don't think you of the slightest consequence. I will go on sitting and drinking, because this is a public-house and I paid my entrance money. I'll sit here and drink, for I look upon you as so
20 many pawns, as inanimate pawns. I'll sit here and drink . . . and sing if I want to, yes, sing, for I have the right to . . . to sing . . . H'm!"

But I did not sing, I simply tried not to look at any of them. I assumed most unconcerned attitudes and waited with impatience for them to speak *first*. But alas, they did not address me! And oh,
25 how I wished, how I wished at that moment to be reconciled to them! It struck eight, at last nine. They moved from the table to the sofa. Zverkov stretched himself on a lounge and put one foot on a round table. Wine was brought there. He did, as a fact, order three bottles on his own account. I, of course, was not invited to join
30 them. They all sat round him on the sofa. They listened to him, almost with reverence. It was evident that they were fond of him. "What for? What for?" I wondered. From time to time they were moved to drunken enthusiasm and kissed each other. They talked of the Caucasus, of the nature of true passion, of snug berths in the
35 service, of the income of an hussar called Podharzhevsky, whom none of them knew personally, and rejoiced in the largeness of it, of the extraordinary grace and beauty of a Princess D., whom none of them had ever seen; then it came to Shakespeare being immortal.

I smiled comtemptuously and walked up and down the other
40 side of the room, opposite the sofa, from the table to the stove and back again. I tried my very utmost to show them that I could do without them, and yet I purposely made a noise with my boots, thumping with my heels. But it was all in vain. They paid no attention. I had the patience to walk up and down in front of them from
45 eight o'clock till eleven, in the same place, from the table to the

stove and back again. "I walk up and down to please myself and no one can prevent me." The waiter who came into the room stopped, from time to time, to look at me. I was somewhat giddy from turning round so often; at moments it seemed to me that I was in delir-
5 ium. During those three hours I was three times soaked with sweat and dry again. At times, with an intense, acute pang I was stabbed to the heart by the thought that ten years, twenty years, forty years would pass, and that even in forty years I would remember with loathing and humiliation those filthiest, most ludicrous, and most
10 awful moments of my life. No one could have gone out of his way to degrade himself more shamelessly, and I fully realised it, fully, and yet I went on pacing up and down from the table to the stove. "Oh, if you only knew what thoughts and feelings I am capable of, how cultured I am!" I thought at moments, mentally addressing the
15 sofa on which my enemies were sitting. But my enemies behaved as though I were not in the room. Once—only once—they turned towards me, just when Zverkov was talking about Shakespeare, and I suddenly gave a contemptuous laugh. I laughed in such an affected and disgusting way that they all at once broke off their con-
20 versation, and silently and gravely for two minutes watched me walking up and down from the table to the stove, *taking no notice of them.* But nothing came of it: they said nothing, and two minutes later they ceased to notice me again. It struck eleven.

"Friends," cried Zverkov getting up from the sofa, "let us all be
25 off now, *there!*"

"Of course, of course," the others assented. I turned sharply to Zverkov. I was so harassed, so exhausted, that I would have cut my throat to put an end to it. I was in a fever; my hair, soaked with per-spiration, stuck to my forehead and temples.
30 "Zverkov, I beg your pardon," I said abruptly and resolutely. Ferfitchkin, yours too, and everyone's, everyone's: I have insulted you all!"

"Aha! A duel is not in your line, old man," Ferfitchkin hissed venomously.
35 It sent a sharp pang to my heart.

"No, it's not the duel I am afraid of, Ferfitchkin! I am ready to fight you tomorrow, after we are reconciled. I insist upon it, in fact, and you cannot refuse. I want to show you that I am not afraid of a duel. You shall fire first and I shall fire into the air."
40 "He is comforting himself," said Simonov.

"He's simply raving," said Trubolyudov.

"But let us pass. Why are you barring our way? What do you want?" Zverkov answered disdainfully.

They were all flushed, their eyes were bright: they had been
45 drinking heavily.

"I ask for your friendship, Zverkov; I insulted you, but . . ."

"Insulted? *You* insulted *me?* Understand, sir, that you never, under any circumstances, could possibly insult *me.*"

"And that's enough for you. Out of the way!" concluded
5   Trudolyubov.

"Olympia is mine, friends, that's agreed!" cried Zverkov.

"We won't dispute your right, we won't dispute your right," the others answered, laughing.

I stood as though spat upon. The party went noisily out of the
10   room. Trudolyubov struck up some stupid song. Simonov remained behind for a moment to tip the waiters. I suddenly went up to him.

"Simonov! give me six roubles!" I said, with desperate resolution.

He looked at me in extreme amazement, with vacant eyes. He, too, was drunk.

15   "You don't mean you are coming with us?"

"Yes."

"I've no money," he snapped out, and with a scornful laugh he went out of the room.

I clutched at his overcoat. It was a nightmare.

20   "Simonov, I saw you had money. Why do you refuse me? Am I a scoundrel? Beware of refusing me: if you knew, if you knew why I am asking! My whole future, my whole plans depend upon it!"

Simonov pulled out the money and almost flung it at me.

"Take it, if you have no sense of shame!" he pronounced pitilessly, and ran to overtake them.

I was left for a moment alone. Disorder, the remains of dinner, a broken wine-glass on the floor, spilt wine, cigarette ends, fumes of
25   drink and delirium in my brain, an agonising misery in my heart and finally the waiter, who had seen and heard all and was looking inquisitively into my face.

"I am going there!" I cried. "Either they shall all go down on their knees to beg for my friendship, or I will give Zverkov a slap in
30   the face!"

V

"So this is it, this is it at last—contact with real life," I muttered as I ran headlong downstairs. "This is very different from the Pope's leaving Rome and going to Brazil, very different from the ball on Lake Como!"

35   "You are a scoundrel," a thought flashed through my mind, "if you laugh at this now."

"No matter!" I cried, answering myself. "Now everything is lost!"

There was no trace to be seen of them, but that made no difference—I knew where they had gone.

At the steps was standing a solitary night sledge-driver in a rough peasant coat, powdered over with the still falling, wet, and as it were warm, snow. It was hot and steamy. The little shaggy piebald horse was also covered with snow and coughing, I remember that very well. I made a rush for the roughly made sledge; but as soon as I raised my foot to get into it, the recollection of how Simonov had just given me six roubles seemed to double me up and I tumbled into the sledge like a sack.

"No, I must do a great deal to make up for all that," I cried. "But I will make up for it or perish on the spot this very night. Start!"

We set off. There was a perfect whirl in my head.

"They won't go down on their knees to beg for my friendship. That is a mirage, cheap mirage, revolting, romantic and fantastical—that's another ball on Lake Como. And so I am bound to slap Zverkov's face! It is my duty to. And so it is settled; I am flying to give him a slap in the face. Hurry up!"

The driver tugged at the reins.

"As soon as I go in I'll give it him. Ought I before giving him the slap to say a few words by way of preface? No. I'll simply go in and give it him. They will all be sitting in the drawing-room, and he with Olympia on the sofa. That damned Olympia! She laughed at my looks on one occasion and refused me. I'll pull Olympia's hair, pull Zverkov's ears! No, better one ear, and pull him by it round the room. Maybe they will all begin beating me and will kick me off. That's most likely, indeed. No matter! Anyway, I shall first slap him; the initiative will be mine; and by the laws of honour that is everything: he will be branded and cannot wipe off the slap by any blows, by nothing but a duel. He will be forced to fight. And let them beat me now. Let them, the ungrateful wretches! Trudolyubov will beat me hardest, he is so strong; Ferfitchkin will be sure to catch hold sideways and tug at my hair. But no matter, no matter! That's what I am going for. The blockheads will be forced at last to see the tragedy of it all! When they drag me to the door I shall call out to them that in reality they are not worth my little finger. Get on, driver, get on!" I cried to the driver. He started and flicked his whip, I shouted so savagely.

"We shall fight at daybreak, that's a settled, thing. I've done with the office. Ferfitchkin made a joke about it just now. But where can I get pistols? Nonsense! I'll get my salary in advance and buy them. And powder, and bullets? That's the second's business. And how can it all be done by daybreak? and where am I to get a second? I have no friends. Nonsense!" I cried, lashing myself up more and more. "It's of no consequence! the first person I meet in the street is

bound to be my second, just as he would be bound to pull a drowning man out of water. The most eccentric things may happen. Even if I were to ask the director himself to be my second tomorrow, he would be bound to consent, if only from a feeling of chivalry, and to
5   keep the secret! Anton Antonitch. . . ."

    The fact is, that at that very minute the disgusting absurdity of my plan and the other side of the question was clearer and more vivid to my imagination than it could be to anyone on earth. But . . .

    "Get on, driver, get on, you rascal, get on!"
10   "Ugh, sir!" said the son of toil.

    Cold shivers suddenly ran down me. Wouldn't it be better . . . to go straight home? My God, my God! Why did I invite myself to this dinner yesterday? But no, it's impossible. And my walking up and down for three hours from the table to the stove?
15   No, they, they and no one else must pay for my walking up and down! They must wipe out this dishonour! Drive on!

    And what if they give me into custody? They won't dare! They'll be afraid of the scandal. And what if Zverkov is so contemptuous that he refuses to fight a duel? He is sure to; but in that
20   case I'll show them . . . I will turn up at the posting station when he is setting off tomorrow, I'll catch him by the leg, I'll pull off his coat when he gets into the carriage. I'll get my teeth into his hand, I'll bite him. "See what lengths you can drive a desperate man to!" He may hit me on the head and they may belabour me from behind. I
25   will shout to the assembled multitude: "Look at this young puppy who is driving off to captivate the Circassian girls after letting me spit in his face!"

    Of course, after that everything will be over! The office will have vanished off the face of the earth. I shall be arrested, I shall be
30   tried, I shall be dismissed from the service, thrown in prison, sent to Siberia. Never mind! In fifteen years when they let me out of prison I will trudge off to him, a beggar, in rags. I shall find him in some provincial, town. He will be married and happy. He will have a grown-up daughter. . . . I shall say to him: "Look, monster, at my
35   hollow cheeks and my rags! I've lost everything—my career, my happiness, art, science, *the woman I loved,* and all through you. Here are pistols. I have come to discharge my pistol and . . . and I . . . forgive you. Then I shall fire into the air and he will hear nothing more of me. . . ."

40   I was actually on the point of tears, though I knew perfectly well at that moment that all this was out of Pushkin's *Silvio* and Lermontov's *Masquerade*. And all at once I felt horribly ashamed, so ashamed that I stopped the horse, got out of the sledge, and stood still in the snow in the middle of the street. The driver gazed at me,
45   sighing and astonished.

What was I to do? I could not go on there—it was evidently stupid, and I could not leave things as they were, because that would seem as though . . . Heavens, how could I leave things! And after such insults!

5 "No!" I cried, throwing myself into the sledge again. "It is ordained! It is fate! Drive on, drive on!"

And in my impatience I punched the sledge-driver on the back of the neck.

"What are you up to? What are you hitting me for?" the peas-
10 ant shouted, but he whipped up his nag so that it began kicking.

The wet snow was falling in big flakes; I unbuttoned myself, regardless of it. I forgot everything else, for I had finally decided on the slap, and felt with horror that it was going to happen *now, at once*, and that *no force could stop it*. The deserted street lamps
15 gleamed sullenly in the snowy darkness like torches at a funeral. The snow drifted under my great-coat, under my coat, under my cravat, and melted there. I did not wrap myself up—all was lost, anyway.

At last we arrived. I jumped out, almost unconscious, ran up
20 the steps and began knocking and kicking at the door. I felt fearfully weak, particularly in my legs and knees. The door was, opened quickly as though they knew I was coming. As a fact, Simonov had warned them that perhaps another gentleman would arrive, and this was a place in which one had to give notice and to observe cer-
25 tain precautions. It was one of those "millinery establishments" which were abolished by the police a good time ago. By day it really was a shop; but at night, if one had an introduction, one might visit it for other purposes.

I walked rapidly through the dark shop into the familiar draw-
30 ing-room, where there was only one candle burning, and stood still in amazement: there was no one there. "Where are they?" I asked somebody.

But by now, of course, they had separated. Before me was standing a person with a stupid smile, the "madam" herself, who
35 had seen me before. A minute later a door opened and another person came in.

Taking no notice of anything I strode about the room, and, I believe, I talked to myself. I felt as though I had been saved from death and was conscious of this, joyfully, all over: I should have
40 given that slap, I should certainly, certainly have given it! But now they were not here and . . . everything had vanished and changed! I looked round. I could not realise my condition yet. I looked mechanically at the girl who had come in: and had a glimpse of a fresh, young, rather pale face, with straight, dark eyebrows, and
45 with grave, as it were wondering, eyes that attracted me at once; I

should have hated her if she had been smiling. I began looking at her more intently and, as it were, with effort. I had not fully collect- ed my thoughts. There was something simple and good-natured in her face, but something strangely grave. I am sure that this stood in
5 her way here, and no one of those fools had noticed her. She could not, however, have been called a beauty, though she was tall, strong-looking, and well built. She was very simply dressed. Something loathsome stirred within me. I went straight up to her. I chanced to look into the glass. My harassed face struck me as revolt-
10 ing in the extreme, pale, angry, abject, with dishevelled hair. "No matter, I am glad of it," I thought; "I am glad that I shall seem repul- sive to her; I like that."

VI

. . . Somewhere behind a screen a clock began wheezing, as though oppressed by something, as though someone were stran-
15 gling it. After an unnaturally prolonged wheezing there followed a shrill, nasty, and as it were unexpectedly rapid, chime—as though someone were suddenly jumping forward. It struck two. I woke up, though I had indeed not been asleep but lying half-conscious.

It was almost completely dark in the narrow, cramped, low-
20 pitched room, cumbered up with an enormous wardrobe and piles of cardboard boxes and all sorts of frippery and litter. The candle end that had been burning on the table was going out and gave a faint flicker from time to time. In a few minutes there would be complete darkness.

25 I was not long in coming to myself; everything came back to my mind at once, without an effort, as though it had been in ambush to pounce upon me again. And, indeed, even while I was unconscious a point seemed continually to remain in my memory unforgotten, and round it my dreams moved drearily. But strange
30 to say, everything that had happened to me in that day seemed to me now, on waking, to be in the far, far away past, as though I had long, long ago lived all that down.

My head was full of fumes. Something seemed to be hovering over me, rousing me, exciting me, and making me restless. Misery
35 and spite seemed surging up in me again and seeking an outlet. Suddenly I saw beside me two wide open eyes scrutinising me curi- ously and persistently. The look in those eyes was coldly detached, sullen, as it were utterly remote; it weighed upon me.

A grim idea came into my brain and passed all over my body,
40 as a horrible sensation, such as one feels when one goes into a damp and mouldy cellar. There was something unnatural in those two eyes, beginning to look at me only now. I recalled, too, that during those two hours I had not said a single word to this creature, and

had, in fact, considered it utterly superfluous; in fact, the silence had for some reason gratified me. Now I suddenly realised vividly the hideous idea—revolting as a spider—of vice, which, without love, grossly and shamelessly begins with that in which true love

5   finds its consummation. For a long time we gazed at each other like that, but she did not drop her eyes before mine and her expression did not change, so that at last I felt uncomfortable.

"What is your name?" I asked abruptly, to put an end to it.

"Liza," she answered almost in a whisper, but somehow far

10   from graciously, and she turned her eyes away.

I was silent.

"What weather! The snow . . . it's disgusting!" I said, almost to myself, putting my arm under my head despondently, and gazing at the ceiling. She made no answer. This was horrible.

15   "Have you always lived in Petersburg?" I asked a minute later, almost angrily, turning my head slightly towards her.

"No."

"Where do you come from?"

"From Riga," she answered reluctantly.

20   "Are you a German?"

"No, Russian."

"Have you been here long?"

"Where?"

"In this house?"

25   "A fortnight."

She spoke more and more jerkily. The candle went out; I could no longer distinguish her face.

"Have you a father and mother?"

"Yes . . . no . . . I have."

30   "Where are they?"

"There . . . in Riga."

"What are they?"

"Oh, nothing."

"Nothing? Why, what class are they?"

35   "Tradespeople."

"Have you always lived with them?"

"Yes."

"How old are you?"

"Twenty."

40   "Why did you leave them?"

"Oh, for no reason."

That answer meant "Let me alone; I feel sick, sad."

We were silent.

God knows why I did not go away. I felt myself more and more

45   sick and dreary. The images of the previous day began of them-

selves, apart from my will, flitting through my memory in confusion. I suddenly recalled something I had seen that morning when, full of anxious thoughts, I was hurrying to the office.

5   "I saw them carrying a coffin out yesterday and they nearly dropped it," I suddenly said aloud, not that I desired to open the conversation, but as it were by accident.

    "A coffin?"

    "Yes, in the Haymarket; they were bringing it up out of a cellar."

10   "From a cellar?"

    "Not from a cellar, but a basement. Oh, you know . . . down below . . . from a house of ill-fame. It was filthy all round . . . Eggshells, litter . . . a stench. It was loathsome."

    Silence.

15   "A nasty day to be buried," I began, simply to avoid being silent.

    "Nasty, in what way?"

    "The snow, the wet." (I yawned.)

    "It makes no difference," she said suddenly, after a brief
20 silence.

    "No, it's horrid." (I yawned again). "The gravediggers must have sworn at getting drenched by the snow. And there must have been water in the grave."

    "Why water in the grave?" she asked, with a sort of curiosity,
25 but speaking even more harshly and abruptly than before.

    I suddenly began to feel provoked.

    "Why, there must have been water at the bottom a foot deep. You can't dig a dry grave in Volkovo Cemetery."

    "Why?"

30   "Why? Why, the place is waterlogged. It's a regular marsh. So they bury them in water. I've seen it myself . . . many times."

    (I had never seen it once, indeed I had never been in Volkovo, and had only heard stories of it.)

    "Do you mean to say, you don't mind how you die?"

35   "But why should I die?" she answered, as though defending herself.

    "Why, some day you will die, and you will die just the same as that dead woman. She was . . . a girl like you. She died of consumption."

40   "A wench would have died in hospital. (She knows all about it already: she said "wench," not "girl.")

    "She was in debt to her madam," I retorted, more and more provoked by the discussion, "and went on earning money for her up to the end, though she was in consumption. Some sledge-driv-
45 ers standing by were talking about her to some soldiers and telling

them so. No doubt they knew her. They were laughing. They were going to meet in a pot-house to drink to her memory."

A great deal of this was my invention. Silence followed, profound silence. She did not stir.

5 "And is it better to die in a hospital?"

"Isn't it just the same? Besides, why should I die?" she added irritably.

"If not now, a little later."

"Why a little later?"

10 "Why, indeed? Now you are young, pretty, fresh, you fetch a high price. But after another year of this life you will be very different—you will go off."

"In a year?"

"Anyway, in a year you will be worth less," I continued malig-
15 nantly. "You will go from here to something lower, another house; a year later—to a third, lower and lower, and in seven years you will come to a basement in the Haymarket. That will be if you were lucky. But it would much worse if you got some disease, consumption, say . . . and caught chill, or something or other. It's not easy to
20 get over an illness in your way of life. If you catch anything you may not get rid of it. And so you would die."

"Oh, well, then I shall die," she answered, quite vindictively, and she made a quick movement.

"But one is sorry."

25 "Sorry for whom?"

"Sorry for life."

Silence.

"Have you been engaged to be married? Eh?"

"What's that to you?"

30 "Oh, I am not cross-examining you. It's nothing to me. Why are you so cross? Of course you may have had your own troubles. What is it to me? It's simply that I felt sorry."

"Sorry for whom?"

"Sorry for you."

35 "No need," she whispered hardly audibly, and again made a faint movement.

That incensed me at once. What! I was so gentle with her, and she . . .

"Why, do you think that you are on the right path?"

40 "I don't think anything."

"That's what's wrong, that you don't think. Realise it while there is still time. There still is time. You are still young, good-looking; you might love, be married, be happy. . . ."

"Not all married women are happy," she snapped out in the
45 rude abrupt tone she had used at first.

"Not all, of course, but anyway it is much better than the life here. Infinitely better. Besides, with love one can live even without happiness. Even in sorrow life is sweet; life is sweet, however one lives. But here what is there but . . . foulness? Phew!"

5   I turned away with disgust; I was no longer reasoning coldly. I began to feel myself what I was saying and warmed to the subject. I was already longing to expound the cherished ideas I had brooded over in my corner. Something suddenly flared up in me. An object had appeared before me.

10   "Never mind my being here, I am not an example for you. I am, perhaps, worse than you are. I was drunk when I came here, though," I hastened, however, to say in self-defence. "Besides, a man is no example for a woman. It's a different thing. I may degrade and defile myself, but I am not anyone's slave. I come and

15 go, and that's an end of it. I shake it off, and I am a different man. But you are a slave from the start. Yes, a slave! You give up everything, your whole freedom. If you want to break your chains afterwards, you won't be able to; you will be more and more fast in the snares. It is an accursed bondage. I know it. I won't speak of any-

20 thing else, maybe you won't understand, but tell me: no doubt you are in debt to your madam? There, you see," I added, though she made no answer, but only listened in silence, entirely absorbed, "that's a bondage for you! You will never buy your freedom. They will see to that. It's like selling your soul to the devil. . . . And

25 besides . . . perhaps, I too, am just as unlucky—how do you know—and wallow in the mud on purpose, out of misery? You know, men take to drink from grief; well, maybe I am here from grief. Come, tell me, what is there good here? Here you and I . . . came together . . . just now and did not say one word to one another all the time,

30 and it was only afterwards you began staring at me like a wild creature, and I at you. Is that loving? Is that how one human being should meet another? It's hideous, that's what it is!"

"Yes!" she assented sharply and hurriedly.

I was positively astounded by the promptitude of this "Yes." So

35 the same thought may have been straying through her mind when she was staring at me just before. So she, too, was capable of certain thoughts? "Damn it all, this was interesting, this was a point of likeness!" I thought, almost rubbing my hands. And indeed it's easy to turn a young soul like that!

40   It was the exercise of my power that attracted me most.

She turned her head nearer to me, and it seemed to me in the darkness that she propped herself on her arm. Perhaps she was scrutinising me. How I regretted that I could not see her eyes. I heard her deep breathing.

45   "Why have you come here?" I asked her, with a note of author-

ity already in my voice.

"Oh, I don't know."

"But how nice it would be to be living in your father's house!
It's warm and free; you have a home of your own."

5   "But what if it's worse than this?"

"I must take the right tone," flashed through my mind. "I may
not get far with sentimentality." But it was only a momentary
thought. I swear she really did interest me. Besides, I was exhausted and moody. And cunning so easily goes hand-in-hand with feel-

10   ing.

"Who denies it!" I hastened to answer. "Anything may happen.
I am convinced that someone has wronged you, and that you are
more sinned against than sinning. Of course, I know nothing of
your story, but it's not likely a girl like you has come here of her

15   own inclination. . . ."

"A girl like me?" she whispered, hardly audibly; but I heard it.

Damn it all, I was flattering her. That was horrid. But perhaps
it was a good thing. . . . She was silent.

"See, Liza, I will tell you about myself. If I had had a home from

20   childhood, I shouldn't be what I am now. I often think that.
However bad it may be at home, anyway they are your father and
mother, and not enemies, strangers. Once a year at least, they'll
show their love of you. Anyway, you know you are at home. I grew
up without a home; and perhaps that's why I've turned

25   so . . . unfeeling."

I waited again. "Perhaps she doesn't understand," I thought,
"and, indeed, it is absurd—it's moralising."

"If I were a father and had a daughter, I believe I should love
my daughter more than my sons, really," I began indirectly, as

30   though talking of something else, to distract her attention. I must
confess I blushed.

"Why so?" she asked.

Ah! so she was listening!

"I don't know, Liza. I knew a father who was a stern, austere

35   man, but used to go down on his knees to his daughter, used to kiss
her hands, her feet, he couldn't make enough of her, really. When
she danced at parties he used to stand for five hours at a stretch,
gazing at her. He was mad over her: I understand that! She would
fall asleep tired at night, and he would wake to kiss her in her sleep

40   and make the sign of the cross over her. He would go about in a
dirty old coat, he was stingy to everyone else, but would spend his
last penny for her, giving her expensive presents, and it was his
greatest delight when she was pleased with what he gave her.
Fathers always love their daughters more than the mothers do.

45   Some girls live happily at home! And I believe I should never let my

daughters marry."

"What next?" she said, with a faint smile.

"I should be jealous, I really should. To think that she should kiss anyone else! That she should love a stranger more than her father! It's painful to imagine it. Of course, that's all nonsense, of course every father would be reasonable at last. But I believe before I should let her marry, I should worry myself to death; I should find fault with all her suitors. But I should end by letting her marry whom she herself loved. The one whom the daughter loves always seems the worst to the father, you know. That is always so. So many family troubles come from that."

"Some are glad to sell their daughters, rather than marrying them honourably."

Ah, so that was it!

"Such a thing, Liza, happens in those accursed families in which there is neither love nor God," I retorted warmly, "and where there is no love, there is no sense either. There are such families, it's true, but I am not speaking of them. You must have seen wickedness in your own family, if you talk like that. Truly, you must have been unlucky. H'm! . . . that sort of thing mostly comes about through poverty."

"And is it any better with the gentry? Even among the poor, honest people who live happily?"

"H'm . . . yes. Perhaps. Another thing, Liza, man is fond of reckoning up his troubles, but does not count his joys. If he counted them up as he ought, he would see that every lot has enough happiness provided for it. And what if all goes well with the family, if the blessing of God is upon it, if the husband is a good one, loves you, cherishes you, never leaves you! There is happiness in such a family! Even sometimes there is happiness in the midst of sorrow; and indeed sorrow is everywhere. If you marry *you will find out for yourself*. But think of the first years of married life with one you love: what happiness, what happiness there sometimes is in it! And indeed it's the ordinary thing. In those early days even quarrels with one's husband end happily Some women get up quarrels with their husbands just because they love them. Indeed, I knew a woman like that: she seemed to say that because she loved him, she would torment him and make him feel it. You know that you may torment a man on purpose through love. Women are particularly given to that, thinking to themselves, 'I will love him so, I will make so much of him afterwards, that it's no sin to torment him a little now.' And all in the house rejoice in the sight of you, and you are happy and gay and peaceful and honourable. . . . Then there are some women who are jealous. If he went off anywhere—I knew one such woman, she couldn't restrain herself, but would jump up at

night and run off on the sly to find out where he was, whether he
was with some other woman. That's a pity. And the woman knows
herself it's wrong, and her heart fails her and she suffers, but she
loves—it's all through love. And how sweet it is to make up after
5   quarrels, to own herself in the wrong or to forgive him! And they
both are so happy all at once—as though they had met anew, been
married over again; as though their love had begun afresh. And no
one, no one should know what passes between husband and wife if
they love one another. And whatever quarrels there may be
10   between them they ought not to call in their own mother to judge
between them and tell tales of one another. They are their own
judges. Love is a holy mystery and ought to be hidden from all
other eyes, whatever happens. That makes it holier and better. They
respect one another more, and much is built on respect. And if once
15   there has been love, if they have been married for love, why should
love pass away? Surely one can keep it! It is rare that one cannot
keep it. And if the husband is kind and straightforward, why
should not love last? The first phase of married love will pass, it is
true, but then there will come a love that is better still. Then there
20   will be the union of souls, they will have everything in common,
there will be no secrets between them. And once they have children,
the most difficult times will seem to them happy, so long as there is
love and courage. Even toil will be a joy, you may deny yourself
bread for your children and even that will be a joy. They will love
25   you for it afterwards; so you are laying by for your future. As the
children grow up you feel that you are an example, a support for
them; that even after you die your children will always keep your
thoughts and feelings, because they have received them from you,
they ill take on your semblance and likeness. So you see this is a
30   great duty. How can it fail to draw the father and mother nearer?
People say it's a trial to have children. Who says that? It is heavenly happiness! Are you fond of little children, Liza? I am awfully
fond of them. You know—a little rosy baby boy at your bosom, and
what husband's heart is not touched, seeing is wife nursing his
35   child! A plump little rosy baby, sprawling and juggling, chubby little hands and feet, clean tiny little nails, so tiny that makes one
laugh to look at them; eyes that look as if they understand everything. And while it sucks it clutches at your bosom with its little
hands, plays. When its father comes up, the child tears itself away
40   from the bosom, flings itself back, looks at its father, laughs, as
though it were fearfully funny, and falls to sucking again. Or it will
bite its mother's breast when its little teeth are coming, while it
looks sideways at her with its little eyes as though to say, 'Look, I
am biting!' Is not all that happiness when they are the three togeth-
45   er, husband, wife and child? One can forgive a great deal for the

sake of such moments. Yes, Liza, one must first learn to live oneself before one blames others!"

"It's by pictures, pictures like that one must get at you," I thought to myself, though I did speak with real feeling, and all at 5 once I flushed crimson. "What if she were suddenly to burst out laughing, what should I do then?" That idea drove me to fury. Towards the end of my speech I really was excited, and now my vanity was somehow wounded. The silence continued. I almost nudged her.

10 "Why are you—" she began and stopped. But I understood: there was a quiver of something different in her voice, not abrupt, harsh and unyielding as before, but something soft and shame-faced, so shamefaced that I suddenly felt ashamed and guilty.

"What?" I asked, with tender curiosity.

15 "Why, you . . ."

"What?"

"Why, you . . . speak somehow like a book," she said, and again there was a note of irony in her voice.

That remark sent a pang to my heart. It was not what I was 20 expecting.

I did not understand that she was hiding her feelings under irony, that this is usually the last refuge of modest and chaste-souled people when the privacy of their soul is coarsely and intrusively invaded, and that their pride makes them refuse to surrender 25 till the last moment and shrink from giving expression to their feelings before you. I ought to have guessed the truth from the timidity with which she had repeatedly approached her sarcasm, only bringing herself to utter it at last with an effort. But I did not guess, and an evil feeling took possession of me.

30 "Wait a bit!" I thought.

VII

"Oh, hush, Liza! How can you talk about being like a book, when it makes even me, an outsider, feel sick? Though I don't look at it as an outsider, for, indeed, it touches me to the heart. . . . Is it possible, is it possible that you do not feel sick at being here your-35 self? Evidently habit does wonders! God knows what habit can do with anyone. Can you seriously think that you will never grow old, that you will always be good looking, and that they will keep you here for ever and ever? I say nothing of the loathsomeness of the life here. . . . Though let me tell you this about it—about your present 40 life, I mean; here though you are young now, attractive, nice, with soul and feeling, yet you know as soon as I came to myself just now I felt at once sick at being here with you! One can only come here

when one is drunk. But if you were anywhere else, living as good people live, I should perhaps be more than attracted by you, should fall in love with you, should be glad of a look from you, let alone a word; I should hang about your door, should go down on my knees
5   to you, should look upon you as my betrothed and think it an honour to be allowed to. I should not dare to have an impure thought about you. But here, you see, I know that I have only to whistle and you have to come with me whether you like it or not. I don't consult your wishes, but you mine. The lowest labourer hires himself as
10 a workman, but he doesn't make a slave of himself altogether; besides, he knows that he will be free again presently. But when are you free? Only think what you, are giving up here? What is it you are making a slave of? It is your soul, together with your body; you are selling your soul which you have no right to dispose of! You
15 give your love to be outraged by every drunkard! Love! But that's everything, you know, it's a priceless diamond, it's a maiden's treasure, love—why, a man would be ready to give his soul, to face death to gain that love. But how much is your love worth now? You are sold, all of you, body and soul, and there is no need to strive for
20 love when you can have everything without love. And you know there is no greater insult to a girl than that, do you understand? To be sure, I have heard that they comfort you, poor fools, they let you have lovers of your own here. But you know that's simply a farce, that's simply a sham, it's just laughing at you, and you are taken in
25 by it! Why, do you suppose he really loves you, that lover of yours? I don't believe it. How can he love you when he knows you may be called away from him any minute? He would be a low fellow if he did! Will he have a grain of respect for you? What have you in common with him? He laughs at you and robs you—that is all his love
30 amounts to! You are lucky if he does not beat you. Very likely he does beat you, too. Ask him, if you have got one, whether he will marry you. He will laugh in your face, if he doesn't spit in it or give you a blow—though maybe he is not worth a bad halfpenny himself. And for what have you ruined your life, if you come to think of
35 it? For the coffee they give you to drink and the plentiful meals? But with what object are they feeding you up? An honest girl couldn't swallow the food, for she would know what she was being fed for. You are in debt here, and, of course, you will always be in debt, and you will go on in debt to the end, till the visitors here begin to scorn
40 you. And that will soon happen, don't rely upon your youth—all that flies by express train here, you know. You will be kicked out. And not simply kicked out; long before that she'll begin nagging at you, scolding you, abusing you, as though you had not sacrificed your health for her, had not thrown away your youth and your soul
45 for her benefit, but as though you had ruined her, beggared her,

robbed her. And don't expect anyone to take your part: the others,
your companions, will attack you, too, win her favour, for all are in
slavery here, and have lost all conscience and pity here long ago.
They have become utterly vile, and nothing on earth is viler, more
5   loathsome, and more insulting than their abuse. And you are laying
down everything here, unconditionally, youth and health and beauty and hope, and at twenty-two you will look like a woman of five-
and-thirty, and you will be lucky if you are not diseased, pray to
God for that! No doubt you are thinking now that you have a gay
10   time and no work to do! Yet there is no work harder or more dreadful in the world or ever has been. One would think that the heart
alone would be worn out with tears. And you won't dare to say a
word, not half a word when they drive you away from here; you
will go away as though you were to blame. You will change to
15   another house, then to a third, then somewhere else, till you come
down at last to the Haymarket. There you will be beaten at every
turn; that is good manners there, the visitors don't know how to be
friendly without beating you. You don't believe that it is so hateful
there? Go and look for yourself some time, you can see with your
20   own eyes. Once, one New Year's Day, I saw a woman at a door.
They had turned her out as a joke, to give her a taste of the frost
because she had been crying so much, and they shut the door
behind her. At nine o'clock in the morning she was already quite
drunk, dishevelled, half-naked, covered with bruises, her face was
25   powdered, but she had a black-eye, blood was trickling from her
nose and her teeth; some cabman had just given her a drubbing. She
was sitting on the stone steps, a salt fish of some sort was in her
hand; she was crying, wailing something about her luck and beating with the fish on the steps, and cabmen and drunken soldiers
30   were crowding in the doorway taunting her. You don't believe that
you will ever be like that? I should be sorry to believe it, too, but
how do you know; maybe ten years, eight years ago that very
woman with the salt fish came here fresh as a cherub, innocent,
pure, knowing no evil, blushing at every word. Perhaps she was
35   like you, proud, ready to take offence, not like the others; perhaps
she looked like a queen, and knew what happiness was in store for
the man who should love her and whom she should love. Do you
see how it ended? And what if at that very minute when she was
beating on the filthy steps with that fish, drunken and dishev-
40   elled—what if at that very minute she recalled the pure early days
in her father's house, when she used to go to school and the neigh-
bour's son watched for her on the way, declaring that he would love
her as long as he lived, that he would devote his life to her, and
when they vowed to love one another for ever and be married as
45   soon as they were grown up! No, Liza, it would be happy for you if

you were to die soon of consumption in some corner, in some cellar like that woman just now. In the hospital, do you say? You will be lucky if they take you, but what if you are still of use to the madam here? Consumption is a queer disease, it is not like fever. The
5   patient goes on hoping till the last minute and says he is all right. He deludes himself. And that just suits your madam. Don't doubt it, that's how it is; you have sold your soul, and what is more you owe money, so you daren't say a word. But when you are dying, all will abandon you, all will turn away from you, for then there will
10   be nothing to get from you. What's more, they will reproach you for cumbering the place, for being so long over dying. However you beg you won't get a drink of water without abuse: 'Whenever are you going off, you nasty hussy, you won't let us sleep with your moaning, you make the gentlemen sick.' That's true, I have heard
15   such things said myself. They will thrust you dying into the filthi-est corner in the cellar—in the damp and darkness; what will your thoughts be, lying there alone? When you die, strange hands will lay you out, with grumbling and impatience; no one will bless you, no one will sigh for you, they only want to get rid of you as soon as
20   may be; they will buy a coffin, take you to the grave as they did that poor woman today, and celebrate your memory at the tavern. In the grave, sleet, filth, wet snow—no need to put themselves out for you—'Let her down, Vanuha; it's just like her luck—even here, she is head-foremost, the hussy. Shorten the cord, you rascal.' 'It's all
25   right as it is.' 'All right, is it? Why, she's on her side! She was a fel-low-creature, after all! But, never mind, throw the earth on her.' And they won't care to waste much time quarrelling over you. They will scatter the wet blue clay as quick as they can and go off to the tav-ern . . . and there your memory on earth will end; other women
30   have, children to go to their graves, fathers, husbands. While for you neither tear, nor sigh, nor remembrance; no one in the whole world will ever come to you, your name will vanish from the face of the earth—as though you had never existed, never been born at all! Nothing but filth and mud, however you knock at your coffin
35   lid at night, when the dead arise, however you cry: 'Let me out, kind people, to live in the light of day! My life was no life at all; my life has been thrown away like a dishcloth; it was drunk away in the tavern at the Haymarket; let me out, kind people, to live in the world again.'"
40   And I worked myself up to such a pitch that I began to have a lump in my throat myself, and . . . and all at once I stopped, sat up in dismay and, bending over apprehensively, began to listen with a beating heart. I had reason to be troubled.

    I had felt for some time that I was turning her soul upside
45   down and rending her heart, and—and the more I was convinced of

it, the more eagerly I desired to gain my object as quickly and as effectually as possible. It was the exercise of my skill that carried me away; yet it was not merely sport. . . .

5   I knew I was speaking stiffly, artificially, even bookishly, in fact, I could not speak except "like a book." But that did not trouble me: I knew, I felt that I should be understood and that this very bookishness might be an assistance. But now, having attained my effect, I was suddenly panic-stricken. Never before had I witnessed such despair! She was lying on her face, thrusting her face into the pillow

10   and clutching it in both hands. Her heart was being torn. Her youthful body was shuddering all over as though in convulsions. Suppressed sobs rent her bosom and suddenly burst out in weeping and wailing, then she pressed closer into the pillow: she did not want anyone here, not a living soul, to know of her anguish and her

15   tears. She bit the pillow, bit her hand till it bled (I saw that afterwards), or, thrusting her fingers into her dishevelled hair, seemed rigid with the effort of restraint, holding her breath and clenching her teeth. I began saying something, begging her to calm herself, but felt that I did not dare; and all at once, in a sort of cold shiver,

20   almost in terror, began fumbling in the dark, trying hurriedly to get dressed to go. It was dark: though I tried my best I could not finish dressing quickly. Suddenly I felt a box of matches and a candlestick with a whole candle in it. As soon as the room was lighted up, Liza sprang up, sat up in bed, and with a contorted face, with a half

25   insane smile, looked at me almost senselessly. I sat down beside her and took her hands; she came to herself, made an impulsive movement towards me, would have caught hold of me, but did not dare, and slowly bowed her head before me.

    "Liza, my dear, I was wrong . . . forgive me, my dear," I began,

30   but she squeezed my hand in her fingers so tightly that I felt I was saying the wrong thing and stopped.

    "This is my address, Liza, come to me."

    "I will come," she answered resolutely, her head still bowed.

    "But now I am going, good-bye . . . till we meet again."

35   I got up; she, too, stood up and suddenly flushed all over, gave a shudder, snatched up a shawl that was lying on a chair and muffled herself in it to her chin. As she did this she gave another sickly smile, blushed and looked at me strangely. I felt wretched; I was in haste to get away—to disappear.

40   "Wait a minute," she said suddenly, in the passage just at the doorway, stopping me with her hand on my overcoat. She put down the candle in hot haste and ran off; evidently she had thought of something or wanted to show me something. As she ran away she flushed, her eyes shone, and there was a smile on her lips—

45   what was the meaning of it? Against my will I waited: she came

back a minute later with an expression that seemed to ask forgiveness for something. In fact, it was not the same face, not the same look as the evening before: sullen, mistrustful and obstinate. Her eyes now were imploring, soft, and at the same time trustful, caressing, timid. The expression with which children look at people they are very fond of, of whom they are asking a favour. Her eyes were a light hazel, they were lovely eyes, full of life, and capable of expressing love as well as sullen hatred.

Making no explanation, as though I, as a sort of higher being, must understand everything without explanations, she held out a piece of paper to me. Her whole face was positively beaming at that instant with naïve, almost childish, triumph. I unfolded it. It was a letter to her from a medical student or someone of that sort—a very high-flown and flowery, but extremely respectful, love-letter. I don't recall the words now, but I remember well that through the high-flown phrases there was apparent a genuine feeling, which cannot be feigned. When I had finished reading it I met her glowing, questioning, and childishly impatient eyes fixed upon me. She fastened her eyes upon my face and waited impatiently for what I should say. In a few words, hurriedly, but with a sort of joy and pride, she explained to me that she had been to a dance somewhere in a private house, a family of "very nice people, *who knew nothing*, absolutely nothing, for she had only come here so lately and it had all happened . . . and she hadn't made up her mind to stay and was certainly going away as soon as she had paid her debt. . ." and at that party there had been the student who had danced with her all the evening. He had talked to her, and it turned out that he had known her in old days at Riga when he was a child, they had played together, but a very long time ago—and he knew her parents, "but *about this* he knew nothing, nothing whatever, and had no suspicion! And the day after the dance (three days ago) he had sent her that letter through the friend with whom she had gone to the party . . . and . . . well, that was all."

She dropped her shining eyes with a sort of bashfulness as she finished.

The poor girl was keeping that student's letter as a precious treasure, and had run to fetch it, her only treasure, because she did not want me to go away without knowing that she, too, was honestly and genuinely loved; that she, too, was addressed respectfully. No doubt that letter was destined to lie in her box and lead to nothing. But none the less, I am certain that she would keep it all her life as a precious treasure, as her pride and justification, and now at such a minute she had thought of that letter and brought it with naïve pride to raise herself in my eyes that I might see, that I, too, might think well of her. I said nothing, pressed her hand and went

out. I so longed to get away. . . . I walked all the way home, in spite
of the fact that the melting snow was still falling in heavy flakes. I
was exhausted, shattered, in bewilderment. But behind the bewilderment the truth was already gleaming. The loathsome truth.

VIII

5   It was some time, however, before I consented to recognise that
truth. Waking up in the morning after some hours of heavy, leaden
sleep, and immediately realising all that had happened on the previous day, I was positively amazed at my last night's *sentimentality*
with Liza, at all those "outcries of horror and pity." "To think of
10   having such an attack of womanish hysteria, pah!" I concluded.
And what did I thrust my address upon her for? What if she comes?
Let her come, though; it doesn't matter. . . . But *obviously*, that was
not now the chief and the most important matter: I had to make
haste and at all costs save my reputation in the eyes of Zverkov and
15   Simonov as quickly as possible; that was the chief business. And I
was so taken up that morning that I actually forgot all about Liza.

First of all I had at once to repay what I had borrowed the day
before from Simonov. I resolved on a desperate measure: to borrow
fifteen roubles straight off from Anton Antonitch. As luck would
20   have it he was in the best of humours that morning, and gave it to
me it once, on the first asking. I was so delighted at this that, as I
signed the IOU with a swaggering air, I told him casually that the
night before "I had been keeping it up with some friends at the
Hôtel de Paris, we were giving a farewell party to a comrade, in fact,
25   I might say a friend of my childhood, and you know—a desperate
rake, fearfully spoilt—of course, he belongs to a good family, and
has considerable means, a brilliant career; he is witty, charming, a
regular Lovelace, you understand; we drank an extra 'half-dozen'
and . . ."

30   And it went off all right; all this was uttered very easily, uncon-
strainedly and complacently.

On reaching home I promptly wrote to Simonov.

To this hour I am lost in admiration when I recall the truly gen-
tlemanly, good-humoured, candid tone of my letter. With tact and
35   good-breeding, and, above all, entirely without superfluous words,
I blamed myself for all that had happened. I defended myself, "if I
really may be allowed to defend myself," by alleging that being
utterly unaccustomed to wine, I had been intoxicated with the first
glass, which I said, I had drunk before they arrived, while I was
40   waiting for them at the Hôtel de Paris between five and six o'clock.
I begged Simonov's pardon especially; I asked him to convey my
explanations to all the others, especially to Zverkov, whom "I

seemed to remember as though in a dream" I had insulted. I added that I would have called upon all of them myself, but my head ached, and besides I had not the face to. I was particularly pleased with a certain lightness, almost carelessness (strictly within the bounds of politeness, however), which was apparent in my style, and better than any possible arguments, gave them at once to understand that I took rather an independent view of "all that unpleasantness last night"; that I was by no means so utterly crushed as you, my friends, probably imagine; but on the contrary, looked upon it as a gentleman serenely respecting himself should look upon it. "On a young hero's past no censure is cast!"

"There is actually an aristocratic playfulness about it!" I thought admiringly, as I read over the letter. "And it's all because I am an intellectual and cultivated man! Another man in my place would not have known how to extricate himself, but here I have got out of it and am as jolly as ever again, and all because I am 'a cultivated and educated man of our day.' And, indeed, perhaps, everything was due to the wine yesterday. H'm!" . . . no, it was not the wine. I did not drink anything at all between five and six when I was waiting for them. I had lied to Simonov; I had lied shamelessly; and indeed I wasn't ashamed now. . . . Hang it all though, the great thing was that I was rid of it.

I put six roubles in the letter, sealed it up, and asked Apollon to take it to Simonov. When he learned that there was money in the letter, Apollon became more respectful and agreed to take it. Towards evening I went out for a walk. My head was still aching and giddy after yesterday. But as evening came on and the twilight grew denser, my impressions and, following them, my thoughts, grew more and more different and confused. Something was not dead within me, in the depths of my heart and conscience it would not die, and it showed itself in acute depression. For the most part I jostled my way through the most crowded business streets, along Myeshtchansky Street, along Sadovy Street and in Yusupov Garden. I always liked particularly sauntering along these streets in the dusk, just when there were crowds of working people of all sorts going home from their daily work, with faces looking cross with anxiety. What I liked was just that cheap bustle, that bare prose. On this occasion the jostling of the streets irritated me more than ever, I could not make out what was wrong with me, I could not find the clue, something seemed rising up continually in my soul, painfully, and refusing to be appeased. I returned home completely upset, it was just as though some crime were lying on my conscience.

The thought that Liza was coming worried me continually. It seemed queer to me that of all my recollections of yesterday this tormented me, as it were, especially, as it were, quite separately.

Everything else I had quite succeeded in forgetting by the evening;
I dismissed it all and was still perfectly satisfied with my letter to
Simonov. But on this point I was not satisfied at all. It was as though
I were worried only by Liza. "What if she comes," I thought inces-
5   santly, "well, it doesn't matter, let her come! H'm! it's horrid that she
should see, for instance, how I live. Yesterday I seemed such a hero
to her, while now, h'm! It's horrid, though, that I have let myself go
so, the room looks like a beggar's. And I brought myself to go out
to dinner in such a suit! And my American leather sofa with the
10   stuffing sticking out. And my dressing-gown, which will not cover
me, such tatters, and she will see all this and she will see Apollon.
That beast is certain to insult her. He will fasten upon her in order
to be rude to me. And I, of course, shall be panic-stricken as usual,
I shall begin bowing and scraping before her and pulling my dress-
15   ing-gown round me, I shall begin smiling, telling lies. Oh, the beastliness! And it isn't the beastliness of it that matters most! There is
something more important, more loathsome, viler! Yes, viler! And
to put on that dishonest lying mask again! . . ."

    When I reached that thought I fired up all at once.
20   "Why dishonest? How dishonest? I was speaking sincerely last
night. I remember there was real feeling in me, too. What I wanted
was to excite an honourable feeling in her. . . . Her crying was a
good thing, it will have a good effect."

    Yet I could not feel at ease. All that evening, even when I had
25   come back home, even after nine o'clock, when I calculated that
Liza could not possibly come, still she haunted me, and what was
worse, she came back to my mind always in the same position. One
moment out of all that had happened last night stood vividly before
my imagination; the moment when I struck a match and saw her
30   pale, distorted face, with its look of torture. And what a pitiful, what
an unnatural, what a distorted smile she had at that moment! But I
did not know then, that fifteen years later I should still in my imagination see Liza, always with the pitiful, distorted, inappropriate
smile which was on her face at that minute.

35   Next day I was ready again to look upon it all as nonsense, due
to overexcited nerves, and, above all, as *exaggerated*. I was always
conscious of that weak point of mine, and sometimes very much
afraid of it. "I exaggerate everything, that is where I go wrong," I
repeated to myself every hour. But, however, "Liza will very likely
40   come all the same," was the refrain with which all my reflections
ended. I was so uneasy that I sometimes flew into a fury: "She'll
come, she is certain to come!" I cried, running about the room, "if
not today, she will come tomorrow; she'll find me out! The
damnable romanticism of these pure hearts! Oh, the vileness—oh,
45   the silliness—oh, the stupidity of these 'wretched sentimental

souls!' Why, how fail to understand? How could one fail to understand? . . ."

But at this point I stopped short, and in great confusion,
indeed.

5   And how few, how few words, I thought, in passing, were
needed; how little of the idyllic (and affectedly, bookishly, artificially idyllic too) had sufficed to turn a whole human life at once
according to my will. That's virginity, to be sure! Freshness of soil!

At times a thought occurred to me, to go to her, "to tell her all,"
10   and beg her not to come to me. But this thought stirred such wrath
in me that I believed I should have crushed that "damned" Liza if
she had chanced to be near me at the time. I should have insulted
her, have spat at her, have turned her out, have struck her!

One day passed, however, another and another; she did not
15   come and I began to grow calmer. I felt particularly bold and cheerful after nine o'clock, I even sometimes began dreaming, and rather
sweetly: I, for instance, became the salvation of Liza, simply
through her coming to me and my talking to her. . . . I develop her,
educate her. Finally, I notice that she loves me, loves me passionate-
20   ly. I pretend not to understand (I don't know, however, why I pretend, just for effect, perhaps). At last all confusion, transfigured,
trembling and sobbing, she flings herself at my feet and says that I
am her saviour, and that she loves me better than anything in the
world. I am amazed, but. . . . "Liza," I say, "can you imagine that I
have not noticed your love? I saw it all, I divined it, but I did not
dare to approach you first, because I had an influence over you and
25   was afraid that you would force yourself, from gratitude, to
respond to my love, would try to rouse in your heart a feeling which
was perhaps absent, and I did not wish that . . . because it would be
tyranny . . . it would be indelicate (in short, I launch off at that point
into European, inexplicably lofty subtleties à la George Sand), but
30   now, now you are mine, you are my creation, you are pure, you are
good, you are my noble wife.

> 'Into my house come bold and free,
> Its rightful mistress there to be'."

Then we begin living together, go abroad and so on, and so on.
35   In fact, in the end it seemed vulgar to me myself, and I began putting out my tongue at myself

Besides, they won't let her out, "the hussy!" I thought. They
don't let them go out very readily, especially in the evening (for
some reason I fancied she would come in the evening, and at seven
40   o'clock precisely). Though she did say she was not altogether a
slave there yet, and had certain rights; so, h'm! Damn it all, she will

come, she is sure to come!

It was a good thing, in fact, that Apollon distracted my attention at that time by his rudeness. He drove me beyond all patience!
He was the bane of my life, the curse laid upon me by Providence.
5 We had been squabbling continually for years, and I hated him. My
God, how I hated him! I believe I had never hated anyone in my life
as I hated him, especially at some moments. He was an elderly, dignified man, who worked part of his time as a tailor. But for some
unknown reason he despised me beyond all measure, and looked
10 down upon me insufferably. Though, indeed, he looked down upon
everyone. Simply to glance at that flaxen, smoothly brushed head,
at the tuft of hair he combed up on his forehead and oiled with sun-
flower oil, at that dignified mouth, compressed into the shape of the
letter V, made one feel one was confronting a man who never doubt-
15 ed of himself. He was a pedant, to the most extreme point, the greatest pedant I had met on earth, and with that had a vanity only befit-
ting Alexander of Macedon. He was in love with every button on
his coat, every nail on his fingers—absolutely in love with them,
and he looked it! In his behaviour to me he was a perfect tyrant, he
20 spoke very little to me, and if he chanced to glance at me he gave
me a firm, majestically self-confident and invariably ironical look
that drove me sometimes to fury. He did his work with the air of
doing me the greatest favour, though he did scarcely anything for
me, and did not, indeed, consider himself bound to do anything.
25 There could be no doubt that he looked upon me as the greatest fool
on earth, and that "he did not get rid of me" was simply that he
could get wages from me every month. He consented to do nothing
for me for seven roubles a month. Many sins should be forgiven me
for what I suffered from him. My hatred reached such a point that
30 sometimes his very step almost threw me into convulsions. What I
loathed particularly was his lisp. His tongue must have been a little
too long or something of that sort, for he continually lisped, and
seemed to be very proud of it, imagining that it greatly added to his
dignity. He spoke in a slow, measured tone, with his hands behind
35 his back and his eyes fixed on the ground. He maddened me particularly when he read aloud the psalms to himself behind his par-
tition. Many a battle I waged over that reading! But he was awfully
fond of reading aloud in the evenings, in a slow, even, sing-song
voice, as though over the dead. It is interesting that that is how he
40 has ended: he hires himself out to read the psalms over the dead,
and at the same time he kills rats and makes blacking. But at that
time I could not get rid of him, it was as though he were chemical-
ly combined with my existence. Besides, nothing would have
induced him to consent to leave me. I could not live in furnished
45 lodgings: my lodging was my private solitude, my shell, my cave,

in which I concealed myself from all mankind, and Apollon seemed to me, for some reason, an integral part of that flat, and for seven years I could not turn him away.

To be two or three days behind with his wages, for instance, was impossible. He would have made such a fuss, I should not have known where to hide my head. But I was so exasperated with everyone during those days, that I made up my mind for some reason and with some object to *punish* Apollon and not to pay him for a fortnight the wages that were owing him. I had for a long time—for the last two years—been intending to do this, simply in order to teach him not to give himself airs with me, and to show him that if I liked I could withhold his wages. I purposed to say nothing to him about it, and was purposely silent indeed, in order to score off his pride and force him to be the first to speak of his wages. Then I would take the seven roubles out of a drawer, show him I have the money put aside on purpose, but that I won't, I won't, I simply won't pay him his wages, I won't just because that is "what I wish," because "I am master, and it is for me to decide," because he has been disrespectful, because he has been rude; but if he were to ask respectfully I might be softened and give it to him, otherwise he might wait another fortnight, another three weeks, a whole month. . . .

But angry as I was, yet he got the better of me. I could not hold out for four days. He began as he always did begin in such cases, for there had been such cases already, there had been attempts (and it may be observed I knew all this beforehand, I knew his nasty tactics by heart). He would begin by fixing upon me an exceedingly severe stare, keeping it up for several minutes at a time, particularly on meeting me or seeing me out of the house. If I held out and pretended not to notice these stares, he would, still in silence, proceed to further tortures. All at once, *à propos* of nothing, he would walk softly and smoothly into my room, when I was pacing up and down or reading, stand at the door, one hand behind his back and one foot behind the other, and fix upon me a stare more than severe, utterly contemptuous. If I suddenly asked him what he wanted, he would make me no answer, but continue staring at me persistently for some seconds, then, with a peculiar compression of his lips and a most significant air, deliberately turn round and deliberately go back to his room. Two hours later he would come out again and again present himself before me in the same way. It had happened that in my fury I did not even ask him what he wanted, but simply raised my head sharply and imperiously and began staring back at him. So we stared at one another for two minutes; at last he turned with deliberation and dignity and went back again for two hours.

If I were still not brought to reason by all this, but persisted in

my revolt, he would suddenly begin sighing while he looked at me,
long, deep sighs as though measuring by them the depths of my
moral degradation, and, of course, it ended at last by his triumph-
ing completely: I raged and shouted, but still was forced to do what
5   he wanted.

This time the usual staring manœuvres had scarcely begun
when I lost my temper and flew at him in a fury. I was irritated
beyond endurance apart from him.

"Stay," I cried, in a frenzy, as he was slowly and silently turn-
10   ing, with one hand behind his back, to go to his room. "Stay! Come
back, come back, I tell you!" and I must have bawled so unnaturally, that he turned round and even looked at me with some wonder.
However, he persisted in saying nothing, and that infuriated me.

"How dare you come and look at me like that without being
15   sent for? Answer!"

After looking at me calmly for half a minute, he began turning
round again.

"Stay!" I roared, running up to him, "don't stir! There. Answer,
now: what did you come in to look at?"

20   "If you have any order to give me it's my duty to carry it out,"
he answered, after another silent pause, with a slow, measured lisp,
raising his eyebrows and calmly twisting his head from one side to
another, all this with exasperating composure.

"That's not what I am asking you about, you torturer!" I shout-
25   ed, turning crimson with anger. "I'll tell you why you came here
myself: you see, I don't give you your wages, you are so proud you
don't want to bow down and ask for it, and so you come to punish
me with your stupid stares, to worry me and you have no
sus . . . pic . . . ion how stupid it is—stupid, stupid, stupid, stu-
30   pid! . . ."

He would have turned round again without a word, but I
seized him.

"Listen," I shouted to him. "Here's the money, do you see, here
it is," (I took it out of the table drawer); "here's the seven roubles
35   complete,   but   you   are   not   going   to   have   it,
you . . . are . . . not . . . going . . . to . . . have it until you come respectfully with bowed head to beg my pardon. Do you hear?"

"That cannot be," he answered, with the most unnatural self-
confidence.

40   "It shall be so," I said, "I give you my word of honour, it shall
be!"

"And there's nothing for me to beg your pardon for," he went
on, as though he had not noticed my exclamations at all. "Why,
besides, you called me a 'torturer,' for which I can summon you at
45   the police-station at any time for insulting behaviour."

"Go, summon me," I roared, "go at once, this very minute, this very second! You are a torturer all the same! a torturer!"

But he merely looked at me, then turned, and regardless of my loud calls to him, he walked to his room with an even step and
5   without looking round.

"If it had not been for Liza nothing of this would have happened," I decided inwardly. Then, after waiting a minute, I went myself behind his screen with a dignified and solemn air, though my heart was beating slowly and violently.
10   "Apollon," I said quietly and emphatically, though I was breathless, "go at once without a minute's delay and fetch the police-officer."

He had meanwhile settled himself at his table, put on his spectacles and taken up some sewing. But, hearing my order, he burst
15   into a guffaw.

"At once, go this minute! Go on, or else you can't imagine what will happen."

"You are certainly out of your mind," he observed, without even raising his head, lisping as deliberately as ever and threading
20   his needle. "Whoever heard of a man sending for the police against himself? And as for being frightened—you are upsetting yourself about nothing, for nothing will come of it."

"Go!" I shrieked, clutching him by the shoulder. I felt I should strike him in a minute.
25   But I did not notice the door from the passage softly and slowly open at that instant and a figure come in, stop short, and begin staring at us in perplexity. I glanced, nearly swooned with shame, and rushed back to my room. There, clutching at my hair with both hands, I leaned my head against the wall and stood motionless in
30   that position.

Two minutes later I heard Apollon's deliberate footsteps. "There is some woman asking for you," he said, looking at me with peculiar severity. Then he stood aside and let in Liza. He would not go away, but stared at us sarcastically.
35   "Go away, go away," I commanded in desperation. At that moment my clock began whirring and wheezing and struck seven.

IX

Into my house come bold and free,
Its rightful mistress there to be.

I stood before her crushed, crestfallen, revoltingly confused,
40   and I believe I smiled as I did my utmost to wrap myself in the skirts of my ragged wadded dressing-gown—exactly as I had imag-

ined the scene not long before in a fit of depression. After standing over us for a couple of minutes Apollon went away, but that did not make me more at ease. What made it worse was that she, too, was overwhelmed with confusion, more so, in fact, than I should have

5 expected. At the sight of me, of course.

"Sit down," I said mechanically, moving a chair up to the table, and I sat down on the sofa. She obediently sat down at once and gazed at me open-eyed, evidently expecting something from me at once. This naïveté of expectation drove me to fury, but I restrained

10 myself.

She ought to have tried not to notice, as though everything had been as usual, while instead of that, she . . . and I dimly felt that I should make her pay dearly for *all this.*

"You have found me in a strange position, Liza," I began, stam-

15 mering and knowing that this was the wrong way to begin. "No, no, don't imagine anything," I cried, seeing that she had suddenly flushed. "I am not ashamed of my poverty. . . . On the contrary, I look with pride on my poverty. I am poor but honourable. . . . One can be poor and honourable," I muttered. "However . . . would you

20 like tea? . . ."

"No," she was beginning.

"Wait a minute."

I leapt up and ran to Apollon. I had to get out of the room somehow.

25 "Apollon," I whispered in feverish haste, flinging down before him the seven roubles which had remained all the time in my clenched fist, "here are your wages, you see I give them to you; but for that you must come to my rescue: bring me tea and a dozen rusks from the restaurant. If you won't go, you'll make me a miser-

30 able man! You don't know what this woman is. . . . This is—everything! You may be imagining something. . . . But you don't know what that woman is! . . ."

Apollon, who had already sat down to his work and put on his spectacles again, at first glanced askance at the money without

35 speaking or putting down his needle; then, without paying the slightest attention to me or making any answer, he went on busying himself with his needle, which he had not yet threaded. I waited before him for three minutes with my arms crossed *à la Napoléon.* My temples were moist with sweat. I was pale, I felt it. But, thank

40 God, he must have been moved to pity, looking at me. Having threaded his needle he deliberately got up from his seat, deliberately moved back his chair, deliberately took off his spectacles, deliberately counted the money, and finally asking me over his shoulder: "Shall I get a whole portion?" deliberately walked out of the room.

45 As I was going back to Liza, the thought occurred to me on the way:

shouldn't I run away just as I was in my dressing-gown, no matter where, and then let happen what would?

I sat down again. She looked at me uneasily. For some minutes we were silent.

5   "I will kill him," I shouted suddenly, striking the table with my fist so that the ink spurted out of the inkstand.

"What are you saying!" she cried, starting.

"I will kill him! kill him!" I shrieked, suddenly striking the table in absolute frenzy, and at the same time fully understanding
10   how stupid it was to be in such a frenzy. "You don't know, Liza, what that—torturer is to me. He is my torturer . . . He has gone now to fetch some rusks; he . . ."

And suddenly I burst into tears. It was an hysterical attack. How ashamed I felt in the midst of my sobs; but still I could not
15   restrain them.

She was frightened.

"What is the matter? What is wrong?" she cried, fussing about me.

"Water, give me water, over there!" I muttered in a faint voice,
20   though I was inwardly conscious that I could have got on very well without water and without muttering in a faint voice. But I was, what is called, *putting it on,* to save appearances, though the attack was a genuine one.

She gave me water, looking at me in bewilderment. At that
25   moment Apollon brought in the tea. It suddenly seemed to me that this commonplace, prosaic tea was horribly undignified and paltry after all that had happened, and I blushed crimson. Liza looked at Apollon with positive alarm. He went out without a glance at either of us.

30   "Liza, do you despise me?" I asked, looking at her fixedly, trembling with impatience to know what she was thinking.

She was confused, and did not know what to answer.

"Drink your tea," I said to her angrily. I was angry with myself, but, of course, it was she who would have to pay for it. A horrible
35   spite against her suddenly surged up in my heart; I believe I could have killed her. To revenge myself on her I swore inwardly not to say a word to her all the time. "She is the cause of it all," I thought.

Our silence lasted for five minutes. The tea stood on the table; we did not touch it. I had got to the point of purposely refraining
40   from beginning in order to embarrass her further; it was awkward for her to begin alone. Several times she glanced at me with mournful perplexity. I was obstinately silent. I was, of course, myself the chief sufferer, because I was fully conscious of the disgusting meanness of my spiteful stupidity, and yet at the same time I could not
45   restrain myself.

"I want to . . . get away . . . from there altogether," she began, to break the silence in some way, but, poor girl, that was just what she ought not to have spoken about at such a stupid moment to a man so stupid as I was. My heart positively ached with pity for her
5   tactless and unnecessary straightforwardness. But something hideous at once stifled all compassion in me; it even provoked me to greater venom. I did not care what happened. Another five minutes passed.

"Perhaps I am in your way," she began timidly, hardly audibly,
10 and was getting up.

But as soon as I saw this first impulse of wounded dignity I positively trembled with spite, and at once burst out.

"Why have you come to me, tell me that, please?" I began, gasping for breath and regardless of logical connection in my
15 words. I longed to have it all out at once, at one burst; I did not even trouble how to begin. "Why have you come? Answer, answer," I cried, hardly knowing what I was doing. "I'll tell you, my good girl, why you have come. You've come because I talked sentimental stuff to you then. So now you are soft as butter and longing for fine sen-
20 timents again. So you may as well know that I was laughing at you then. And I am laughing at you now. Why are you shuddering? Yes, I was laughing at you! I had been insulted just before, at dinner, by the fellows who came that evening before me. I came to you, mean- ing to thrash one of them, an officer; but I didn't succeed, I didn't
25 find him; I had to avenge the insult on someone to get back my own again; you turned up, I vented my spleen on you and laughed at you. I had been humiliated, so I wanted to humiliate; I had been treated like a rag, so I wanted to show my power. . . . That's what it was, and you imagined I had come there on purpose to save you.
30 Yes? You imagined that? You imagined that?"

I knew that she would perhaps be muddled and not take it all in exactly, but I knew, too, that she would grasp the gist of it, very well indeed. And so, indeed she did. She turned white as a hand- kerchief, tried to say something, and her lips worked painfully; but
35 she sank on a chair as though she had been felled by an axe. And all the time afterwards she listened to me with her lips parted and her eyes wide open, shuddering with awful terror. The cynicism, the cynicism of my words overwhelmed her. . . .

"Save you!" I went on, jumping up from my chair and running
40 up and down the room before her. "Save you from what? But per- haps I am worse than you myself. Why didn't you throw it in my teeth when I was giving you that sermon: 'But what did you come here yourself for? was it to read us a sermon?' Power, power was what I wanted then, sport was what I wanted, I wanted to wring out
45 your tears, your humiliation, your hysteria—that was what I want-

ed then! Of course, I couldn't keep it up then, because I am a wretched creature, I was frightened, and, the devil knows why, gave you my address in my folly. Afterwards, before I got home, I was cursing and swearing at you because of that address, I hated

5   you already because of the lies I had told you. Because I only like playing with words, only dreaming, but, do you know, what I really want is that you should all go to hell. That is what I want. I want peace; yes, I'd sell the whole world for a farthing, straight off, so long as I was left in peace. Is the world to go to pot, or am I to go

10   without my tea? I say that the world may go to pot for me so long as I always get my tea. Did you know that, or not? Well, anyway, I know that I am a blackguard, a scoundrel, an egoist, a sluggard. Here I have been shuddering for the last three days at the thought of your coming. And do you know what has worried me particu-

15   larly for these three days? That I posed as such a hero to you, and now you would see me in a wretched torn dressing-gown, beggarly, loathsome. I told you just now that I was not ashamed of my poverty; so you may as well know that I am ashamed of it; I am more ashamed of it than of anything, more afraid of it than of being

20   found out if I were a thief, because I am as vain as though I had been skinned and the very air blowing on me hurt. Surely by now you must realise that I shall never forgive you for having found me in this wretched dressing-gown, just as I was flying at Apollon like a spiteful cur. The saviour, the former hero, was flying like a mangy,

25   unkempt sheep-dog at his lackey, and the lackey was jeering at him! And I shall never forgive you for the tears I could not help shedding before you just now, like some silly woman put to shame! And for what I am confessing to you now, I shall never forgive *you* either! Yes—you must answer for it all because you turned up like this,

30   because I am a blackguard, because I am the nastiest, stupidest, absurdest and most envious of all the worms on earth, who are not a bit better than I am, but, the devil knows why, are never put to confusion; while I shall always be insulted by every louse, that is my doom! And what is it to me that you don't understand a word

35   of this! And what do I care, what do I care about you, and whether you go to ruin there or not? Do you understand? How I shall hate you now after saying this, for having been here and listening. Why, it's not once in a lifetime a man speaks out like this, and then it is in hysterics! . . . What more do you want? Why do you still stand con-

40   fronting me, after all this? Why are you worrying me? Why don't you go?"

     But at this point a strange thing happened. I was so accustomed to think and imagine everything from books, and to picture everything in the world to myself just as I had made it up in my dreams

45   beforehand, that I could not all at once take in this strange circum-

stance. What happened was this: Liza, insulted and crushed by me, understood a great deal more than I imagined. She understood from all this what a woman understands first of all, if she feels genuine love, that is, that I was myself unhappy.

5 The frightened and wounded expression on her face was followed first by a look of sorrowful perplexity. When I began calling myself a scoundrel and a blackguard and my tears flowed (the tirade was accompanied throughout by tears) her whole face worked convulsively. She was on the point of getting up and stop-
10 ping me; when I finished she took no notice of my shouting: "Why are you here, why don't you go away?" but realised only that it must have been very bitter to me to say all this. Besides, she was so crushed, poor girl; she considered herself infinitely beneath me; how could she feel anger or resentment? She suddenly leapt up
15 from her chair with an irresistible impulse and held out her hands, yearning towards me, though still timid and not daring to stir. . . . At this point there was a revulsion in my heart too. Then she sudden-ly rushed to me, threw her arms round me and burst into tears. I, too, could not restrain myself, and sobbed as I never bad before.
20 "They won't let me . . . I can't be good!" I managed to articu-late; then I went to the sofa, fell on it face downwards, and sobbed on it for a quarter of an hour in genuine hysterics. She came close to me, put her arms round me and stayed motionless in that position. But the trouble was that the hysterics could not go on for ever, and
25 (I am writing the loathsome truth) lying face downwards on the sofa with my face thrust into my nasty leather pillow, I began by degrees to be aware of a far-away, involuntary but irresistible feel-ing that it would be awkward now for me to raise my head and look Liza straight in the face. Why was I ashamed? I don't know, but I
30 was ashamed. The thought, too, came into my overwrought brain that our parts now were completely changed, that she was now the heroine, while I was just a crushed and humiliated creature as she had been before me that night—four days before. . . . And all this came into my mind during the minutes I was lying on my face on
35 the sofa.

My God! surely I was not envious of her then.

I don't know, to this day I cannot decide, and at the time, of course, I was still less able to understand what I was feeling than now. I cannot get on without domineering and tyrannising over someone, but . . . there is no explaining anything by reasoning and so it is useless to reason.

I conquered myself, however, and raised my head; I had to do
40 so sooner or later . . . and I am convinced to this day that it was just because I was ashamed to look at her that another feeling was sud-denly kindled and flamed up in my heart . . . a feeling of mastery

and possession. My eyes gleamed with passion, and I, gripped her hands tightly. How I hated her and how I was drawn to her at that minute! The one feeling intensified the other. It was almost like an act of vengeance. At first there was a look of amazement, even of
5   terror on her face, but only for one instant. She warmly and rapturously embraced me.

X

A quarter of an hour later I was rushing up and down the room in frenzied impatience, from minute to minute I went up to the screen and peeped through the crack at Liza. She was sitting on the
10   ground with her head leaning against the bed, and must have been crying. But she did not go away, and that irritated me. This time she understood it all. I had insulted her finally, but . . . there's no need to describe it. She realised that my outburst of passion had been simply revenge, a fresh humiliation, and that to my earlier, almost
15   causeless hatred was added now a *personal hatred*, born of envy. . . . Though I do not maintain positively that she understood all this distinctly; but she certainly did fully understand that I was a despicable man, and what was worse, incapable of loving her.

I know I shall be told that this is incredible—but it is incredible
20   to be as spiteful and stupid as I was; it may be added that it was strange I should not love her, or at any rate, appreciate her love. Why is it strange? In the first place, by then I was incapable of love, for I repeat, with me loving meant tyrannising and showing my moral superiority. I have never in my life been able to imagine any
25   other sort of love, and have nowadays come to the point of sometimes thinking that love really consists in the right—freely given by the beloved object—to tyrannise over her.

Even in my underground dreams I did not imagine love except as a struggle. I began it always with hatred and ended it with moral
30   subjugation, and afterwards I never knew what to do with the subjugated object. And what is there to wonder at in that, since I had succeeded in so corrupting myself, since I was so out of touch with "real life," as to have actually thought of reproaching her, and putting her to shame for having come to me to hear "fine sentiments";
35   and did not even guess that she had come not to hear fine sentiments, but to love me, because to a woman all reformation, all salvation from any sort of ruin, and all moral renewal is included in love and can only show itself in that form.

I did not hate her so much, however, when I was running about
40   the room and peeping through the crack in the screen. I was only insufferably oppressed by her being here. I wanted her to disappear. I wanted "peace," to be left alone in my underground world. Real

life oppressed me with its novelty so much that I could hardly breathe.

But several minutes passed and she still remained, without stirring, as though she were unconscious. I had the shamelessness to
5   tap softly at the screen as though to remind her. . . . She started,
sprang up, and flew to seek her kerchief, her hat, her coat, as though
making her escape from me. . . . Two minutes later she came from
behind the screen and looked with heavy eyes at me. I gave a spiteful grin, which was forced, however, to *keep up appearances*, and I
10   turned away from her eyes.

"Good-bye," she said, going towards the door.

I ran up to her, seized her hand, opened it, thrust something in
it and closed it again. Then I turned at once and dashed away in
haste to the other corner of the room to avoid seeing, anyway. . . .
15   I did mean a moment since to tell a lie—to write that I did this
accidentally, not knowing what I was doing through foolishness,
through losing my head. But I don't want to lie, and so I will say
straight out that I opened her hand and put the money in it . . . from
spite. It came into my head to do this while I was running up and
20   down the room and she was sitting behind the screen. But this I can
say for certain: though I did that cruel thing purposely, it was not an
impulse from the heart, but came from my evil brain. This cruelty
was so affected, so purposely made up, so completely a product of
the brain, of books, that I could not even keep it up a minute—first
25   I dashed away to avoid seeing her, and then in shame and despair
rushed after Liza. I opened the door in the passage and began listening.

"Liza! Liza!" I cried on the stairs, but in a low voice, not boldly.

There was no answer, but I fancied I heard her footsteps, lower
30   down on the stairs.

"Liza!" I cried, more loudly.

No answer. But at that minute I heard the stiff outer glass door
open heavily with a creak and slam violently; the sound echoed up
the stairs.

35   She had gone. I went back to my room in hesitation. I felt horribly oppressed.

I stood still at the table, beside the chair on which she had sat
and looked aimlessly before me. A minute passed, suddenly I started; straight before me on the table I saw. . . . In short, I saw a crum-
40   pled blue five rouble note, the one I had thrust into her hand a
minute before. It was the same note; it could be no other, there was
no other in the flat. So she had managed to fling it from her hand on
the table at the moment when I had dashed into the further corner.

Well! I might have expected that she would do that. Might I
45   have expected it? No, I was such an egoist, I was so lacking in

respect for my fellow-creatures that I could not even imagine she would do so. I could not endure it. A minute later I flew like a madman to dress, flinging on what I could at random and ran headlong after her. She could not have got two hundred paces away when I
5   ran out into the street.

It was a still night and the snow was coming down in masses and falling almost perpendicularly, covering the pavement and the empty street as though with a pillow. There was no one in the street, no sound was to be heard. The street lamps gave a disconsolate and
10   useless glimmer. I ran two hundred paces to the cross-roads and stopped short.

Where had she gone? And why was I running after her?

Why? To fall down before her, to sob with remorse, to kiss her feet, to entreat her forgiveness! I longed for that, my whole breast
15   was being rent to pieces, and never, never shall I recall that minute with indifference. But—what for? I thought. Should I not begin to hate her, perhaps, even tomorrow, just because I had kissed her feet today? Should I give her happiness? Had I not recognised that day, for the hundredth time, what I was worth? Should I not torture her?
20   I stood in the snow, gazing into the troubled darkness and pondered this.

"And will it not be better?" I mused fantastically, afterwards at home, stifling the living pang of my heart with fantastic dreams. "Will it not be better that she should keep the resentment of the
25   insult for ever? Resentment—why, it is purification; it is a most stinging and painful consciousness! Tomorrow I should have defiled her soul and have exhausted her heart, while now the feeling of insult will never die in her heart, and however loathsome the filth awaiting her—the feeling of insult will elevate and purify
30   her . . . by hatred . . . h'm! . . . perhaps, too, by forgiveness. . . . Will all that make things easier for her though? . . ."

And, indeed, I will ask on my own account here, an idle question: which is better—cheap happiness or exalted sufferings? Well, which is better?

So I dreamed as I sat at home that evening, almost dead with
35   the pain in my soul. Never had I endured such suffering and remorse, yet could there have been the faintest doubt when I ran out from my lodging that I should turn back half-way? I never met Liza again and I have heard nothing of her. I will add, too, that I remained for a long time afterwards pleased with the phrase about
40   the benefit from resentment and hatred in spite of the fact that I almost fell ill from misery.

* * * * *

Even now, so many years later, all this is somehow a very evil memory. I have many evil memories now, but . . . hadn't I better end

my "Notes" here? I believe I made a mistake in beginning to write them, anyway I have felt ashamed all the time I've been writing this story; so it's hardly literature so much as a corrective punishment. Why, to tell long stories, showing how I have spoiled my life
5   through morally rotting in my corner, through lack of fitting environment, through divorce from real life, and rankling spite in my underground world, would certainly not be interesting; a novel needs a hero, and all the traits for an anti-hero are *expressly* gathered together here, and what matters most, it all produces an unpleasant
10 impression, for we are all divorced from life, we are all cripples, every one of us, more or less. We are so divorced from it that we feel at once a sort of loathing for real life, and so cannot bear to be reminded of it. Why, we have come almost to looking upon real life as an effort, almost as hard work, and we are all privately agreed
15 that it is better in books. And why do we fuss and fume sometimes? Why are we perverse and ask for something else? We don't know what ourselves. It would be the worse for us if our petulant prayers were answered. Come, try, give any one of us, for instance, a little more independence, untie our hands, widen the spheres of our
20 activity, relax the control and we . . . yes, I assure you . . . we should be begging to be under control again at once. I know that you will very likely be angry with me for that, and will begin shouting and stamping. Speak for yourself, you will say, and for your miseries in your underground holes, and don't dare to say all of us—excuse
25 me, gentlemen, I am not justifying myself with that "all of us." As for what concerns me in particular I have only in my life carried to an extreme what you have not dared to carry halfway, and what's more, you have taken your cowardice for good sense, and have found comfort in deceiving yourselves. So that perhaps, after all,
30 there is more life in me than in you. Look into it more carefully! Why, we don't even know what living means now, what it is, and what it is called? Leave us alone without books and we shall be lost and in confusion at once. We shall not know what to join on to, what to cling to, what to love and what to hate, what to respect and what
35 to despise. We are oppressed at being men—men with a real individual body and blood, we are ashamed of it, we think it a disgrace and try to contrive to be some sort of impossible generalised man. We are stillborn, and for generations past have been begotten, not by living fathers, and that suits us better and better. We are devel-
40 oping a taste for it. Soon we shall contrive to be born somehow-from an idea. But enough; I don't want to write more from "Underground."

[*The notes of this paradoxalist do not end here, however. He could not refrain from going on with them, but it seems to us that we may stop here.*]